Culture and Self

Culture and Self

Philosophical and Religious Perspectives, East and West

edited by
Douglas Allen
with the assistance of Ashok Malhotra

WestviewPress
A Division of HarperCollinsPublishers

Copyright © 1997 by Westview Press, A Division of HarperCollins Publishers, Inc., except for Chapter Two, which is © 1995 by Alan Roland.

Published in 1997 in the United States of America by Westview Press, 5500 Central Avenue, Boulder, Colorado 80301-2877, and in the United Kingdom by Westview Press, 12 Hid's Copse Road, Cumnor Hill, Oxford OX2 9JJ

A CIP catalog record for this book is available from the Library of Congress.
ISBN 0-8133-2673-7 (hc)—ISBN 0-8133-2674-5 (pb)

The paper used in this publication meets the requirements of the American National Standard for Permanence of Paper for Printed Library Materials Z39.48-1984.

10   9   8   7   6   5   4   3   2   1

In memory of Nina J. Malhotra and for Ilze

Contents

Preface   ix
Introduction, Douglas Allen   xi

PART 1
MULTIPLE ASIAN AND WESTERN PERSPECTIVES

1 Social Constructions of Self: Some Asian, Marxist,
   and Feminist Critiques of Dominant Western Views
   of Self, *Douglas Allen*   3

2 How Universal Is Psychoanalysis? The Self in India,
   Japan, and the United States, *Alan Roland*   27

PART 2
CHINESE AND WESTERN PERSPECTIVES

3 Ethics, Relativism, and the Self, *Mary I. Bockover*   43

4 Classical Confucian and Contemporary Feminist Perspectives
   on the Self: Some Parallels and Their Implications,
   Henry Rosemont, Jr.   63

5 Buddho-Taoist and Western Metaphysics of the Self,
   Kenneth K. Inada   83

PART 3
INDIAN AND WESTERN PERSPECTIVES

6 Reducing Concern with Self: Parfit and the Ancient Buddhist
   Schools, *Ananyo Basu*   97

7 Sartre and Samkhya-Yoga on Self, *Ashok K. Malhotra*   111

PART 4
JAPANESE AND WESTERN PERSPECTIVES

8 Nietzsche and Nishitani on Nihilism and Tradition,
Graham Parkes 131

9 Views of Japanese Selfhood: Japanese and Western Perspectives,
Mara Miller 145

Bibliography 163
About the Book and Editor 173
About the Contributors 175
Index 177

Preface

A major reason for publishing this book arose from the recognition that contemporary scholars are investigating the nature of "the self" in radically new ways. Indeed, they now usually approach their subject matter from nontraditional scholarly perspectives, cognizant that they must do justice to the specific cultural and historical contexts within which specific concepts of self are formulated. Investigation of "the self" has, of course, been a major philosophical and religious concern throughout both the East and the West. But traditional Eastern and Western philosophies and religions have generally been concerned with establishing the true, objective self, free from all cultural determinants. By way of contrast, the contributors to this book assume that views of self must be historically and culturally situated. Yet because they also want to avoid the sort of facile relativism and subjectivism whereby "anything goes," their studies are replete with value judgments.

An unusual feature of this book is that all of its chapters focus on traditions and individuals, East and West, yet also emphasize comparative philosophy, religion, and culture. Unlike collections that include sections on Chinese concepts of self, Indian concepts of self, and so forth, the present volume brings specific Eastern and Western perspectives into a dynamic comparative relation.

This comparative orientation emphasizes the sense of interrelatedness and interdependency increasingly being felt throughout the world. Not only must we attempt to do justice to the other *as* other, but it is only in relation to that which is other that we can truly understand ourselves. In addition, this comparative approach emphasizes a view of individual and cultural creativity. It is through the encounter with the other that we are provided with the means for overcoming our self-imposed isolation and cultural provincialism and for realizing our potential as self-transcending creative beings.

This volume is intended to appeal not just to specialists but to general readers across a variety of disciplines. Among such disciplines are Eastern philosophy and religion in particular and Asian studies in general; comparative philosophy, religion, and cultural studies; and investigations of "the self" and "the person." Indeed, the audience for the book potentially extends far beyond the disciplinary boundaries of philosophy and religion.

So that nonspecialists can more easily read and pronounce the Sanskrit and other Asian terms used throughout, the editor has spelled them out and eliminated their diacritical marks.

I wish to thank the editors of the *Journal of Chinese Philosophy* and *International Studies in Philosophy* for permission to use parts of Kenneth A. Inada's "The Challenge of Buddho-Taoist Metaphysics of Experience," *Journal of Chinese Philosophy* 21/1 (1994): 27–47, and Graham Parkes's "Nietzsche and Nishitani on the Self-Overcoming of Nihilism," *International Studies in Philosophy* 25/2 (1993): 51–60. These articles appear in revised and enlarged form as Chapters 5 and 8, respectively.

I also thank Spencer Carr, Michelle Baxter, and other editors at Westview Press for their cooperative attitude and constructive suggestions at various stages of this book project.

Douglas Allen

Introduction

DOUGLAS ALLEN

Traditional scholars of philosophy and religion, in both the East and the West, have often placed a major emphasis on analyzing the nature of self. But with a few significant exceptions, they have dismissed or devalued the role of culture in their specific formulations of "the self," arguing instead for some view of an objective, ahistoric, universal self. When they have cited cultural conditionings and variables, moreover, these scholars have usually described them as subjective, illusory, and distorting influences, thus obscuring the deeper, underlying, objective view of "the self" that transcends all such particular historical and cultural expressions.

With the exception of European and other Western phenomenology and existentialism, which have always centered on an analysis of the constitution and functioning of the self, much of twentieth-century Western philosophy has lost interest in the traditional philosophical focus on the self. Logical positivism and analytic philosophy—utilizing what were taken to be more rigorous scientific approaches and methods of verification—often dismissed traditional concerns about "the self" as based on intellectual confusion, category mistakes, and unscientific, subjective, obsolete metaphysics.

A renewed interest in analyzing the self has emerged in recent decades, but most scholars have not adopted the traditional orientations that claim knowledge of some ahistorical, transcultural, universal, objective self. On the contrary, most contemporary scholars, including the contributors to this volume, have recognized that specific concepts of self must be historically and culturally situated. In this regard, many recent studies of self share an anti-essentialist orientation in the sense of critiquing the dominant essentialist approaches to self that have defined much of traditional Eastern and Western philosophy and religion. Indeed, the majority of the studies presented in this volume emphasize something usually neglected by the traditional approaches to self: the need to contextualize specific views of self and to analyze such views in terms of the dynamic, dialectical relations between self and culture.

The chapters of this book—with their primary emphasis on comparative philosophy, religion, and culture—have been divided into four parts: Multiple Asian and Western Perspectives, Chinese and Western Perspectives, Indian and Western Perspectives, and Japanese and Western Perspectives. Included among these analyses are Vedanta, Samkhya-Yoga, and other Hindu approaches; Buddhist, Confucian, Taoist, and other Indian, Chinese, and Japanese perspectives; Cartesian and other dominant Western perspectives; and Marxist, Nietzschean, Sartrean, feminist, and other challenges to dominant Western interpretations of culture and self.

In Chapter 1, "Social Constructions of Self: Some Asian, Marxist, and Feminist Critiques of Dominant Western Views of Self," Douglas Allen argues against a traditional philosophical orientation, in the East and West, that maintains that philosophers uncover the "true," "objective," eternal nature of "the self" by penetrating beneath layers of ignorance and illusion. After analyzing some of the complex relations among texts, contexts, and interpretations, Allen formulates a modern, post-Cartesian view of self as the autonomous individual that has dominated Western socioeconomic, political, and cultural life. Then he presents four alternative concepts of self: the Hindu *karma yoga* of the *Bhagavad-Gita,* the Buddha's teaching of *anatta* (no-self), Marx's analysis of the historical constitution of the modern capitalist self, and the approaches of de Beauvoir and other feminists to masculinist formulations of self. Next, after reviewing various critiques of a construction of self that has dominated much of Western culture, he considers the differences among these four concepts as well as the ways in which they may be complementary and integrated in more comprehensive formulations. And finally, though he concurs with the recent philosophical assertion that no specific concepts of self may claim exclusivistic, ahistoric, universal truth, Allen argues against certain extreme relativisms that insist on the primacy and absoluteness of difference. Upholding the principle of "commonality with differences," he argues for the existence of a deep level of commonality among humans and their need to empathize with and relate to other concepts of self created by other cultures—concepts that, in turn, may function as catalysts to our own creative process of self-development.

In Chapter 2, "How Universal Is Psychoanalysis? The Self in India, Japan, and the United States," Alan Roland asks whether human nature is universal or culturally variable and, more particularly, whether psychoanalysis is universal in encompassing an understanding of persons from radically different cultures such as India and Japan. He focuses on these issues as they are involved in major psychoanalytic studies of South Asians by Sudhir Kakar and Catherine Ewing and of Japanese by Takeo Doi. From cultural anthropology Roland borrows the orientations of universalism, evolutionism, and relativism, along with their underlying philosophical assumptions, to demonstrate how these orientations are integral to the psychological explorations of the aforementioned analysts. From their work, he evaluates whether the current assumption of universal validity of psychoanalytic theory is helpful or problematic for understanding the self of Indians and Japanese as compared to that of Westerners. As a practicing psychoanalyst himself, Roland then turns to his own resolution of various thorny problems involving modern Western philosophical assumptions integral to psychoanalysis—assumptions that can confound the understanding of others from radically different cultures.

In Chapter 3, "Ethics, Relativism, and the Self," Mary I. Bockover presents a comparative study of traditional Western ethics and Confucian philosophy. Specifically, she formulates a major critique of traditional philosophy and ethics by reference to ethical relativism, especially as conceptualized in the works of Bernard Williams and other recent Western philosophers. Bockover argues that Confucian philosophy and some Western approaches can meet the challenges posed by relativism. She also discusses the way in which these Eastern and Western orientations generate fundamentally different conceptions of morality and, in turn, different conceptions of "self." In the process, Bockover explains how all the various systems of Western ethics embrace a central objective and challenge that give rise to a concept of person qua abstract individual. By way of contrast, she then examines the main concern and challenge of "ethics" according to Confucian philosophy and describes how the concept of person qua inherently social being emerges in this system of thought. Finally, she argues that even these clearly differing views of ethics and self share a common predicament: ethical indeterminacy.

In Chapter 4, "Classical Confucian and Contemporary Feminist Perspectives on the Self: Some Parallels and Their Implications," Henry Rosemont, Jr., considers several recent feminist critiques of philosophy, finding many parallels with classical Confucianism. In most contemporary Western discourse in moral and political philosophy, the self is characterized as an autonomous, rights-bearing individual. Rosemont contrasts this view of the self with the ancient Confucian concept of the role-carrying person, claiming, first, that the latter closely approximates the caring person described in much current feminist writing in the West and, second, that this Confucian/feminist person is more appropriate to the analysis of moral problems than is the autonomous, rights-bearing individual.

In Chapter 5, "Buddho-Taoist and Western Metaphysics of the Self," Kenneth K. Inada claims that our experiential locus stems from the nature of becoming. But whereas the discourse of Western philosophers is grounded in the concept of being, that of Buddhists and Taoists is grounded in the concept of nonbeing. The difference is great, and in many ways it informs us of the subtle variations in Eastern and Western cultures. Indeed, the tension between being and nonbeing has never been resolved. Inada further probes the nature of becoming by introducing the novel concepts of symmetric and asymmetric components. These components, he argues, form the foundation of becoming prior to the rise of being and nonbeing, and in doing so they help us to understand the being-nonbeing dynamics in our approach to the metaphysics of the self.

In Chapter 6, "Reducing Concern with Self: Parfit and the Ancient Buddhist Schools," Ananyo Basu compares Derek Parfit's reductionist view of self with various Buddhist perspectives on the self. Basu begins with an exegesis of Parfit's perspectives on personal identity and self and cites some of Parfit's responses to his critics. In particular, he considers the attempt by David Bastow to expand Parfit's reductionist view along Buddhist lines and indicates some of the weaknesses in that approach. Basu's survey of competing, early Buddhist schools demonstrates that there is no perfect fit between Parfit's view of self and the Buddhist views of same. Basu concludes by advocating reliance on the Madhyamika school so as to provide a reliable reductionist, anti-essentialist approach to self. He believes that this form of Buddhism will provide the best insights and most promising directions for contemporary philosophical approaches to self.

In Chapter 7, "Sartre and Samkhya-Yoga on Self," Ashok Malhotra delineates six perspectives on the self presented by Jean-Paul Sartre in his work *Being and Nothingness.* Sartre views the self as a consciousness, an ego, a body, a social entity, a value, and an egoless being. Malhotra compares and contrasts Sartre's position with the Samkhya-Yoga view of the self as consciousness, *buddhi, ahamkara, manas,* the sense-motor organ complex, and ego-less reality. Although there are major ontological differences between the two positions, Malhotra submits that they are similar in spirit.

In Chapter 8, "Nietzsche and Nishitani on Nihilism and Tradition," Graham Parkes describes the profound influence of Friedrich Nietzsche on Nishitani Keiji, a Kyoto School philosopher in the tradition of Zen. It is clear from Nishitani's 1949 text, *The Self-Overcoming of Nihilism,* that he shares with Nietzsche the idea that the self "becomes what it is" through the confrontation with nihilism. The realization that "the highest values have devalued themselves"—as Nietzsche characterized the nihilistic condition—frees one from the bonds of cultural tradition, thus, in a sense, relieving one of the burden of the past. Similarly, according to Nishitani, the confrontation with nihilism effects a realization of the self's identity with *mu,* or nothingness, which in turn distances the self from the conditioning factors of the past. In short, Nietzsche and Nishitani concur that if one is able to sustain the confrontation with nihilism, letting the self plumb the phenomenon to its utmost depths, a kind of turn takes place in which nihilism ultimately "overcomes itself." For Parkes, the interesting question to be asked regarding this commonality is, What does each thinker regard as the appropriate relationship to one's traditional culture after the break occasioned by nihilism has taken place? Nietzsche is often misunderstood to have been advocating a completely new start, untrammeled by tradition of any kind. But a comparison with Nishitani's prescriptions for the successful self-overcoming of nihilism shows us that what Nietzsche really had in mind was a "reappropriation" of the tradition through a kind of "intellectual nomadism."

In Chapter 9, "Views of Japanese Selfhood: Japanese and Western Perspectives," Mara Miller argues that scholars (and others) often mistakenly claim that selfhood in Japan is completely unlike selfhood in the West. As a partial explanation for this error, Miller cites the popular as well as scholarly misconception of the Japanese as lacking in creativity, originality, independence, and moral autonomy. She also examines some of the theoretical problems, solutions, and critiques regarding the study of Japanese selfhood by social scientists. Finally, Miller points to examples of autonomy and creativity in traditional Japanese religion and language, noting that many such instances have been hidden from Western observers by our methodologies or theoretical assumptions and preferences. What emerges from Miller's chapter, then, is a recognition of the complexities of the Japanese self, which, at least in some respects, comes closer to Western views of self than we might think.

Culture and Self

Part One

Multiple Asian and Western Perspectives

Chapter One

Social Constructions of Self: Some Asian, Marxist, and Feminist Critiques of Dominant Western Views of Self

DOUGLAS ALLEN

Examination of the nature of self has been one of the key concerns of both Eastern and Western philosophers.[1] With a few significant exceptions, such as the teachings of the Buddha or various forms of relativism and skepticism, traditional philosophers have argued in favor of views upholding the reality of an ahistoric, objective, universal, "true," or authentic, self.[2] Traditional philosophers could not avoid recognizing that various concepts of self were historically and culturally constituted; but they typically described these concepts as subjective, superficial, illusory, and inadequate, as veiling or distorting the deeper, underlying, objective view of the self that transcended such historical and cultural expressions.

My approach to uncovering and analyzing constructions of self differs from that of most traditional philosophers. Concepts and images of self appear in the most privileged texts. They are "given" in the sense of being constructed by dominant socioeconomic, cultural, scientific, philosophical, religious, and other social forces. These constructions of self are presented in traditional philosophies as expressing the objective, universal, true self. Alternative, even oppositional, self-images also appear in less privileged texts.

Not all self-images are such apparent dominant or secondary "givens." Many must be uncovered and deciphered. Often we are unaware of the extent to which our own self-images have been assumed and internalized, having been socialized into a world of given images not of our own making. But we do not simply incorporate those images of particular self-constructions in a passive, static, completely deterministic manner. There remains the complex question of how such self-images are mediated, contextualized, and reinterpreted.

Philosophical, religious, and cultural self-images are reconstituted, revalorized, and reinterpreted in many different ways. To understand how given self images have been constructed, interpreted, and lived, one must grasp specific, dynamic variables defining one's historical and cultural context and shedding light on how given self-images have been reconstituted in new creative ways.

Toward this end, I initially present some general, nontraditional observations on the dynamic relation of texts, contexts, and interpretation. I then briefly formulate a "traditional" philosophical approach to "the self" by focusing on the most influential philosophical orientation: "modern," Western views of self, especially arising from the orientation of René Descartes, for whom a correct analysis of the self constituted the foundation of his entire philosophy. This "modern" Western philosophical tradition was developed through the key contributions of such formative philosophers as Thomas Hobbes, John Locke, and David Hume. These philosophers rejected the particular Cartesian metaphysics underlying Descartes' view of self, and they disagreed with each other, even to the extent that a Humean critique raised doubt as to whether "the self" had any objective status. But they all assumed a general, shared orientation, expressing highly atomistic, individualistic, essentially nonsocial, egoistic views of the self—an orientation that has defined most of "modern philosophy."[3]

Next I present four alternative approaches to the self: Hinduism, especially the analysis of the path of *karma yoga* in the *Bhagavad-Gita;* Buddhism, especially the Buddha's analysis of *anatta;* Marxism, especially Marx's analysis of the modern capitalist self; and feminism, especially de Beauvoir's analysis of the patriarchal or masculinist self. For those familiar with these four approaches, my brief presentations may seem rather undeveloped and noncontroversial.

My use of these four alternative analyses of self suggests that such a modern, Western, philosophical orientation is historically and culturally constituted. Although my position avoids unilinear reductionism and facile relativism, I submit that one cannot understand concepts of self without also understanding the historical, cultural, social, economic, moral, and aesthetic contexts within which such concepts are constituted and verified philosophically and experientially.

In a subsequent section, I attempt to relate the Hindu, Buddhist, Marxist, and feminist approaches to self with their critiques of the dominant, modern, Western constructions of self. These approaches are significantly different from one another, yet also complementary. Moreover, each approach contributes to the development of a more adequate analysis of self in areas where the others are undeveloped or reveal deficiencies.

Another section follows in which I delineate several respects in which one can speak of a commonality of humanity, but a commonality with a respect for differences. Through a series of fragmented points, I suggest that much recent scholarship may have gone too far in insisting on the primacy of cultural diversity and differences in our constructions of self. But such discussions of the commonality of humankind tend to be on a rather abstract level of analysis. We must reaffirm and strengthen our profound sense of commonality while at the same time recognizing that different concepts of self reflect changing historical and cultural conditions, allowing no specific concept of self to claim exclusive, eternal, ahistoric, universal, objective truth.

In the concluding section, I distinguish between the two aims developed in this chapter: the major aim of presenting a variety of critiques of a dominant, modern Western approach to "the self"; and a second, less developed aim of offering some suggestions as to what alternative approach or direction might be taken in providing a more adequate approach to self.

Texts, Contexts, and Interpretation

During my research in India in 1992, the most interesting challenges to my attempt to relate Hindu, Buddhist, Marxist, and feminist critiques concerned the nature of texts, contexts, and interpretation. For example, an economist in Calcutta claimed that "the ideas of the *Bhagavad-Gita* should be analyzed on their own terms," as differentiated from attempts to contextualize them. And a philosopher at Banaras Hindu University forcefully argued that I was "totally confused," that I was mixing texts that had nothing to do with each other. "The *Gita*," he said, "has nothing to do with feminist perspectives. . . . We know what the Buddha was thinking from the original Pali texts." These criticisms reflected traditional philosophical and scholarly approaches to texts that I once accepted.

To the same criticisms I responded by asking "Which *Bhagavad-Gita?*" The contemplative monistic text of Shankara Vedanta philosophy? The metaphysically dualistic text of Sankhya philosophy? The emotionally charged, devotional, theistic, *bhakti* text? The action-oriented *karma yoga* text of Mohandas Gandhi? The various twentieth-century, nationalistic readings of the text? The *Gita* of two thousand years ago or of today? The text of various religious elites or of diverse masses of peasants? If the *Gita* does not present feminist perspectives, are questions about sexism and other hierarchical forms of domination irrelevant to self-constructions in the text? Aren't textual silences and omissions often pregnant with meaning and significant in interpreting texts?

My view is that Cartesian and other modern Western formulations, as well as the *Gita,* the teachings of Buddha, and Marxist and feminist writings, involve struggle and contestation, with some insights and interpretations being suppressed and silenced and others being textualized and gaining authority. My experiences in Sri Lanka and India made clear that people in different historical and cultural contexts have interpreted the Buddhist Pali Canon or the Hindu *Ramayana* in radically different ways. To abstract and fetishize a text as free from all contextual determinants and then to contend that masses of peasants or Sinhalese Buddhists or Ayodhya Hindus "got it wrong" or "got it right" does not seem to be an adequate approach to the nature of self-constructions or even to the nature of texts.

What I concluded from such challenges in India and elsewhere is that there exists a dynamic, complex, dialectical relationship between texts and contexts. When we read texts, we are continually rereading, retelling, recreating, and reinterpreting—processes that are based, at least partially, on changing cultural, socioeconomic, religious, philosophical, and other contextual influences. My reading of the *Gita* is not identical with the reading of an orthodox, Vedantic Shankara almost twelve hundred years ago. Rather, to some extent my reading is always something new. It is informed by my understanding of Shankara's interpretation, as taught to me at a young age by orthodox Hindus in Banaras, but it is also informed by the more socially activist readings of Mohandas Gandhi and by gender, caste, class, and other voices that were silenced or camouflaged in earlier cultural contexts. When I try to compare and contrast alternative self-constructions, I would agree that I am "confusing" the issue by "mixing" different perspectives, but only if I were to retain some inadequate, essentialist, ahistorical, absolute, decontextualized interpretation of texts. What I am trying to do instead is to provide new, creative readings, interpretations, and constructions of texts that are always to some extent contextualized.

At the same time, I do not want to assume the rather fashionable, subjectivist position that "anything goes": To privilege certain criteria and argue that certain readings or interpretations are more adequate than others would be to impose a view made possible by a relatively superior position in the context of contemporary power relations. Texts are always contextualized and are continually created and recreated as part of a dynamic cultural process; but texts are not infinitely malleable. They are extremely flexible and can be revalorized in the most unexpected ways, but specific texts have forms and structures, serve functions, and disclose limits and boundaries in their constructions of self.

"Modern" Western Concepts of the Self

What comes to mind when we think of our own "self" or of some other "person"?[4] Jitendra Nath Mohanty indicates that the systematically ambiguous first-person pronoun *I* refers, first, to the person I am; second, to my self; third, to the subject that I also am; and fourth, to my ego.[5] But for the purposes of this chapter, I'll emphasize that human beings in the modern industrial and technological societies of the West have tended to assume, both for one's own self and for other selves, some view of a person as a separate, independent, autonomous, I-me individual or ego. Most of our modern Western concepts of self have had Cartesian epistemological roots.[6]

Let us simply note several characteristics defining this Cartesian approach to self.[7] First, in developing an ancient philosophical tradition that assumes that the real is the rational—so that the more rational we become, the more in touch with reality we are—Descartes accepted as true only what is "clear and distinct" to the rational mind, and he privileged mind over body. Indeed, having a body is not essential to Descartes' analysis of the self as a thinking thing. Second, this thinking thing of which I can be certain is a separate and individual self, rather than a social and relational self. I come to know this self in isolation, independent of other persons. Indeed, all of my relations to others have been subjected to methodological doubt. Third, this thinking thing or mind can be more certain of its own existence than of the existence of anything else; thus established is knowledge of my own separate self as the starting point and foundation of my philosophy. Fourth, since I can be certain only of my own existence and even then only when I am doubting or thinking, I am threatened by a pervasive skepticism and the prospect of a self-imprisoned solipsism. This is why so much of Western philosophy since Descartes has been defined by the attempt to overcome an ego-defined solipsism and to formulate and verify an objective, ego-oriented world of meaning.

Finally, knowledge of the self as separate, autonomous, thinking thing is not historically and culturally constituted. The essential self is something one has, observes, and analyzes—not something one creates. Claims involving historical and cultural variables can be subjected to methodological doubt, but any rational person will accept the existence of the self as an individual thinking thing.

Modern Western social and political philosophies, especially those with Hobbesian and Lockean roots, have usually started with an assumed condition of rather isolated and insulated individuals, existing in some "state of nature," and have then postulated how these atomistic selves could come together through some "social contract" to establish a legitimate state. Influential capitalist political economists, such as Adam Smith and David Ricardo, have also assumed a human condition of separate I-me individuals and then theorized how these atomistic selves could interact to establish a rationally ordered economy.

Those of us in the West are socialized to accept variations of the concept of the modern self, the autonomous individual, as an integral part of our political, legal, economic, cultural, and educational systems. We have an educational system in which students are assigned separate grades for their separate work. We have an economic system in which individuals sell their labor power for a separate wage and are bombarded with commercials that present models of individual success by maximizing separate ego possession and consumption of commodities. In all such contexts, we carry within ourselves variations of the autonomous individual as inseparable from what it is to be a true self. Most of us assume that our views of the self are not culturally and historically constituted but are "natural," objective, ahistorical, nonpolitical, rational, ethical, and universally applicable.

When missionaries (including contemporary political and economic "missionaries" in Washington and elsewhere), anthropologists, philosophers, and other westerners have encountered Asian, African, Latin American, Native American, and other views of self (including many female views of self in the West), they have often dismissed or devalued these other views—which seem to lack a separate, independent, I-me self—as premodern, backward, subjective, irrational, immoral, and relegated to a lower evolutionary stage of development.

There have been many recent critiques of this construction of self as the "modern," "liberal," largely isolated and insulated autonomous individual— namely, socialist, Marxist, anarchist, feminist, Third Worldist, pragmatist, "poststructuralist," and "postmodernist" critiques; but also various "conservative" critiques, such as those implicit in Alasdair MacIntyre's essentially neo-Aristotelian social ideal and in Thomist and other theological positions, especially militant fundamentalisms that reflect precapitalist and premodern concepts of self. Contemporary feminists have analyzed dominant concepts of the "nonrelational," individual self as "patriarchal" and "masculinist." Marxists and socialists have analyzed such self concepts as reflecting capitalist historical developments. And many Asian, African, Latin American, and Native American scholars have analyzed such concepts as "Western" or "Eurocentric."

In this section I have examined aspects of the dominant, modern, Western approach to self with its hegemonic claims toward ahistoric, transcultural objectivity and universality. The fact that so many modern Western philosophers have assumed that their concepts of self were not socially, culturally, and historically constituted may seem to have some basis in common sense. Each of us does have a separate body, a separate nervous system, a separate physical identity. But the existence of a separate biological or physical identity does not in itself account for an ahistoric and universal concept of "the self" or "the person." Such a concept always involves a filling in, a completion, an interpretation. The concept of self as separate, atomistic, private, autonomous individual has been constituted by specific, complex, social, economic, historical, cultural, and psychological relations. It is my position that such a modern, Western self-claim to ahistoric rationality and universal objectivity not only is philosophically inadequate but also serves neo-colonial and imperial goals of domination.

"Alternative" Concepts of the Self

Hinduism: The Bhagavad-Gita

In the *Bhagavad-Gita*,[8] Arjuna is visited by fears and doubts, having become immobilized as he considers whether to fight or withdraw from the battlefield—a decision for which either outcome is likely to have negative results. Krishna instructs Arjuna that he has no choice but to act, since even inaction is itself an action. Arjuna's action must be based on accurate self-knowledge of his *karma* and on fulfilling his *dharma* without allowing egoistic inclinations to interfere with his sense of duty. His must be a selfless attitude with no ego-attachment to the results of his actions. Krishna describes many yogas—including *karma* (action), *bhakti* (devotion), and *jñana* (knowledge)—all of which deny that the finite, empirical, separate ego is the permanent self and offer paths to ego-transcendence. In other words, characteristics usually essential to modern concepts of the self are presented in the *Gita* as defining the constitution of a false or illusory self, and the *Gita* proposes means for transcending such self-constitutions as essential to spiritual liberation.

The nature of the relative world, unlike the spiritual reality of *purusha* or *Atman/Brahman,* is mutability, and the individual person is constituted by one's "consciousness of ego" (VIII.3–4). The true devotee must free oneself "from the delusion of 'I' and 'mine,'" from the ego and its selfishness (XII.13–14). A yogi must gain total "control over one's ego," "caring nothing for the fruit of action" (VI.1, 36).

The actions of those who have not renounced the self and its desires bring the fruit of *karma* and continued bondage in the world of *maya,* "but those who have renounced the ego and desire will reap no fruit at all, either in this world or in the next" (XVIII.12). By dedicating all actions to Krishna, with consciousness fixed in the true, nonegoistic Self (*Atman*), "being free from desire and egoism," Arjuna is to fulfill his duty by fighting (III.30). And according to the *Gita*'s distinctive analysis of *karma yoga,* such selfless action, free from characteristics that define modern Western concepts of the self, involves renunciation of any ego-attachment to the fruit of one's action (e.g., II.47–52, III.7, 19, IV.19–23).

One who has abandoned ego-desires and cravings and is free from self/ego and "any sense of mineness and egotism" transcends karmic bondage and experiences peace (II.71; XVIII.17). "And casting aside self-sense, force, arrogance, desire, anger, possession, egoless and tranquil of mind, [such a person] becomes worthy of becoming one with *Brahman*" (XVIII.53).

Unlike the self described by Cartesian and other modern views, the true immutable Self actually "does nothing"; egoistic orientations create the "delusion" that our individual self is the doer. Actions are performed by the *gunas*, but a person, "deluded by one's egoism, thinks: 'I am the doer'" (e.g., III.27, XIII.20–21, XVIII.16).

Many passages of the *Gita* (e.g., III.30, VII.4–5, 13–14), utilizing Sankhya cosmology, analyze this "delusion" in terms of the *ahamkara* ("I-maker," the ego). The *ahamkara*, part of the evolution of *prakriti* (nature), is constituted by the three *gunas* and expresses our "lower nature" in *maya*. It is the ego-function at the center of the "delusion" in which we mistakenly refer experiences to an "I," thus confusing *prakriti* with the true Self or spirit (*purusha*). Whether we emphasize the path of selfless action, selfless knowledge, or selfless devotion to God, the *Gita* insists on the need to overcome our egoistic desires and attachments and to transcend our identification with the ego/separate self.

We need not focus on the *Gita*'s metaphysics, which, in several differing formulations, maintains that there is a true eternal Self free from historical and cultural constitutions. Rather, the key point here is that according to the *Gita*, modern Western concepts of the separate, atomistic, egoistic, I-me, autonomous, individual self should be analyzed as historically and culturally constituted, as illusory creations arising from ignorance and veiling knowledge of our true Self.

Mohandas Gandhi wrote of the *Gita*'s distinctive path of *karma yoga* in terms that clearly contrast with the ego-oriented, ego-attached world of the modern Western self. The practitioner of *karma yoga*, he said, "is a devotee who is jealous of none, who is a fount of mercy, who is without egotism, who is selfless, who treats alike cold and heat, happiness and misery." Such a person is one who acts with a spirit of nonattachment to results, "good or bad, who treats friend and foe alike, who is untouched by respect and disrespect, who is not puffed up by praise, who does not go under when people speak ill of him [or her]." Gandhi concluded that such a philosophical and religious approach "is inconsistent with the existence at the same time of strong attachments."[9]

Buddhism: The Buddha's Teaching of Anatta

Perhaps more than any other major figure in the history of philosophy and religion, Siddhartha Gautama, the Buddha, emphasized that our concepts of the self or ego are illusory, that an ego-constructed world is essential to our

ignorance and suffering, and that freedom or liberation entails self-transcendence—or, since there is no substantial self, transcendence of the illusion of
the self. Many interpreters thus define Buddhism as a philosophy of "not-
self." Here we shall briefly consider the Buddha's foundational teaching of
no-self (*anatta*) in terms of the concepts of self/ego that are analyzed as illusory constructions essential to our suffering and mode of being in the realm
of *samsara* (the worldly cycles of birth and rebirth).

In "The Three Characteristics" ("Signs of Being," or "Signata") of all finite phenomena in the cycles of existence, the Buddha states: "It remains a
fact, and the fixed and necessary constitution of being, that all its elements
are lacking in an ego."[10] Representative of critiques of self/ego found in the
canonical literature on no-self (*anatta*)[11] is the following: The Buddha does
not deem it fitting to consider any of the five aggregates of attachment (i.e.,
the body, feeling, perception, the predispositions/impressions, and consciousness), "which are impermanent, painful, and subject to change," as
"this is mine, this am I, this is my ego (soul, self)."

According to the "Characteristic" of *anicca,* everything is "impermanent";
in the continuous becoming of lived experience, we find no permanent, unchanging, everlasting entity such as a self or soul. That which we tend to call
an ego or self is merely a combination of ever-changing physical and mental
states. The composite constructed self or person creates the illusion of a permanent individual self, thus preventing us from experiencing the flow of
continuous becoming. This imaginary false belief in an independent separate
self is essential to the generation of our selfish desires, greed, craving, hatred,
and ego-attachments.

In the Buddha's teachings of the Four Noble Truths,[12] we find that the aggregates of attachment, which create the illusion of the "individual" or "I,"
are *dukkha* (suffering, impermanence, the human condition); that *tanha*
(craving, desiring), as the immediate cause of *dukkha,* has at its center of attachment (*upadana*) the false concept of a self; and that the overcoming of
dukkha, by eliminating *tanha,* consists in the extinction of the illusory concept of an individual self. This experiential realization of reality is denoted in
Pali texts as *nana-dassana:* insight, "seeing with wisdom," "seeing things as
they really are."

Also according to the Buddha's teachings, this imaginary false belief in a
self/ego, far from being a harmless epistemological error, "produces harmful
thoughts of 'me' and 'mine,' selfish desire, craving, attachment, hatred, ill-
will, conceit, pride, egoism, and other defilements, impurities and problems.
It is the source of all the troubles in the world from personal conflicts to
wars between nations. In short, to this false view can be traced all the evil in
the world."[13]

Both the Hindu and the Buddhist critiques we have considered maintain
that our modern concepts of a separate individual self are finite, empirical,
and temporal constructions of the world of *maya* or *samsara.* Such histori-

cally and culturally constituted concepts create a world of bondage and illusion through the generation of ego-desires and attachments. According to the *Gita,* the constituted, unstable, false self, structured by the *gunas,* disguises the basic unity and permanence of unchanging *purusha* or *Brahman/Atman;* and through illusion, it fragments and renders impermanent the immutable nature of the true Self. For the Buddha, the constituted concepts of an unstable, false self, structured by the aggregates of attachment or *skandhas,* disguise the basic flow of continuous becoming of lived experience; in short, such concepts unify and create a static illusion that there is some reality corresponding to the belief in a permanent individual self or ego.

While maintaining that concepts of self are historically and culturally constituted, these traditional Hindu and Buddhist critiques of the construction of the individual separate self are very general and abstract and reflect what is essentially an ahistorical approach. The analysis of the illusory concepts of self really transcends any specific historical and cultural conditions and expresses the general human condition within the context of the world of *maya* or *samsara,* the karmic cycles of ignorance and bondage. We now turn to a very different approach to the analysis of self concepts—one that includes modern Western formulations as constituted by specific historical and cultural developments.

Marxism: Marx's Analysis of the Capitalist Self

Like Krishna and the Buddha in their analyses of the humanly constructed self or ego, Karl Marx maintained that our concepts of the self are socially and historically constituted; that our egoistic orientation is central to suffering and bondage; and, at least in terms of class societies, that such self-constructions must be transcended if we are to experience higher stages of human realization.

In *The Ethnological Notebooks,* Marx demonstrated that individualism dominated by egoism and greed is premodern, but he usually focused on modern capitalism as representing the culmination of this historical development. In this connection, the factors he considered included the destruction of traditional social bonds; the dominance of concepts emphasizing isolated, self-sufficient, ego-oriented individuals; and the hegemony of theories of modern individualism assuming, justifying, and promoting such historically constituted concepts.

Marx criticized the adherents of such modern theories for assuming what needs to be explained. Political economists and social contract theorists assume modern forms of alienated labor, property relations, competition, selfishness, and the capitalist division of labor to be ahistorical eternal laws of nature; they falsely universalize the specific historically and culturally formed characteristics of the modern, isolated, independent, egoistic individual as constituting human nature as such.[14]

In *Capital* and elsewhere, Marx analyzed capitalism as a mode of production in which egoistic individuals exploit the labor of others in order to extract surplus value, which is the basis of profit and the key to the accumulation of capital and wealth. It is not some ahistoric, eternal aspect of the self to be egoistic and exploitative. The laws of capital accumulation, especially those structures essential to the mechanism for extracting surplus value, ensure that capitalists must function in this manner or else be driven from the market. Capitalist relations of production constitute a system of human relations of separate selves with their egoistic desires, needs, and attachments. Marx presents the foregoing analysis at length in the first of three volumes of *Capital*.[15]

In his "German Ideology," Marx provided a historical materialist basis for analyzing specific concepts of the self.[16] The nature of individuals, he wrote, depends on the material conditions determining their production. Therefore, modern Western constructions of self must be socially and historically situated in terms of the primacy of capitalist production. For example, capitalism could not develop until feudal and other precapitalist modes had been undermined so that individuals as "modern" human beings conceived of themselves—or, more often, were coerced into acting—as atomistic, separate selves "free" to sell their labor power for a wage. The primacy of the modern ego or self in culture and ideology, in the legal and educational systems as well as in philosophy and religion, expresses specific concepts of self consistent with capitalist production. The revolutionary transcendence of capitalism thus requires the transcendence of the "modern" self or person with its intended world.

Indeed, in a claim that would have surprised neither Buddha nor Krishna in the *Gita,* Marx submitted that the transcendence of the separate, egoistic self will result in a state of liberation in which there is a qualitative difference in our human faculties and in our concept of what it is to be a fulfilled self. In our egoistic orientation, clearly expressed in modern constructions of self, all of our physical and mental senses have been reduced to "the sense of having," of possessing, of consuming. In transcending the modern ego and its private property relations, need and enjoyment will have "lost their egotistical nature"; the human senses and attributes will become completely "emancipated"; they will become truly "human."[17]

In short, Marx would have regarded modern Western constructions of self dialectically, revealing positive historical developments, inherent structures of oppression, exploitation, and alienation, and contradictions allowing for their reconstitution and transcendence. He also would have regarded any assumption of an ahistoric, static view of the self as revealing a hidden agenda, usually grounded today in a context of modern capitalist relations of production and ideologies. Marx would have emphasized that modern Western and other specific concepts of self must be situated and interpreted as being historically and culturally constituted.

Feminism: De Beauvoir's Analysis of the Masculinist Self

As with the other "alternative" formulations considered in this chapter, we must be selective in dealing with the concept of the masculinist self.[18] There are many kinds of feminists, but no single unifying feminist construction of self and, for that matter, no single feminist critique of modern Western concepts of self.[19]

A well-known anti-essentialist, anti-Cartesian approach was taken by Simone de Beauvoir in *The Second Sex,* probably the most influential, feminist theoretical work. In her existentialist feminist approach, de Beauvoir upheld the Sartrean principle that "existence precedes essence"; in other words, there are no ahistoric, immutable, eternal, universal essences, whether of "the feminine," "the masculine," or "the self." Hence all constituted essences, including those expressed in modern Western concepts of the self, have to be situated as specific historical and cultural creations.

In contrast to Descartes' concept of the isolated, self-sufficient, reflecting ego is de Beauvoir's relational view of self: "The other," she argued, is a necessary structure of human consciousness, and one can define oneself as a self and develop as a self-transcending self only in relation to that which is other or not-self.[20] What concerns de Beauvoir about the history of sexist human relations is that "male" has been constituted (by men) as "the self," "the subject," "the absolute," and "the essential," whereas "female" has been constituted (again, by men) as "the other," "the object," "the relative," and "the inessential." Woman, in her "immanence," has been historically and culturally defined and objectified as "the other," and thus denied the capacity and power for self-transcendence as an "autonomous being."

Further, since woman has been constituted as "the other," as not-self, it is not surprising that the essential characteristics defining modern Western concepts of "the self"—rationality, objectivity, autonomy, independence, and so on—have been socialized by a male-dominated sexist society as more essential or characteristic of men than of women. Accordingly, de Beauvoir's feminist project, at least in *The Second Sex,* is to establish more symmetrical self-other relations so that both women and men have the capacity to realize their potential for freedom as self-transcending subjects.[21]

Carol Gilligan, in her widely read and influential book, *In a Different Voice,* illustrates de Beauvoir's general claim that women have been defined and interpreted as less developed selves or not-selves.[22] Gilligan focuses on the psychological-development framework of Lawrence Kohlberg, who posits six stages of moral development with corresponding progressive developments in how one views oneself. Many characteristics of modern, Western constructions of self are reflected on this scale: autonomous thinking, abstract rationality, "postconventional" universality (which frees one from culturally constituted limitations), and recognition of and respect for individual rights, dignity, and justice. What initially troubled Gilligan, however, is that Kohlberg's studies and her own seemed to confirm a contention made by Freud: that women, who rarely exceed stage 3 of Kohlberg's scale, are less morally developed than men.

The problem, Gilligan later proposed, lies with Kohlberg's scale and not women's lack of morality. Through her interviews with women about abortion, she concluded that women are just as concerned as men about moral reasoning, but they tend to characterize moral and self-development "in a different voice." In other words, women tend to be concerned with specific, concrete situations rather than with principles of abstract rationality and universality; with functioning as interdependent selves-in-relations rather than as autonomous independent individuals; with maintaining caring relations and determining how their actions might affect everyone involved rather than with making decisions based on noncontextualized principles of justice and duty.

Although Gilligan does not want to posit an essentialist ahistoric theory of female and male moralities, she also does not explore the basis of these differently gendered constructions of self and moral development.[23] Nancy Chodorow, Nancy Hartsock, and other feminists argue that differently gendered relations of production and reproduction, different resolutions of childhood psychological conflicts over sexual and gender identity, and different patterns of male-dominated socialization establish specific contexts within which concepts of self, including characteristics of post-Cartesian Western formulations, are historically and culturally constituted.

Relating the Critiques: Several Suggestions

We have briefly considered several traditional as well as recent critiques of a construction of self that has dominated much of modern Western cultural, political, economic, social, ethical, and philosophical life. According to these critiques, all of which view freedom and liberation in terms of ego-transcendence, our egoistic cultural orientation is central to suffering, oppression, exploitation, alienation, bondage, and illusion.

Again, I must emphasize the degree to which I have oversimplified the great diversity of critiques of the ego/self within Hindu, Buddhist, Marxist, and feminist philosophies. In actuality, of course, there are significant differences among these four "alternative" approaches to the modern Western self. Some theorists critique the historical and cultural construction of the ego and argue the essentialist position that posits a true, transcultural self or non-

self. Others argue that all concepts of self are historically and culturally constituted and that none is justified in claiming that it expresses the "true" or
"essential" self. I will now briefly suggest a few possible relations among
Hindu-Buddhist, Marxist, and feminist approaches as represented by
Krishna in the *Gita,* the teachings of Buddha, and the writings of Karl Marx
and Simone de Beauvoir.

For Buddha and Krishna, the ego and its egoistic orientation have epistemic but not ontological status. Right knowledge destroys the illusory belief in the reality of the ego and its intended world. We experience a nonegoistic reality that was always "there"; it is our perspective, not reality, that has
changed. For Marx and de Beauvoir, the modern ego may be "illusory" in
the sense of being a constructed alienated self, but it is "real" as the creation
of an ongoing human project. For all of its negativity, the modern capitalist
and masculinist ego is a cultural and historical development and creates specific preconditions for its transcendence and the experience of less oppressive, less exploitative, more fulfilling constructions of self.

Krishna and Buddha, while agreeing with much of Marx's and many feminist critiques of the nature of an ego-structured world, would have con-
tended that formulations of nonegoistic feminist and communist selves are
still constructions within *maya* and *samsara,* the cycles of karmic bondage.
From their perspectives, Marx and de Beauvoir appear naive in not fully understanding our human mode of being in the word; their communism and
feminism, with nonegoistic individuals, are illusory utopias, unattainable
human projections.

Marx and de Beauvoir, while agreeing with much of the Hindu-Buddhist
analyses of ego-craving and attachment, would have countered that such
spiritual perspectives remain deficient. Ahistorical abstractions do not allow
for the specificity necessary to understand particular cultural, social, historical, and material conditions within which the ego is constructed and transcended. These Asian spiritual goals do little to overcome real oppression
and exploitation. Rather, our project is to constitute a world that is more
genuinely human—a constructed world in which those obstacles that pre-
vent the realization of our potential as new, more developed selves have been
overcome.

But traditional perspectives of the *Gita* and the Buddha, in their analyses
of the ego and their goals of ego-transcendence, are not primarily interested
in establishing a world that is "genuinely human." Nonegoistic freedom
from suffering and bondage entails the transcendence of even those conditions essential to Marxist and feminist imaginative idealizations of unalien-
ated, nonexploitative, nonsexist selves.

The four alternative approaches discussed here are, as noted, not only significantly different from one another in their critiques of the construction of
the modern self, but also complementary. It may be that Hindu and Bud-

dhist perspectives, without more focus on the contextualized specificity of political, economic, cultural, and historical variables, remain incomplete, leaving most human beings oppressed and alienated, inadequate to deal with historical and cultural ego-transcending experiences, and often appearing as escapes from reality. Marx and de Beauvoir's analyses of capitalist and masculinist ego-construction may provide a greater sense of such historical, economic, and cultural specificity.

It may be that Marxist economic and political perspectives, without certain personal and spiritual dimensions, remain incomplete, leaving most human beings alienated and unfulfilled, inadequate to deal with various personal, intersubjective, emotional, imaginative, psychological, and aesthetic ego-transcending experiences. Hindu, Buddhist, and feminist analyses may focus more attention on various "subjective" dimensions of ego-formation and ego-world-structuring, including the need to overcome ego-desiring attachments, a priority usually absent among Marxists, who have often tended to replicate characteristics of the capitalist and masculinist self. Indeed, Asian philosophical analyses may help some Marxists and other westerners understand why they become imprisoned in their own egos and ego-constructions; why, for example, they react to criticism of something they've said or written by feeling personally attacked and vulnerable, and becoming defensive and even aggressive.

Finally, it may be that many recent feminist perspectives, with their emphasis on personal and subjective dimensions of particular embodied selves and, often, their reactions against abstract theorizing, remain incomplete as well, leaving unanalyzed larger economic, political, and cultural structures of domination. Marxist approaches may focus more attention on how specific features of (masculinist) ego-construction are situated within general socio-economic and cultural relations of power and on how gender-construction might be related to class, imperialist, and other historical developments. And in its emphasis on the subjective and psychological dimensions of ego-formation, feminism may learn from centuries of focus on this concern by Hindu and Buddhist philosophies.

Commonality with Differences

In India, responses to my comparative research were often consistent with recent philosophical developments in the West. Occasionally I was challenged by traditional brahmins, Vedantists, and other scholars who emphasized the essential unity and oneness of humankind and rejected as superficial or even illusory any focus on cultural diversity and differences in analyzing constructions of self. Indeed, when I first arrived in India in 1963–1964, these challenges were the most common responses among Indian philosophers; but today the situation is often reversed. Reacting against

"Orientalism" and Western ethnocentrism, and influenced by cultural relativism, multiculturalism, deconstructionism, feminism, and postmodernism, most of those who interacted with my research project were determined to reclaim, construct, and preserve irreducible "differences." They were very suspicious of any discussion of essential unity, commonality, or universality. Some correctly challenged my use of the terms *East, West* and *Indian*, pointing out the tremendous diversity among views of self. Several questioned whether my conclusion regarding our "commonality" as human beings—our "unity with differences"—was just another "modern, Western project."

Through such challenges I have been able to clarify my project as anti-essentialist in traditional terms, yet I want to avoid the rather fashionable, unlimited relativism that I find methodologically, conceptually, and practically inadequate. What I offer in this section is a series of rather fragmented points suggesting that the pendulum may have swung too far in the opposite direction in our insistence on the primacy of cultural diversity and differences in self-constructions.

First, the emphasis on the historical and cultural constitution of concepts of self can lead not only to a critique of modern, Western self-claims to universal ahistoric objectivity but also to a critique of all claims by constituted concepts of self to any sort of commonality, generality, objectivity, or relation to reality. In some of the most influential contemporary philosophical approaches, this emphasis can lead to extreme relativism.

This contemporary philosophical tendency is evident in the writings of many "postmodern feminists," especially those who, in the context of Lacanian and Derridian deconstructionism, identify with the French writers Hélène Cixous, Luce Irigaray, and Julia Kristeva. Such postmodern feminists emphasize differences, multiplicity, and plurality of constructed selves and reject the imposition of any dominant philosophical models that deny the rich plurality of otherness. In doing so, they reject not only modern concepts of "the self" but also the general claims of Hindu, Buddhist, Marxist, and many feminist analyses. Some postmodern feminists even reject certain concepts associated with "feminism" and "women's liberation," per se, as unjustified attempts to impose alternative hegemonic models, thus denying the differences among, and the plurality of, individual selves.

Much can be said for philosophical orientations that insist on the significance of traditionally neglected concepts of other selves outside the dominant relations of power and that resist hegemonic authoritarian claims of modern concepts of the self; but an extreme emphasis on differences and plurality can be self-defeating. As so much contemporary philosophy has demonstrated, one can deconstruct oneself into an intellectually attractive position of powerlessness and irrelevance. For those concerned with the historical, economic, and cultural constitutions of dominant concepts of self and the ways in which certain specific models reflect dominant power relations that must be resisted, an emphasis on the extreme relativism and plurality of differences may lead to a kind of conceptual "tolerance" and perhaps even eclecticism; but it may also prove inadequate for real struggles against general interlocking structures of concentrated power at the heart of exploitation and oppression.

Second, and even more fundamentally, many contemporary philosophical and cultural orientations deny or minimize the real interdependencies, interconnections, and commonality of humankind. Mohandas Gandhi and Martin Luther King, Jr., among others, were correct in emphasizing that there is something fundamental about what unites us as human beings. Racism, sexism, homophobia, classism, ageism, national chauvinism, violence, militarism, war, exploitation, and oppression—all reflect a primary normative focus on differences and what divides us, and thus an undermining or denial of what unites us, a denial of our commonality as human beings. Recognizing our commonality with other human beings allows us to relate to other persons and other cultures in terms of unity with a respect for differences.

Third, in my studies in the phenomenology of religion, I have at times analyzed this sense of commonality in terms of profound mythic and symbolic structures found throughout the world.[24] Such general mythic and symbolic structures arise from and reveal basic existential crises, allowing for general patterns of self-constitution, creativity, and self/ego-transcendence. One cannot decipher the meanings constituted by such essential myths and symbols without acknowledging an underlying dimension of commonality, of general structures and patterns not fully exhausted by or reduced to cultural and historical "boundaries" and differences.

At the same time, if concerned with interpreting the meaning of real lived historical and cultural phenomena, one cannot remain on the rather abstract level of essential mythic and symbolic structures, general or universal existential crises, and patterns of self-constitution. Although the particular qua particular may be unintelligible, people do not live their lives on the level of "pure" universal or general structures and meanings. Such a recognition of "exemplary," "paradigmatic," or "essential" structures involves a process of imaginative and conceptual abstraction, abstracting from concrete, particular variables that define the specific contexts within which general structures of meaning are situated, experienced, and constituted. Even general symbolic structures of self-constitution are always revalorized in new ways; they are reconstituted in terms that express historical and cultural specificity, reflecting culturally constituted self-concepts and differences.

Fourth, the process of relating to others, in terms of both appreciating differences and recognizing commonality, is of the greatest urgency for understanding the contemporary world. The world is rapidly becoming "smaller" and more interdependent. We have no choice but to recognize the historical, political, economic, technological, and ecological structures of increasing global interconnectedness.

In this regard we may point to a paradox of much contemporary life. Premodern, precapitalist, agrarian peoples, though relatively isolated, tended to conceive of themselves in terms of transparently social, interrelated, and interdependent cultural communities, whereas modern urban people, increasingly dependent on others throughout the world for their food, clothing, transportation, information, recreation, and culture, conceive of themselves as isolated, atomistic, nonsocial, egoistic individuals. It is possible to view the recent resurgence of religious and political fundamentalism in South Asia and elsewhere as a resistance to modern Western concepts of the self and their intended worlds of meaning, and as an attempt, at least in part, to reconstitute the essential structures of a premodern, more communal self.

Increasingly, we realize that we are economically, politically, militarily, and culturally interconnected global beings. Our cultures, our views of self, our very existences are shaped and determined by "regional wars" in the Persian Gulf and elsewhere; nuclear and chemical accidents at Chernobyl, Three Mile Island, and Bhopal; the ecological devastation of Brazilian rain forests and of our ozone layer; multinational corporate and international banking; global military-industrial-state complexes; and imperialist exploitation of others. Our mutual *dependence,* then, must be recognized, as when opponents of the nuclear and conventional arms races remind us that we either must learn to live together or we shall perish together. We must communicate on this level of interdependence, empathizing with and relating to other concepts of self, in order to comprehend the necessary conditions for humanity's development and survival.

Fifth, empathizing with and relating to other concepts of self, created by other cultures and even other historical periods, may serve as a catalyst to our own creative process of self-development and self-constitution. My relational view of self is not unrelated to Hegel's general structural analysis of the dialectical process of self-development and self-alienation in *The Phenomenology of Mind.* To become a more sensitive, conscious, and ethical self, Hegel tells us, the self, while maintaining its autonomy as subject, must "objectify" and "externalize" itself in relating to that which is "other." Self-alienation may result either when the self defines itself internally and refuses to externalize itself and relate authentically to the external other; or when the self objectifies itself and then gives up its capacity as an autonomous subject, thus allowing itself to be defined as immanent, nontranscending other. Through this dynamic process of self-externalization, the relation to the other provides the necessary basis for the dialectical movement of self-transcendence—for the reconstitution of the new, more conscious, more fulfilled self.

Today, conceptualization of "the other" must be broadened beyond any modern, Western self-claims to ahistoric, universal objectivity to include other concepts of self with their different worlds of meanings. Such a creative, nonoppressive relation to the other is a necessary condition for our own dynamic process of self-constitution, freedom, and development.

For those of us in the modern, technological, industrialized West, complex nonoppressive encounters with other concepts of self can reveal new worlds of meaning: new ways of freeing our imaginations and of being more in touch with our emotions; of experiencing nature and the cosmos; of relating to death, time, and history; of understanding the myths and symbols often already influencing us; in short, new ways of understanding and creating our own selves and our relations to others.

This process of self-constitution, dependent on providing culturally diverse contexts for creative encounters with worlds of meaning of "the other"—including the disempowered and dispossessed, the oppressed and exploited, those on the "periphery," workers, women, gays and lesbians, and people of color—applies not only to cultures of the West. Indeed, the constructions of "archaic," Hindu, Buddhist, and other non-Western texts are also not free from class, caste, gender, race, and other relations of power. Thus it is important that many contemporary scholars in India, for example, are focusing on culturally defined self-identities of *subalterns*, women, peasants, tribals, and *dalits* (meaning "the oppressed ones" or the "downtrodden" Untouchables).

By establishing creative encounters with "the other," including other cultural creations and concepts of self usually excluded or unrecognized by dominant Western and Eastern traditions, we create the possibility for increasing our sensitivity and awareness, overcoming some of our provincialism, "bursting open" our historically and culturally imposed limitations on what is valuable, significant, and even possible, and reconstituting new views of self.

Concluding Observations

People who have heard some of the foregoing analysis have found it suggestive, thought-provoking, and creative, but also somewhat confusing. They have asked, Just where does this leave us? What precisely am I attempting to do in these formulations?

To the question of whether I am concerned with a metaphysical question of the nature of the self or with "what people have in their heads," I have responded that I am more interested in the latter—namely, with views of self that are assumed and socialized, that lie at the foundation of our economic and political systems and our views of human nature. But I also do not want to draw a simple, sharp dichotomy, since I've tried to show that "what people have in their heads" in modern Western orientations is not unrelated to a certain post-Cartesian philosophical approach to "the self." One can assume this general philosophical approach to self—emphasizing the separate, autonomous, abstract self or ego—without adopting or even being aware of the specific metaphysics formulated by Descartes.

Some have pushed me to define my own personal view of "the self." If I reject the modern, Western claim to some objective, ahistoric, transcultural self, what is my alternative? My inability to provide a concise, alternative formulation of "the self" has produced some impatience and frustration.

Such questioning of my approach to self has led me to clarify two different aims in this approach.[25] First, I am primarily interested in presenting a critique—or a variety of critiques—of the dominant, modern Western perspective on "the self." But, second, I must answer the question invited by this chapter: Beyond critiquing an inadequate modern approach to self, what is *my* concept of "the self"?

In addressing this question, and thus the aim of providing an alternative approach to self, I have found it necessary to avoid typical, traditional, ahistorical, transcultural answers about the true nature of "the self." It is not possible to provide simple, abstract, static, essentialized formulations free from all specific cultural and other contextual variables. Instead, the constitution of self must be seen as part of a complex, dynamic, often contradictory, open-ended, ongoing process. Self is not something abstract, static, ahistoric, and given; it is not something that one has, observes, and analyzes. On the contrary, self is dynamic, complex, and relational; it is socially, culturally, and historically constituted and developed through an ongoing dialectical process.

My own "alternative" view is that we are participants in an ongoing project of constituting and reconstituting selves that are more developed, less alienated, more ethical and humane, less oppressed and exploited, more sensitive and conscious, more free, more creative, and more in harmony with nature and other human beings. In undertaking such a project, we must act to redefine, transform, and transcend the dominant constitution of the modern, abstract, separate, autonomous self or ego. All four alternative approaches discussed in this chapter—the Hindu *karma yoga* of the *Gita*, the Buddha's teaching of *anatta*, Marx's analysis of the historical constitution of the modern capitalist self, and de Beauvoir's and other feminist approaches to masculinist formulations of self—provide valuable insights and contribute to more adequate views of self—insights and views that I have incorporated into my own approach to self. As we have seen, some of the claims from these four alternative approaches are mutually exclusive, but others are complementary and can be integrated in new, more developed, and more comprehensive formulations. In a nonreductionistic, semi-autonomous manner, each perspective will be seen as necessary, but not sufficient, for a comprehensive analysis of self. The constitution of this new relational, ever-changing, dynamic, holistic self, in terms of the emphasis placed on particular interrelated parts, will depend greatly on specific cultural and other contextual variables.

Notes

1. I would like to thank the Smithsonian Institution for a grant on "Views of the Self: East and West" that enabled me to do research on this project in India during 1992. I would also like to thank the University of Maine for a Summer Faculty Research Grant to do research on "Philosophical Analysis of the Transcendence of the Ego: Asian and Marxian Perspectives."

2. Many examples of such a traditional approach can be seen in Hinduism, which, perhaps more than any other philosophical tradition, has focused on investigating the nature of "the self." For instance, Shankara's Vedanta philosophy maintains that our historically and culturally constituted concepts of the spatial, temporal, empirical self or ego are expressions of a mode of "nescience," the "superimposition" of the finite, illusory self on the true Self. By removing the veils of ignorance that constitute the world of *maya,* we come to experience the ahistoric, eternal, unchanging, universal, true Self (*Atman*).

3. My use of the term *Western* in this paragraph and elsewhere is not meant to imply a geographical location. Rather, in a somewhat general and loose manner, I am pointing to a post-Cartesian, post-Enlightenment, "modern" concept of self, as the highly atomistic, separate, I-me, autonomous individual or ego, that underlies modern Western economic, political, legal, cultural, and educational approaches. Studies have shown that many people in the modern West—especially those who are oppressed and exploited (women, Native Americans, African Americans)—do not always express modern Western concepts of self. On the contrary, such people may resist viewing themselves as independent, separate, autonomous individuals and thus retain a social, relational view of self. In addition, there are views of self, often accepted by the more privileged and "Westernized" classes in India and other Asian societies, that incorporate features of modern Western concepts of self.

4. The terms *self* and *person* are used interchangeably in this chapter, but these concepts need not be identical. There have been many cultures in which the concept of self is recognized but the concept of person is not. "The person" is a specific way of constituting "the self" that has dominated much of modern, Western epistemological, ethical, political, and legal thought.

5. Jitendra Nath Mohanty presents this analysis in "Layers of Selfhood" (unpublished paper).

6. It may be objected that much contemporary Western philosophy on the self has been anti-Cartesian. For example, many books in British and U.S. analytic philosophy have focused on the problem of "personal identity." The most influential of these is Derek Parfit's *Reasons and Persons* (Oxford: Clarendon Press, 1984). The majority of the analytic philosophers focus on a technical epistemological problem of memory and personal identity, largely derived from Locke, that tells us little or nothing about actual Western views of self and culture. Accordingly, this section of the

chapter is concerned with modern concepts of self that shape our economic, political, legal, and cultural institutions, religious ideologies, assumptions about human nature, and so forth.

7. The passages from *Meditations on First Philosophy* that I cite in this section are taken from "Meditation II: Of the Nature of the Human Mind; and that it is more easily known than the Body."

8. As with other "alternative" constructions from Buddhism, Marxism, and feminism, it should be obvious that there is no single Hindu concept of self and no single Hindu critique of modern Western concepts of self. Most of the quotations in this section are taken from Radhakrishnan's translation of the *Gita* in Sarvepalli Radhakrishnan and Charles A. Moore, eds., *A Source Book in Indian Philosophy* (Princeton: Princeton University Press, 1957), pp. 101–163.

9. M. K. Gandhi, "The Message of the Gita," in Mahadev Desai, *The Gita According to Gandhi* (Ahmedabad: Navajivan Publishing House, 1946), p. 130.

10. *Anguttara-nikaya* 3.134, in Henry Clarke Warren, ed., *Buddhism in Translations* (New York: Atheneum, 1963), p. xiv. "The Three Characteristics" are *anatta*, *anicca*, and *dukkha*.

11. *Samyutta-nikaya* 3.66, in Radhakrishnan and Moore, eds., *A Source Book in Indian Philosophy*, pp. 280–281; *Samyutta-nikaya* 22.85 and 22.22, in Warren, ed., *Buddhism in Translations*, 138–145, 159–160. My brief formulation of *anatta* is typical of the Buddhist scriptural teachings of "no-self." In recent years, studies have challenged such unqualified scriptural interpretations as reflecting the hegemonic social position of the Buddhist monkhood, given its interlocking power relations with the privileged classes of society, and as ignoring very different religious orientations of mass or "popular Buddhism." In *Selfless Persons* (Cambridge: Cambridge University Press, 1982), Steven Collins convincingly argues that the strict canonical analysis of "no-self" was intended only for elite monks or specialists and that Buddhism itself always made provision for other interpretations of self. Elsewhere ("Religious-Political Conflict in Sri Lanka: Philosophical Considerations," in *Religion and Political Conflict in South Asia: India, Pakistan, and Sri Lanka,* ed. Douglas Allen [Westport, Conn.: Greenwood Publishers, 1992; Delhi: Oxford University Press, 1993], pp. 181–203 in both publications), I try to make sense of the contradictions between contemporary (Sri Lankan) cultural and historical constructions of the Sinhala Buddhist "self," on the one hand, and the *anatta* and other scriptural teachings of the Buddha, on the other.

12. *Samyutta-nikaya* v.420 and *Majjhima-nikaya* 3.248–252, in Radhakrishnan and Moore, eds., *A Source Book in Indian Philosophy*, pp. 274–275, 275–278.

13. Walpola Rahula, *What the Buddha Taught* (New York: Grove Press, 1959), p. 51.

14. See, for example, Karl Marx, "The Economic and Philosophic Manuscripts of 1844," in *The Marx-Engels Reader*, ed. Robert Tucker (New York: Norton, 1972), pp. 55–56; and Karl Marx, *Grundrisse*, trans. Martin Nicolaus (New York: Random House/Vintage Books, 1973), p. 83. Similarly, in his "Theses on Feuerbach" (also in *The Marx-Engels Reader*, p. 109), Marx criticized Feuerbach for presupposing an abstract isolated individual and not realizing that his abstract individual "belongs in reality to a particular form of society."

15. One of many translations of this work is Karl Marx, *Capital*, Vol. 1, trans. Ben Fowkes (New York: Random House/Vintage Books, 1977).

16. Karl Marx, "Germany Ideology," in Tucker, ed., *The Marx-Engels Reader*, pp. 114ff.

17. Marx, "The Economic and Philosophic Manuscripts of 1844," in Tucker, ed., *The Marx-Engels Reader*, pp. 73–74.

18. As a parallel to the term *feminist* I prefer to use *masculinist* rather than *male*. Moreover, *masculinist* and *feminist* need not be identical with *male* and *female sexual identity*. A minority of women, especially those who have achieved some success in terms of standards applicable to the contexts of a male-dominated world, have incorporated into their own lives characteristics of the masculinist self. And a minority of men, especially those who have reacted strongly against specific contexts of their male-dominated patterns of socialization, have incorporated into their own lives characteristics of the feminist self.

19. Certain kinds of "liberal feminism" have accepted characteristics of the modern post-Cartesian, post-Enlightenment self. The problem, then, has to do not so much with modern concepts of self as with sexual, economic, political, cultural, and other obstacles that have prevented many women from developing themselves as separate, autonomous individuals. We may also note that certain kinds of "radical feminism" have rejected such characteristics of the autonomous, separate, rational, ego-oriented individual as those at the foundation of a male-dominated and -justified system of aggressiveness and violence, selfishness and lack of caring—a system that represses much that is human, values abstract rationality, devalues the body, and fosters nonrelational alienation and oppressive hierarchical relations of domination and control. (Of course, this observation is not unique to radical feminism; socialist and other feminists have come to a similar conclusion.)

20. See Simone de Beauvoir's analysis of the constitution of the self in terms of self-other relations in her Introduction to *The Second Sex*, trans. and ed. H. M. Parshley (New York: Random House/Vintage Books, 1974), pp. xv–xxxv.

21. There is considerable tension and ambiguity in de Beauvoir's writings between the concept of an autonomous, separate, individual self and that of a more social self, as well as between the liberal reformist and more radical restructuring solutions that she proposes. For example, on a general structural level, she often presents the model of "the self" or "the subject" as "male," and seems to propose that women can refuse to be "the other" by adopting the model of the autonomous, transcending, male self. But as many feminists have maintained, this strategy might, at best, result in the reformist "solution" of dividing the "sexist pie" more equitably, such that women, too, acquire the opportunity to function as oppressing, exploiting, alienated selves.

22. Carol Gilligan, *In a Different Voice: Psychological Theory and Women's Development* (Cambridge, Mass.: Harvard University Press, 1982). See also Carol Gilligan, "Concepts of the Self and of Morality," *Harvard Educational Review* 47 (November 1977): 481–517.

23. Such constructions have given rise to heated debate among feminists and other scholars. For example, in an observation equally applicable to de Beauvoir's "self" equals "male" and "other" equals "female," commentators have questioned Gilligan's lumping together of females and males under female and male moralities and concepts of self without taking into consideration racial, class, and other variables. Some have submitted that African-American, Native American, Chinese, and

impoverished working-class subjects, among others, do not so clearly display Gilligan's specifically differentiated male-female scales of moral and self development.

24. See, for example, Douglas Allen, *Structure and Creativity in Religion* (The Hague: Mouton Publishers, 1978); Douglas Allen, *Mircea Eliade et le phénomène religieux* (Paris: Payot Editions, 1982); and Douglas Allen, *Mircea Eliade on Myth and Religion* (New York: Garland Publishers, 1997).

25. I would like to thank my colleague Michael Howard for bringing this distinction to my attention.

Chapter Two

How Universal Is Psychoanalysis? The Self in India, Japan, and the United States

ALAN ROLAND

Hardly anyone today would gainsay the common humanity among people from diverse cultures and civilizations. Some kind of psychological universalism is clearly in evidence. But what kind becomes the question. Even more to the point, to what extent do current psychological theories that have originated in the West, such as psychoanalysis, encompass this common humanity as well as the considerable differences that are easily observed?

Not all theorists are so sanguine about the search for psychological universals across cultures. Clifford Geertz, the noted anthropologist, sees little use in trying to ascertain psychological universals, as he considers them to be the lowest common denominator of human nature.[1] Human nature, in his view, only realizes itself in diversity through culture. As Geertz explains: "The Western conception of the person as a bounded, unique, more or less integrated motivational and cognitive universe, a dynamic center of awareness, emotion, judgment, and action organized into a distinctive whole and against a social and natural background is, however incorrigible it may seem to us, a rather peculiar idea within the context of the other world cultures."[2]

An even more radical view is that of A. K. Ramanujan, who views the very tendency toward the universal and unique as rooted in Western philosophical assumptions, quite at odds with a Hindu cultural emphasis on contextualization.[3] Ramanujan cites, for instance, the Hindu moral code of *dharma*, whereby proper behavior is contextually based on the place, the time, the kind of relationship, and the nature of the persons involved. He further delineates the contextual nature of time (auspicious and inauspicious), of place (sacred and mundane), and of aesthetics (specific *ragas* of music are to be played only at particular times of day or during certain seasons). To be sure, Ramanujan acknowledges the important search for the universal or ultimate (*moksha*) in Hindu spiritual culture, but this he sees as a counterpoint to the contextual involvement in the social world; and *moksha* is arrived at only by first going through the latter. He thus implies that the search for psychological universals in the sociocultural world is not at all a universal approach for understanding human nature but, rather, one based on Western culture.

But there is another, even more significant issue that psychoanalytic universalism raises: To what extent does psychoanalysis, deeply rooted in the Northern European/North American culture of individualism[4] and formulated on the basis of data on Euro-American personality, encompass an understanding of psyches from radically different civilizations such as Asian ones? Older psychoanalytic approaches, such as those of Erik Erikson and Abraham Kardiner, proposed that different cultures interplay with what were assumed to be a basic groundplan of human development, structuralization, and functioning.[5] But the groundplan itself, as outlined in current-day Freudian psychoanalysis of whichever model (classical drive theory, structural theory, ego psychology, self psychology, and object relations theory), still encompasses many basic assumptions and values of individualism, even while critiquing notions of individualism's self-contained, self-reliant, rational individual.

Freud, for instance, initiated the psychological critique of individualism by undermining the Enlightenment idea of the human being's inherent rationality through his formulation of the unconscious and primary process thinking. But he then restored a central value of individualism, Kant's ideal of rational autonomy, through his theory of resolving unconscious conflicts. "Where id was, ego shall be." Further, one can easily see individualism's paradigm of the self-contained individual in Freud's drive and structural theories, whereby all motivation originates within the intrapsychic drives and structures of the person. The social surround receives scant attention from Freud except as the aim of the drives, as gratifiers or frustrators, as the source of superego and especially ego-ideal contents through parental carriers of the culture, and as the reality principle of what an individual can or cannot do in the social world. Freud presents a one-person psychology.

What is true of Freud is also true of major innovative theorists within the Freudian genre, such as Erikson, Melanie Klein, D. W. Winnicott, and Heinz Kohut. All have critiqued one or another major dimension of individualism while carrying over its basic assumptions and values. A simple example of an important critique of the self-contained individual is Winnicott's famous dictum "There is no such thing as a baby," meaning that a baby cannot exist without a mothering person.[6] Simultaneously, he develops a theory of transitional objects (e.g., a security blanket) and transitional phenomena that details the internalization of the mothering person, which allows the young child to be separate and alone at times without experiencing a devastating loneliness. This is another central value in individualism. Transitional objects are not nearly so much in evidence in Asian societies, where there is far more symbiotic mothering and emotional enmeshment within the extended family and less sense of a separate individualistic self.[7]

Psychoanalysis and Asian Cultures

Given this kind of cultural baggage of individualism along with its assumptions of universalism, how has psychoanalysis approached understanding those from radically different cultures such as Asian ones? And what kinds of problems are engendered by the use of a theory and therapy so steeped in individualism? To answer these questions, one would do well to borrow a leaf from anthropology, which has had decades of experience in investigating different cultures. Anthropologists have interpreted these other cultures in three essential ways, each with its own underlying premises: evolutionism, universalism, and relativism.[8] All three approaches are equally relevant to the small but increasing number of psychoanalysts and psychoanalytic anthropologists who themselves have worked in radically different cultures, and also to psychoanalysts in the United States working with patients from significantly to radically different cultures. The theoretical dilemmas involved in each of these three orientations will become readily apparent when we consider the psychoanalytic approach to Asian cultures, and they will have to be resolved if a viable theoretical perspective is to emerge.

Evolutionism as applied to psychoanalysis posits definitive norms for what healthy human nature should be and how it develops in contrast to psychopathology. These norms, which invariably constitute a contemporary normative model of the Northern European/North American individualized self as formulated in current psychoanalytic theory, are assumed to be universal and superior. Hence others from cultures significantly or radically different who do not measure up to this universal normative model are seen as exhibiting inferior psychological development or psychopathology.

An example of the pitfalls of an evolutionist view of human nature is easily seen in Sudhir Kakar's psychoanalytic work on Indians—a work that unfortunately undermines his many perceptive observations.[9] Kakar well recognizes that the Indians' psychological makeup is modally different from that of Westerners, but he holds to the basic premise of evolutionism—that the theory of human nature in psychoanalysis is universally normative. By subscribing to this normative approach, he invariably assesses Indian personality as modally inferior to the individualism of Westerners. Indians thus emerge in Kakar's analysis as having an underdeveloped ego—that is, as lacking the independent, self-reliant, self-directing ego of Western individualism; as lacking rational, logical, secondary-process thinking, another hallmark value of individualism; as exhibiting vague emotional boundaries between self and other with much less of the self-other demarcation that is also characteristic of individualism; and as having a weak conscience or superego because they follow the highly contextual ethical norms of others rather than the categorical imperative of Western male individualism. A few quotations from Kakar's *The Inner World* will illustrate the problematic aspects of his evolutionism:

> No [Indian] group can survive for long if its members are brought up to neglect the development of those secondary processes through which we mediate and connect outer and inner experience. An [Indian] "underdeveloped ego" in relation to the outer world is a risky luxury. ... Under these "modern" conditions, an individual ego structure, weak in secondary and reality-oriented processes and unsupported by an adequate social organization, may fail to be adaptive (pp. 107, 108).

Kakar claims that "this same intense exclusivity [with the mother in early childhood] tends to hinder the growth of the son's autonomy, therefore leaving the psychic structure relatively undifferentiated, the boundaries of the self vague" (p. 130). He then concludes that in India "the categorical conscience ... does not exist as a psychic structure sharply differentiated from the id and the ego, nor are its parts 'idealized' as they tend to be in Western cultures. ... [T]he communal conscience is a social rather than an individual formation, it is not 'inside' the psyche. ... [I]nstead of having one internal sentinel an Indian relies on many external 'watch men' to patrol his activities" (p. 135). Although he protests to the contrary, Kakar fundamentally accepts the Enlightenment demystification and secularization of religion in psychoanalytic theory whereby spiritual experiences, so valued in Indian society, are viewed as regression to the early mother-infant relationship: "The blissful soothing and nursing associated with the mother of earliest infancy ... has been consensually deemed the core of mystical motivation."[10]

The second approach toward assessing the universality and variability of the self in different cultural settings is essentially to search for universals only. Differences are seen as only superficially colored by culture. In universalism, higher-order generalities predominate with specific, culture-rich, thick descriptions of human nature bleached out from consideration.

An example of the pitfalls of psychological universalism is found in the work of Catherine Ewing, an American psychoanalytic anthropologist who has worked in Pakistan.[11] Ewing avoids the pitfalls of evolutionism in Kakar's work, with its value-laden judgments of Indians, by combining the usual cultural relativism of anthropology with the universalism of psycho-analysis—in short, by acknowledging that although cultures vary enor-mously, everyone is essentially the same psychologically. She well recognizes that people in Pakistan behave and interact very differently from people in the United States, attributing this fact solely to the cultural patterns of inter-personal engagement and interpersonal autonomy (individualism), respec-tively. She gives these patterns equal weight, thus avoiding the implicit supe-riority-inferiority norms of evolutionism. Otherwise, Ewing takes the view that Pakistanis are no different psychologically from North Americans, that their selves are basically alike. In this regard, her position is similar to that of many other psychoanalytic anthropologists.

Ewing utilizes an ego psychology framework to focus on the differentia-tion and separateness between inner representations of the self and object (other). However, unlike Kakar, who views Indians' degree of separateness of inner images of self and other (self and object representations) as less than that of Westerners and therefore inferior, Ewing simply emphasizes the ne-cessity for separation to occur so as to avoid psychopathology. She thus ex-tends the usefulness of a psychoanalytic understanding of normality and psychopathology to an Asian culture.

But because she is so completely oriented toward the universal—in this case, in terms of the necessity for separation between inner images of self and object—Ewing completely ignores the different degrees of separation be-tween inner representations of self and other in Pakistanis as contrasted to North Americans. She therefore does not see that Pakistanis have an experi-ential sense of a we-self that includes inner images of others of the extended family and community as part of the self to a much greater extent than does the highly individualistic, more self-contained North American I-self. *Thus, modal differences in psychological makeup, or variabilities in the makeup of the self, are completely missing when the focus is on universals.* Wedded to psychological universalism, Ewing is unable to relate how the variability in the self among either Pakistanis or North Americans enables them to func-tion effectively within their own cultural and interpersonal patterns but not as well within those of the other.

Moreover, because of these modal differences in the self, Ewing is unable to see that the norms for psychopathology also vary. Thus, a problem in separa-tion between inner images of self and other that might be considered severe borderline psychopathology in North Americans might fall along the neu-rotic continuum for Pakistanis. For instance, the semi-merger experience of a Pakistani with his or her mother and with others of the extended family, in which he or she has little sense of autonomy and great difficulty making deci-sions, might be perceived by a North American psychoanalyst as encompass-ing much more severe psychopathology than it might actually be. Thus, if evolutionism is a sin of commission, then universalism is one of omission.

The third theoretical approach for evaluating the universality and variability of the self in diverse settings is relativism. As applied to psychological phenomena, relativism entails highly differing views of human nature in different cultures, but these are analyzed within a framework entirely different from Western individualism, each having its own internal consistency and validity related to the indigenous culture and its social patterns. The only problem with relativism, however, is that it provides no common categories or standards for comparison or criticism across cultures.

Perhaps the best example of relativism in the psychological realm is Takeo Doi's use of it in his seminal psychoanalytic work in Japan on dependency relationships (*amae*) and the dual self-structure of a public and a highly private self (*omote/ura*).[12] Doi jettisoned psychoanalytic theory because its norms of individualism are too Western-centric and its categories do not encompass central dimensions of the Japanese psyche. The *amae* kind of dependency relationship, in which you presume that the other will take care of you without your having to ask or to articulate your needs, is something that is almost completely missing in psychoanalytic theory. Similarly, the dual self-structure, in which a person's public presentation of self (*omote*) is oriented toward fulfilling a rigorous social etiquette while maintaining a highly private self (*ura*) that contains all kinds of unexpressed thoughts, fantasies, and feelings, particularly ambivalent ones, is also foreign to psychoanalytic elaborations of the self.

What Doi does maintain, however, is the psychoanalytic sensibility of exploring the inner world of Japanese people and of probing for its developmental antecedents by delineating the meanings of predominant Japanese linguistic terms. By elaborating the various facets of Japanese dependency relationship (*amae*) and a dual-self structure (*omote/ura*), Doi has been able to formulate a culturally variable psychology of Japanese in many of its important configurations that differs radically from the psychoanalytic self of Northern European/North American individualism.

Doi's basic theoretical approach differs greatly from the evolutionism of Kakar and the universalism of Ewing given his focus on the variabilities of the Japanese self—variabilities that he considers to be on a par with those of individualism. However, after elaborating this modal psychology of the Japanese, Doi searches for the universality of this kind of (*amae*) dependency in persons in the United States. He indeed finds it to be present, but in diminished form, due to the Northern European/North American cultural emphasis on self-reliance; indeed, the *amae* kind of dependency relationship is conceptualized in psychoanalytic theory only in Michael Balint's concept of passive object love. Thus, psychological variabilities hardly present in the Northern European/North American psychological makeup are simply not a salient part of psychoanalytic theory. And then the theory without this kind of category will either completely miss this variability in others or see it as inferior or psychopathological.

A profound insight of Doi's approach is to move from the exploration of psychological variabilities in a given culture (i.e., the Japanese) to the formulation of some of these variabilities, such as the *amae* dependency relationship, as a universal category present in all cultures, but manifesting itself in patterns and configurations significantly different from those of the Japanese without positing any value-laden universal norms. One can see that psychoanalysis itself, having previously entailed extensive investigation into the psychological variability of Northern Europeans and North Americans, now involves the formulation of universal categories. Western psychoanalysts who lack the comparative experience of working in different civilizations, as Doi has done, fail to realize the extent to which the elaboration of the contents and norms of various psychoanalytic categories, as well as the configurations of them, involves the particular variabilities of the highly individualistic Northern European/North American self.

What are the limitations of Doi's psychoanalytic relativism? Most salient is his jettisoning of psychoanalytic theory as too-burdensome baggage. Although this was initially highly liberating to enable Doi to formulate an indigenous psychology of the Japanese, one related to Japanese cultural and social patterns, we are left with an essentially atheoretical approach—that is, one without a variety of universal categories.

What are the drawbacks of Doi's atheoretical psychoanalytic approach? First of all, Doi only explicitly but not implicitly puts aside psychoanalytic categories. He draws not only on his cross-civilizational clinical experience in Japan and the United States but also on North American ego psychology, which so emphasizes the separation-individuation process. In elaborating the psychology of *amae,* Doi implicitly contrasts the Japanese focus on this kind of dependency relationship with the North American psychoanalytic emphasis on individuation, autonomy, and inner separation of images of self and others. And in his elaboration of the Japanese dual-self structure, he utilizes still another dimension of ego psychology: one that explores the organization of the self. Thus, his perceptive elaboration of the psychology of Japanese has to be seen against the theoretical backdrop and concerns of psychoanalytic ego psychology, a salient theory during the 1950s and 1960, when Doi was in training in the United States. Ironically, one critique of Doi's work is that he carried over a too-individualistic set from Western psychoanalysis to the understanding of *amae* dependency relationships. Indeed, the latter are better seen in terms of particular contextualized relationships and situations in which demands for proper social etiquette are temporarily relaxed.[13]

More specifically, Doi's relativism, lacking the benefit of certain psychoanalytic categories and comparative work in other Asian cultures, limits some of his clinical understanding. Doi recognizes the psychopathological forms of *amae*, such as a demanding entitlement. Doi sees this primarily as a result of frustrated *amae* dependency in childhood. However, Indians, who have much the same *amae* dependency psychology as Japanese, rarely exhibit any demanding entitlement, even in cases where dependency needs are deeply frustrated in childhood.

To understand this clinical phenomenon, one must take into account not only the childhood *amae* relationship but also two other factors: a very strict conscience and the presence or absence of maternal empathic attunement with the child. I found demanding entitlement in Japanese to result from childhood situations in which the child has indeed been very dependent on his or her mother, though not always frustrated in terms of dependency needs; and in which the child has also internalized the mother's strong expectations for very high standards of performance but in the presence of poor maternal attunement with the child's nature. In such situations, the lack of gratification was due more often to lack of maternal empathy than to the *amae* relationship itself.

At the point that Doi developed his theory of *amae*, psychoanalytic self psychology, with its strong emphasis on the maternal mirroring relationship, had not yet been formulated. Doi was therefore unable to use this category—a circumstance that, in my view, limited his clinical understanding. As a further result, he was unable to elaborate the central role of self-esteem, or, more accurately, we-self esteem, in Japanese relationships.[14] *My point is that, in the psychoanalytic relativism that Doi developed, general psychoanalytic categories and assumptions are implicitly used, misused, or countered, owing to the absence of such concepts as the maternal mothering relationship and self-esteem.* To the extent that these universals are not acknowledged, they enter unseen into psychoanalytic relativism, for better or worse.

Thus, although Doi's work leaves us with a much fuller understanding of the variability of the self in Japanese, and with a couple of new universal categories minimally present in Westerners, we have no comprehensive theory with which to evaluate both universality and variability in human nature across cultures. This becomes particularly important when we consider how useful it would be, for instance, to compare the configurations of the Japanese self with those of the self of other Asians, who are much closer to the Japanese in psychological makeup than are Westerners, or even with those of the self of Hispanics.

It is evident, then, that evolutionism, universalism, and relativism are beset by their own problems and pitfalls—hence the dilemma involved in using current individualistically oriented psychoanalytic theory across cultures. But because variability, universals, and normality-psychopathology are essential issues in assessing the self across cultures, it is imperative that we develop newer modes of resolving this dilemma.

Toward a Comparative Psychoanalysis

The evolution of a comparative psychoanalysis suitable for patients across a wide variety of cultures requires a new theoretical approach. A new paradigm involves using the varied categories of the psychoanalytic theory of personality and therapy from a variety of psychoanalytic models as universals: superego and ego-ideal, ego boundaries, developmental stages, self-object relationships, self and object representations, self-identity, the internal object world, affects and drives, transference, resistance, and dream-analysis, among others.[15] One must then decontextualize these categories of their current Northern European/North American content and norms, or their variability, as they are now elaborated in psychoanalytic theory; and then recontextualize them based on the clinical data of persons from significantly or radically different cultures. The new contents and norms of each category are then integrated with the social and historical contexts of that culture. This approach would also add new universal categories, as Doi has done with *amae* dependency relationships and the *omote/ura* dual self-structure.

Most important, to capture the true variability of human nature, one must take the further step of putting these recontextualized categories into their unique configurations or organizations of the self in different cultures. As with a painting, whether representational or abstract, such issues as values between darks and lights, color harmonies and contrasts, line, texture, compositional structure, and dissonances, must achieve a unique balance. Artists are well aware of this requirement, and so psychoanalysts must be if they are to understand the universality and variability of the self across cultures.

As a simple example of this new approach, consider the category of ego boundaries. In the North American context, current psychoanalytic norms call for outer ego boundaries between self and other(s) to be relatively firm so that a person can have close relationships without being involved in merger experiences, which constitute psychopathology. Conversely, inner ego boundaries should be somewhat flexible so that a person is in touch with inner feelings, fantasies, and impulses, but not flooded by them. In cultures different from those governed by individualism, such as India and Japan, outer ego boundaries are much vaguer and more permeable. This finding is in keeping with the close emotional enmeshment among family, group, and community members in India and Japan—and the Japanese variant features even vaguer outer boundaries than that of the Indians.

Experientially, I, and others I have known from the United States, have felt swallowed up when living in an Indian or Japanese milieu. In such instances, the normal North American boundaries between self and other(s) disappear, which becomes very threatening to one's sense of self and to one's identity. For example, a well-known Indologist left with her family after a month of living with an Indian family they deeply cherished. The lack of boundaries proved too threatening. The same was true of a young man who married a Japanese woman. He fled from her family in Japan when he felt that his identity was dissolving. Similar experiences have been reported to me by Indians and Japanese who have lived several years in Europe or the United States and then returned home.

One must contextualize this generalization by citing that Indians and Japanese make sharp distinctions between insider and outsider relationships—that is, between one's own people and others in India, and between *uchi* and *soto* in Japan. The more permeable outer ego boundaries occur within the insider relationships characteristic of the extended family and of closely knit groups such as the work group in Japan. In outsider relationships in both cultures, such as different castes or communities in India and others outside of one's family and group in Japan, outer ego boundaries are usually kept very firm with considerable social distance and emotional restraint.

But counterbalancing this permeable outer boundary through semi-merger experiences with others in insider relationships is an inner boundary of a highly private, secret self. More secretive in Japanese than in Indians, this self is a repository of individuality rarely found in North Americans, for whom individuality is characteristically expressed in the social world.[16] The innermost ego boundary varies even more between Indians and Japanese, inasmuch as the former are usually far more in touch with their inner world than the latter, and somewhat more in touch than North Americans. This difference is due to cultural norms. For instance, Japanese have a far more perfectionistic ego-ideal and rigorous social etiquette than Indians and North Americans and so are less in touch with themselves. By contrast, Indians, although their culture insists on proper social etiquette in family and group hierarchical relationships, give considerable latitude to a wide variety of personal ideas, feelings, and fantasies. Thus, North Americans, Indians, and Japanese all have the universal category of ego boundaries; but this category has to be recontextualized for Indians and Japanese from the usual norms of psychoanalysis, adding a new category of an inner boundary involving a highly private self. These three cultures also specify different configurations for outer and inner boundaries.

From the perspective of normality/psychopathology, norms vary considerably from one configuration of ego boundaries to another. Merger or semi-merger experiences that would be considered borderline if not severe psychopathology for most North Americans usually fall within the neurotic range for Japanese. In a group supervisory session in Hiroshima in 1982, Dr. Totoro Ichimaru presented the case of Kiyoshi, a seventeen-year-old boy. His transference to Dr. Ichimaru was such that the latter not only experienced a suffocating closeness and discomfort at the lack of boundaries between himself and Kiyoshi but also felt that he was being given absolutely no opportunity to express himself and, indeed, was being totally disregarded by Kiyoshi. When I mentioned to the group that this kind of symbiotic transference to the therapist, reflective of a pathological symbiotic tie to a mother who disregards her child's inner world, would be regarded in the United States as the severe psychopathology of a borderline patient, the Japanese therapists responded that in Japan it is considered to fall within the category of neurosis. One explanation is the relatively boundaryless nature of the mother-child relationship in Japan.[17] By the same token, the relatively firm outer ego boundary considered to be normal for North Americans is highly maladaptive for Japanese and Indians in their emotionally enmeshed family and group relationships and would therefore be considered indicative of another kind of neurotic psychopathology.

Other categories also enter into unique balances and configurations in the overall organization of the self in a given culture area. For example, verbal and nonverbal modes of communication clearly vary as a function of ego boundaries and the expression of individuality. The firmer the outer ego boundary, as in North Americans, the more reliance there is on verbal communication, as if to balance and bridge the separateness of autonomous individuals and to implement their individuality in the social world.

By contrast, when a highly developed private self is the locus of individuality and balances semi-merger experiences in long-lasting family and group relationships, nonverbal empathic sensing becomes salient. And the more secretive the private self becomes, as in the Japanese (as compared to Indians), the more finely tuned is empathic, intuitive sensing. Verbal expression is then more used to observe proper social etiquette in the hierarchical relationships. Thus, these variabilities of ego boundaries, individuality, and modes of communication enter into special balances with each other, forming unique configurations in persons from radically different cultures.

A new paradigm would also incorporate the sociohistorical experiences of persons from a given civilization, insofar as these experiences have become internalized within the psyche. Certainly, the psychological makeup of women in contemporary North America is profoundly related to the women's movement, which has incorporated and critiqued the values of individualism hitherto reserved for men. Both Indians and Japanese over the past two hundred years have become increasingly exposed to the antithetical values of Western individualism, which has had profound psychological effects. When these values have been posited in the sociopolitical context of colonialism, which is so denigrating to indigenous cultures, the psychological effects have been devastating.

In addition, a new paradigm would include psychological phenomena that psychoanalysis with its Enlightenment philosophical heritage looks askance at. I refer here to the realm of spiritual experiences and disciplines, which, with few exceptions, has been relegated by psychoanalysts from Freud onward to the stage of infant-mother symbiotic, merger states, if not to other forms of psychopathology. Even more disparaged than the spiritual has been the magic-cosmic world of personal destiny, in which patients from a variety of cultures are involved in numerous ways, such as astrology, palmistry, the spirit world, psychics and mediums, and rituals. This is anathema to most psychoanalysts. Those whose tradition posits a self-contained, rational individual simply do not appreciate the fact that patients outside of the Northern European/North American culture belt have a self that is far more enmeshed and embedded in an extended family, group, and community context—or what is now being referred to as sociocentric/organic societies[18]—but also often exists in a world of invisible influences and spirits as well as sometimes in the spiritual. To assume a denigrating attitude toward these psychological phenomena is to miss a major portion of the patient's psyche.

In conclusion, psychoanalytic universalism in the form of its categories is here to stay, but in a far more circumscribed role whereby the contents of these categories have to be changed and the current norms of normality/psychopathology attached to these contents have to be recognized as culture-bound. When comparing the self from India, Japan, and the United States for a workable analysis, one must integrate the philosophical polarities of Western universalizing assumptions with contextualizing ones, whether one is dealing with Asian modes regarding the social and cosmic worlds or modes of a more recent Western vintage such as social constructionism or feminist theory. A further integration must also be made of the spiritual self, one that transcends and encompasses both universalizing categories and contextualized views of the self. This integration can then form a solid basis for evolving a comparative psychoanalysis of persons from radically different cultures.

Notes

1. Clifford Geertz, *The Interpretation of Cultures* (New York: Basic Books, 1973).

2. Ibid., p. 48.

3. A. K. Ramanujan, "Is There an Indian Way of Thinking? An Informal Essay," in *India Through Hindu Categories*, ed. McKim Marriott (New Delhi and London: Sage Publications, 1990), pp. 41–58.

4. I would argue that in the progression of individualism from the religious to the philosophical, to the social and political, to the economic, and to the cultural and literary theory of Romanticism (Louis Dumont, *Essays on Individualism* [Chicago: University of Chicago Press, 1986]), one can look upon psychoanalysis as the further extension of individualism to the realm of the psychological. If individuals are set on their own in Northern European/North American societies in a way never before done, then psychoanalysis is the psychological theory and therapy par excellence that enables them to be on their own through resolving all kinds of unconscious conflicts and deficits.

5. Erikson's groundplan of development, which emphasizes the striving for autonomy and initiative in childhood and identity conflicts and resolutions in adolescence, is far more oriented toward those in Northern European and North American societies and is not that much in evidence in children and adolescents in Asian societies. Erik Erikson, *Childhood and Society* (New York: W. W. Norton, 1950); and *Identity, Youth, and Crisis* (New York: W. W. Norton, 1968). Abraham Kardiner, *The Psychological Frontiers of Society* (New York: Columbia University Press, 1945).

6. Donald W. Winnicott, "Transitional Objects and Transitional Phenomena," in *Collected Papers* (New York: Basic Books, 1951).

7. Simon Grolnick and Leonard Barkin, editors, *Between Reality and Fantasy* (New York: Jason Aronson, 1978).

8. Richard A. Shweder and Edmund Bourne, Jr., "Does the Concept of the Person Vary Cross-Culturally?" in *Culture Theory: Essays on Mind, Self, and Emotion,* ed. Robert LeVine and Richard A. Shweder (Cambridge/Melbourne/New York: Cambridge University Press, 1984).

9. Sudhir Kakar, *The Inner World: A Psychoanalytic Study of Childhood and Society in India* (Delhi: Oxford University Press, 1978). See also his *Shamans, Mystics and Doctors* (New York: Alfred A. Knopf, 1982); *Intimate Relations: Exploring Indian Sexuality* (Chicago: University of Chicago Press, 1991); and *The Analyst and the Mystic: Psychoanalytic Reflections on Religion and Mysticism* (New Delhi: Penguin Books, 1991).

10. Kakar, *The Analyst and the Mystic,* p. 29.

11. Catherine Ewing, "Can Psychoanalytic Theories Explain the Pakistani Woman? Intrapsychic Autonomy and Interpersonal Engagement in the Extended Family," *Ethos* 19 (1991): 131–160.

12. Takeo Doi, *The Anatomy of Dependence* (Tokyo: Kodansha International, 1973); Takeo Doi, *The Anatomy of Self: The Individual Versus Society* (Tokyo: Kodansha International, 1985).

13. Yasuhiko Taketomo, "*Amae* as Metalanguage: A Critique of Doi's Theory of *Amae,*" *Journal of American Academy of Psychoanalysis* 14 (1986): 525–544.

14. Alan Roland, *Cultural Pluralism and Psychoanalysis: The Asian and North American Experience* (New York and London: Routledge, 1996).

15. Alan Roland, *In Search of Self in India and Japan: Toward a Cross-Cultural Psychology* (Princeton: Princeton University Press, 1988).

16. A Japanese psychoanalyst, Akahisa Kondo, once told me that "our individuality lies in what we do not say" (personal communication).

17. See Roland, *In Search of Self in India and Japan,* pp. 138–140, for a fuller discussion of this case.

18. Hazel Markus and S. Kitayama, "Culture and the Self: Implications for Cognition, Emotion, and Motivation," *Psychological Review* 98 (1991): 224–253.

Part Two

Chinese and Western Perspectives

Chapter Three

Ethics, Relativism, and the Self

MARY I. BOCKOVER

Ethics is one of the most elusive and paradoxical areas of investigation that the human mind has ever tried to master. Ancient or contemporary, from the East or from the West, ethics is distinctive in demanding a clear, solid foundation—but one that it simultaneously defies. Ethics demands such a foundation in entailing principles or rules that justify or condemn our actions. Justification requires a reason; thus, ethics requires something more foundational than its rules if it is not going to simply beg the question of why they are indeed obligatory. At the same time, such a foundation is defied by ultimately having to rely on a "first" principle that is supposed to be self-justifying—a principle whose Moral Truth cannot be proven but is supposed to be self-evident. This *problem of ethical indeterminacy* (PEI), the problem of not being able to conclusively establish that ethics has a universal foundation, is discussed at length in the present chapter. As we will see, it has profound implications for ethics, some of which have been overlooked and others that have not.

One philosophical reaction to the problem of ethical indeterminacy is moral relativism, which, since the pre-Socratics, has offered a kind of challenge to the legitimacy of ethics in one form or another in the West. Because the truth (or falsity) of the foundational first principles of the various ethical systems cannot be determined (by definition), they must simply be assumed or taken on faith. Hence Moral Truth is going to be relative to the foundational principle one happens to adopt—in other words, relative to the principle that seems to be the most self-justifying to a particular person, group, and so on. The moral relativist could then safely conclude that the ultimate justifiability of any given ethical system is indeterminate, for there is no other principle more foundational than the one taken to be self-evident. Therefore, there is no way to establish that one internally consistent ethical system is better than another conflicting one of equal consistency. From this, however, the moral relativist could also conclude that there is no such thing as Moral Truth; hence, a universal ethic is not possible since the foundation that would make moral claims universally or objectively true does not exist. Instead, Moral Truth and moral falsity are taken to be exclusively relative to the particular system that entails them.[1] There simply is no "higher truth," even in principle, that could resolve conflicts between incompatible ethical systems.

I will argue later that this conclusion is too strong. Just because the actual truth of ethical principles cannot be determined (i.e., from PEI), it does not follow that such a standard does not exist. Paradoxically, we cannot conclude that moral relativism is true, for the very reason that Moral Truth cannot be determined. All that follows from the premises stated above is that we cannot *prove* whether or not Moral Truth exists. But this conclusion merely amounts to PEI, which is not what distinguishes the relativist. It is my contention that moral relativism is not merely moral skepticism; it is a stronger view maintaining that universal ethics altogether lacks the foundation it requires, in principle and in practice. Hence one who believes in the possibility of universal ethics must at least hold the "morally agnostic" view that Moral Truth *might* exist; and one can even believe more strongly that it does exist while consistently believing that it is impossible to know what that Moral Truth is. The relativist is distinguished by the stronger claim that Moral Truth *does not exist*—a claim that implies not only that the tenets of a particular ethical system can be judged only by virtue of its own terms or principles but also that so-called universal principles are not universal at all. Indeed, they are not universal because the first principles of the various systems of universal ethics are not understood as self-justifying. They are therefore understood as unjustified and question-begging, from a relativist perspective. To the contrary, PEI implies only that the "ultimate" moral status of any given moral claim will remain a mystery—which is why ethics defies the very foundation it demands.

This conclusion leads to an implication of PEI that has previously been overlooked. Ethics is not defeated by indeterminacy, as many moral relativists suggest. Besides appraising the debate between universal ethics and relativism, a key aim of this chapter is to show how PEI is essential for framing the objectives and challenges of any given ethical system. In addition, because of PEI we are assured that substantive moral debates can go on indefinitely.

So far, I have spoken of ethics in a most general way. As the chapter progresses, however, I will more specifically explicate PEI through an analysis of Western ethics (mainly, the ethical theories of Aristotle, Kant, and Mill) and the moral teachings of Confucius. I will also briefly examine how these ethical systems have engendered different concepts of self. Whereas Kantian and utilitarian ethics treat the self abstractly or impersonally, the ethics of

Aristotle and Confucius treat the self nonabstractly—in conceiving of morality as an activity defined by and incorporated into the very fabric of personal life. In the end, PEI is a problem for all of these ethical systems. I will show that PEI is a feature of any rationally acceptable ethical system, although it has mainly theoretical implications for the West and exclusively practical implications for Confucian ethics. Regardless, we can presume that ethics will continue to thrive, since it is not defeated by indeterminacy or diversity. Stated bluntly, the perplexing variety of ethical perspectives that so often promotes conflict can also serve to enrich ethics. It is for the latter reason that I see comparative ethics as occupying an important and increasingly larger role within the discipline.

Western Ethics

The Problem of Ethical Indeterminacy and the Relativists' Challenge to Ethics

The mere fact that one cannot prove something is true does not mean it is false. This bit of logic has been used by many to fallaciously "justify" claims that cannot be falsified. It also points to a potentially vast number of reasonable beliefs—about the world, human nature, morality, and so on—that we may simply assume are true. For example, we may presume that one cannot be in two places at the same time, that something cannot be both true and false at the same time, that 2 + 2 will always equal 4, and the like. Yet such claims cannot be proven because they cannot, in principle, be falsified. Nothing could count as evidence against them. The truth of such claims are nonetheless taken to be obvious or self-evident, based purely on intuition.

It may take a serious breakdown of one's intuitions to bring into question the self-evidence of these claims. But even under cognitively healthy conditions, what may be obvious to one person may not be so obvious to another, even when the truth of the matter is supposed to be self-evident. Thus, although the aforementioned claims may be self-evident to almost everyone, a problem emerges: For many "self-justifying" claims that cannot be proven (or falsified), one will always find it difficult to know just where to draw the line between those that are obviously true and those that are not.

This conclusion leads directly to PEI. Note, however, that the foundational (allegedly self-justifying) first principles of the various Western ethical systems are even more dubious than the claims above. Two central examples from the history of Western ethics support this point.

Let's begin with Kant's Categorical Imperative: Act only on that maxim that you can will to be universal law (i.e., on a maxim that is valid for all rational, free beings). In the *Groundwork of the Metaphysic of Morals,* Kant attempted to justify the Categorical Imperative by "transcendentally proving" that reason and freedom are necessary conditions for morality. More specifically, he claimed that the Categorical Imperative is justified precisely because reason and freedom form its foundation—and ethical action cannot consistently undermine its own foundation. From a reasonably skeptical point of view, however, one could say that Kant failed to prove that the Categorical Imperative is truly obligatory, since he failed to show that reason and freedom have *absolute* moral value. For even if reason and freedom are "necessary" for morality to be possible, this contention does not prove that they *alone* have inherent moral value and, hence, that they must *always* be respected.

But instead of thinking of Kant's Categorical Imperative as being justified by an unconvincing proof, one can conceive of it as inherently self-justifying or foundational. That is, one can think of the Categorical Imperative as a kind of moral assumption—as long as one values reason and freedom highly enough. In this case, one must be sufficiently persuaded that the capacities to reason and act freely are uniquely "good-in-themselves" and, therefore, that compromising them in any way would be morally inconsistent. The Categorical Imperative itself would then be understood as a first principle—a perfectly reasonable move for those who think of reason and free will as having such a high moral value. The self-evident way to proceed would require one to consistently justify and condemn actions for all rational, free beings, regardless of differences in culture and personal taste. Or to put it crudely, one has come to assume the truth of the "golden rule" that whatever is justified for one person is justified for another, all other things being equal.

So Kant's ethics will be most attractive to those who take freedom to be the central moral value; and its categorical demands might even be convincing to those who take freedom to be the only genuine moral value. But now consider a second example: Bentham and Mill's Principle of Utility. According to this principle, the only thing that has inherent moral worth is happiness, so actions are considered moral only in proportion to the happiness, benefit, or utility they produce. Happiness therefore constitutes the only "proof" this utilitarian ethic can appeal to, since "ultimate ends are not amenable to direct proof."[2] Stated more accurately, then, the Principle of Utility can be thought of as a self-justifying first principle for those who are persuaded that happiness alone is desirable in itself.[3] In that case, happiness would be the sole end of human action and, therefore, the only thing that has intrinsic moral worth. The moral necessity of bringing about the greatest amount of happiness (general happiness) is taken to follow, even if this can be brought about only at the expense of one's own happiness.

At this point, I hope it is clear that there can be—and often is—a conflict between Kantian and utilitarian principles. Indeed, different assumptions about what has intrinsic moral worth can take us down very different moral paths. What if happiness for thousands can be maximized by infringing on only one person's freedom? The utilitarian answer is frequently reflected in social decisions for which it would be utterly impractical to consider the will of one person over so many. The Kantian answer is that one is never justified in acting against the Categorical Imperative or in violating a person's will to achieve practical gains, or even to avoid great harm. One must choose either to be a good utilitarian and minimize unhappiness, or to be a good Kantian and respect free will despite the consequences. Most crucially, one ultimately decides which choice is morally preferable, in virtue of the value taken to be most self-evident at the time.

This conflict illustrates the moral relativist's point. Here are two moral theories, both of which are internally logically consistent, and both of which appeal to allegedly self-justifying first principles that often generate mutually exclusive but allegedly obligatory courses of action.

Much more recently, Bernard Williams has accounted for this kind of dilemma in "The Truth in Relativism."[4] Williams explains the "truth" in relativism by laying out the parameters of conflict for mutually exclusive ethical systems. In short, he says, there must be at least two systems of belief, say, S1 and S2, that are (a) to some extent self-contained and (b) exclusive of one another. The most straightforward case is one in which S1 and S2 entail conflicting consequences, C1 and C2, respectively. S1 yields one consequence (e.g., by answering "yes" to a yes/no question), and S2 yields another (by answering "no" to the same question). Of course, there must be a "vocabulary of appraisal" in order for these systems of belief to be engaged in such a confrontation. Simply stated, each must know what the other is saying, to be able to disagree. Hence we have the parameters of a system-based conflict, whereby fundamentally different belief systems lead to very different conclusions about what is, and what is not, obligatory. Finally, it is worth mentioning that for Williams, moral relativism applies only to ethical confrontations that are "real," or that present a reasonable option for "going over" from one system to another.

What would be the basis for "going over" from one belief system to another? The answer is simply that one must be sufficiently persuaded to do so. The dispute cannot be reasonably settled by appealing to what I have been calling a "higher" Moral Truth. A person is sufficiently persuaded by another belief system (or not), depending on what he or she values.

Williams's claim that a confrontation has to be "real" and not just conceivable (or "notional") is open to question, but I think his account of ethical confrontation is excellent. However, his account of real confrontation between exclusive ethical systems does not show that moral relativism is true, strictly speaking. What Williams has shown is that moral relativism is *plausible*, but no more plausible than another belief system—such as Kantian ethics or utilitarianism—that is internally consistent and self-contained, yet assumes that (some) Moral Truth exists.

Indeed, the same reasoning that Williams uses to show that relativism is "true" (i.e., that real confrontations between exclusive ethical systems cannot be resolved) can also be applied to the dispute between moral relativism and universal ethics. On the one hand, those who believe that a certain ethical theory is universally valid cannot appeal to Moral Truth to prove this. They cannot even show that there *is* a Moral Truth and will always seem to beg the question in assuming that it exists. On the other hand, the "truth" in relativism—that there is no Moral Truth—does not follow from PEI—that is, from the fact that there are real confrontations that cannot be resolved. All that follows is that an *appeal* to Moral Truth cannot be used as a "proof" for settling ethical disputes. Therefore, relativism also seems to beg the question in concluding what it ultimately must assume: that there is no such thing as Moral Truth.

Paradoxically, then, the force of PEI is as follows: We cannot appeal to Moral Truth *even if it does exist.* Indeed, we cannot determine anything substantive about Moral Truth, including whether (or not) it exists. Hence the debate between universal ethics and moral relativism could continue indefinitely, for the very reason that Moral Truth is so indeterminate.[5] In effect, it is reasonable to believe that relativism is *true* only as long as one considers it obvious that a universal basis for ethics is *not possible.* In this case, one would take the truth of relativism to be self-justifying, just as a proponent of universal ethics takes the foundational principle of her belief system to be self-justifying.

To make this point another way, the "truth" in relativism simply does not follow from PEI. Relativism rests on the stronger assumption that Moral Truth is nonexistent rather than merely indeterminate[6]—an assumption that constitutes the relativist's first principle, considered by this perspective to be self-justifying as well as necessary if one is to conclusively deny that a universal ethic is possible. Once we understand that the truth of relativism does not follow from PEI,[7] then we can see just how strong a commitment the relativist is making to an assumption he cannot prove—that there is no such thing as Moral Truth or, in effect, no universal foundation for ethics. But this assumption is just as reasonable as being committed to the equally unprovable assumption that Moral Truth (of some form or another) does exist. What does PEI leave us with, then, besides the fact that there is no way of proving or disproving that Moral Truth exists and, hence, no way to *truly* resolve this dispute? The answer is: real confrontation between equally plausible but mutually exclusive systems of belief—one that takes the possibility of Moral Truth (and thus universal ethics) for granted[8] and the other that denies precisely this possibility. It just depends on what one takes to be more or less obvious.

The Problem of Ethical Indeterminacy and the Western Concept of Self

We have seen that a belief in (some) Moral Truth is as plausible as the belief that it does not exist. We have also seen that even a belief that Moral Truth is possible (or that it may exist) is strong enough to support the possibility of a universal ethic and is therefore to be distinguished from moral relativism. There is just no way to decide which of these beliefs is ultimately correct, and thus no way to resolve this debate. One must simply make a conceptual commitment one way or the other. The point of this discussion has been to show that in the stronger cases—namely, those in which one either has come to believe in and live by a specific ethical view or has come to flat-out deny the universal validity of such a commitment—a belief must be held in something that cannot be proven but that ultimately must be taken on faith.

In addition, we have seen that conflicts can abound among those who believe in some kind of Moral Truth. Clearly, disparate accounts of Moral Truth produce conflicting accounts of moral action. Kant's ethics and utilitarianism[9] are two such conflicting theories: They disagree about what has intrinsic moral worth, and, at some level, both take their point of view to be self-evident. But it also seems self-evident to the relativist that there is no objective foundation for any ethical theory. In this case, one presumes that personal and cultural boundaries distinguish moral values so thoroughly that the resolution of conflicts between them is theoretically impossible (since it is assumed that Moral Truth does not exist) as well as practically impossible (since moral values are indeed so disparate). The only option is to "go over" from one system to another.

Simply stated, one puts relativism aside by assuming that PEI does not provide a good enough reason to abandon the pursuit of Moral Truth. And it is precisely in the *theoretical* pursuit of this indeterminate principle that Western ethics has developed. Kant used lofty, metaphysical terms in his attempt to define morality. Recall that he argued "transcendentally" to show that reason and freedom are necessary features of morality. More specifically, in recognizing that an empirical proof was not possible Kant argued that we can "conceive of the necessity" of this Moral Truth but we cannot conceive of the thing itself. This is so because the "thing itself" was taken to exist in the realm of noumena, a purely intelligible realm that is inaccessible to us sensible beings who gain knowledge only through experience. For Kant, noumena were to be distinguished from phenomena—the objects that we can come to know a posteriori or "after the fact." Thus he offered an a priori principle whose Truth exists "before the fact," but whose moral value we must understand as being categorically imperative in the world of experience.[10] To state the matter boldly, the Truth of the Categorical Imperative is actually indeterminate, but one may come to "conceive of its necessity" in holding with Kant's appeal to the a priori—that is, to the claim that it is our rational and free nature that makes morality possible. Kant's view may still be taken to beg the question of whether reason and freedom alone have intrinsic moral worth, or whether they have unconditional moral value.

By way of contrast, Bentham and Mill used an empirical approach to Moral Truth, offering a "greatest happiness" principle that may also be thought of as appealing to our nature. In this case, however, the appeal is to our natural tendency to pursue pleasure and avoid pain. This is why happiness is thought to have intrinsic moral worth and, hence, why the principle of utility can be considered self-justifying. But an empirical approach does not constitute an empirical proof, and the aforementioned appeal, like any claiming that something has *intrinsic* value, can be accused of simply begging the question. Despite these differences, though, the basic point here is that both utilitarianism and Kantian ethics depend on indeterminacy. Their foundational principles are defined by their assumptions about Moral Truth and, hence, about what is considered to be "self-justifying" in having "intrinsic" moral value. Meanwhile, PEI guarantees that Truth, if it exists, will forever remain a mystery. Likewise, Western ethics will forever remain a *speculative* discipline, within which system-based conflicts can continue indefinitely— that is, between conflicting ethical systems and their respective versions of Moral Truth.[11]

So in the West, speculative ethics has been the tradition; since its inception in Greece, the pursuit of Truth has been central. But it wasn't until Descartes conceptually isolated the cogito, or "thing which thinks," that ethics embraced an abstract concept of self.[12] This development is clearly seen in Kant's ethics, whereby a moral action is motivated *solely* by reason, independent of personal or subjective considerations. More specifically, through "pure" reason one determines which actions can be universalized and, hence, which actions are moral. Here is a perfect picture of an utterly impersonal, abstract self, one who chooses to act only in ways that are "valid for everyone."

Even utilitarianism, which holds that the "subjective consideration" of happiness alone has intrinsic moral worth, requires judgments that maximize it from an abstract, impersonal point of view.[13] Being a good utilitarian obliges one to think like a "benevolent spectator"; in fact, one must often choose the "greater good" in spite of one's personal needs, desires, and relationships. This choice is considered a necessary feature of doing a cost/benefit analysis fairly, so that the scale is not tipped in favor of maximizing one's own happiness at the expense of the "greater good." The right choice must always be made by one who conceives of personal happiness abstractly—in order to put the "greater good" before all else.

Kantian and utilitarian ethics have been unquestionably influential theories in the West and are typical in employing an abstract concept of self. But before Descartes, ethics did not conceptually separate the self from the actual contingencies of personal life. Just consider Aristotle's account of morality found in the *Nicomachean Ethics,* which defines the first principle of all human activity as eudaemonia or "happiness." This notion of happiness is nothing like the utilitarians', however; it refers to a balanced state of personal integrity and well-being that develops out of repeated, virtuous action. Virtuous action is important primarily because it becomes a part of a person's character, if repeated often enough. A virtuous character leads, in turn, to greater personal stability, harmony, or "happiness."

One clear implication of Aristotle's ethics is that one can engage in a moral action without being a moral person. For being a moral person requires that moral action has become a deliberate habit. Aristotle offered a kind of moral psychology whereby morality is defined as an *essentially personal* achievement. A person becomes virtuous only by acting virtuously, and a virtuous person becomes "happier" and more balanced. Personal integrity therefore depends on moral integrity. Clearly, then, Aristotle's account does not abstract the self away from the person, for one's personal history is the very basis for saying that the person is moral or not.

In summary, Western ethics has been pursuing Moral Truth since its inception, but after Descartes it did so by abstracting the self away from the contingencies of personal life. The concept of self as an utterly impersonal ego or "thing which thinks" went right to the heart of Western ethics. Western ethics has also been bound by PEI from its inception. On the one hand, I have shown that this relationship to PEI may be less of a problem than the relativist thinks it is, since the claim that "there is no Moral Truth" is as unprovable as the claim that "Moral Truth exists." On the other hand, since Moral Truth is indeterminate even if it does exist, the following question will always remain for ethics: Are the moral claims that derive from its various systems *truly* justified—or just question-begging? This question is especially plausible, since so many ethical systems conflict. In effect, since PEI and the ethical conflicts it entails can never truly be resolved, one can just as reasonably opt for relativism as for some ethical theory.[14] It all depends on what is more or less self-evident to the (nonabstract) person making the decision.

For those who opt for some ethical system, recognizing the force of PEI will have great advantages. Besides the obvious benefit of promoting tolerance of diversity (which relativism does too), one can appreciate that believing in (some) Moral Truth is made reasonable by accepting its indeterminacy. This leads to a *paradox of ethics* for the moral person: One fully embraces an ethic—one believes that it is true and lives by it even in the face of conflict, while accepting that its Truth cannot be proven.[15] In effect, one accepts that one's own position can be reasonably questioned, even while embracing it as ultimate. One advantage of understanding PEI and this paradox it generates, then, is that specific moral claims are tempered by a healthy skepticism. This skepticism is particularly important since such claims are, after all, about what *ought* to be done. More than anything else, though, one comes to understand that others—other *nonabstract* persons—hold different, equally unprovable first principles, depending upon what *they* value most highly at the time. For a commitment to some Moral Truth, even one allegedly "valid for everyone," is a *personal choice* made for one's own reasons. Even in embracing principles assumed to be self-evident or self-justifying, one must recognize that people often have good reasons for valuing different things. Again, just consider the conflicting assumptions entailed by Kantian and utilitarian ethics. The paradox, generally stated, is that conflicting conclusions about the same moral problem *can both be right,* as long as they are reasonably guided by different moral assumptions.[16]

Yet this paradox is not so much of a threat to universal Moral Truth if PEI is properly understood. To the contrary, the fact that the foundation of ethics is unprovable is a central theoretical advantage, for this unprovability is precisely what provides the catalyst for further moral thought. In accepting that its various foundational principles are indeterminate, universal ethics can continue to be questioned and challenged, *even* by those who believe in it. (Such questioning can be done either generally or with a specific system of universal ethics in mind.) In other words, acknowledging that a belief in Moral Truth is an article of faith should vitiate the dogmatism often exhibited by those who think they have complete and final knowledge of morality. In thinking that one has arrived at Moral Truth, one often stops asking the most pivotal ethical questions (e.g., Am I really right?). In believing that evaluating one's own first principles is no longer necessary, one's *moral thinking* stops. PEI has given us sufficient reason to be sure that moral reevaluation is necessary, since moral intuitions often change. In turn, we have reason to question the universality of our moral claims. If nothing else, we must admit that there is no proof that they are rationally justified.

The central issue, then, is that understanding PEI entails understanding the role of intuition and self-justification in ethics as well as the role that confrontation plays in stimulating further moral thought. And now with a system of communication that literally spans the globe, it should come as no surprise that comparative ethics is steadily on the rise. Indeed, what a fine way for ethics to thrive in this ever-changing, diverse world. But what about all the individuals who must choose in the face of a moral dilemma or confrontation? Ours is a personal choice as much about *how* to be moral as why, if we are really thinking morally. Only then can we act on what we think is *ultimately* right—paradoxically, with the knowledge that conflicting moral choices may be equally reasonable and with the faith that our choice is the right one.

Confucian Ethics and Comparative Philosophy

Confucius and the Absence of an Abstract Concept of Self

In general, the Western approach to morality is markedly different from that of Confucius.[17] For one thing, unlike Western ethics, Confucius's teachings are not theoretical. Instead, he provided a timelessly influential and nonabstract method for living a good life—a *humane* life. This teaching is something that Westerners can (and indeed have) come to understand and value. Specifically, Confucius employed "down to earth" language to describe how human beings can interact with each other in a harmonious, civilized way. His teaching can be explained in terms of two ideas central to Confucian philosophy: *li* and *jen*.[18] For the Chinese these principles are essentially manifest in *interpersonal* conduct.

Li has been translated as rite, ritual, ceremony, propriety, and right conduct; and *jen*, as goodness, nobility, benevolence, and humaneness. But most important, the concepts of *li* and *jen* are essentially related and cannot be fully understood independently from one another. Confucius sometimes spoke of them separately, however, as we will see in various passages from the *Analects*. For this reason I, too, will examine *li* and *jen* as separately as possible by discussing the major themes of each as they are derived from Confucius's work.

The following are some themes of *li* found in the *Analects* (Book:Section). (a) *Li* is used as a guide to govern or to rule: (2:3), (3:19), (4:13), (13:6), (15:4), (15:17). (b) *Li* is a ritual vessel (utensil): (5:3), (15:1). (c) Those who are *jen* (good, noble, benevolent) are restrained by *li,* and submission to *li* is needed in order to be *jen:* (3:3), (6:25), (8:2), (9:10), (12:1). (d) *Li* is more than the behavior; it requires the right emotion and reverence: (2:7), (2:8), (3:4), (3:11), (3:12), (3:26), (9:3), (17:11). (e) *Li* establishes one as a human being; it gives one firm footing: (2:4), (8:8), (16:13), (20:3). And (f) *li* generates a power; that is, it establishes *te* ("moral"[19] power): (2:1), (3:11), (4:11), (12:19).

We are informed in the *Analects* that *li* or ritual is essential to living a distinctively human life. And most crucially, living a distinctively human life means living in dignified harmony with others. *Li* is thus *relational:* It entails appropriate patterns of conduct for the great variety of human relationships.[20] Of course, *li* will vary, depending on the relation at hand. Confucius believed that our distinctively human roles were defined by our relation to others and, moreover, that these roles define the "person" him- or herself. For example, to be a mother, one must have a child; to be a teacher, one must have a student; to be a friend, one must have a friend. And insofar as one is a mother, a teacher, a friend, there are certain ways in which she should conduct herself—ways that are "prescribed by *li."*

In essence, then, *li* not only defines "moral" or proper human conduct; it also defines what it means to be a person (or a human being), from a Confucian point of view. As for the "moral" features of *li,* human beings should engage only in conduct appropriate to their relationships with others. But this prescription has direct bearing on what it means to be a human being, as we are inherently *social* beings who are *not* defined by some abstract intrapersonal characteristic. Instead, we are defined by actual relationships that vary from person to person and, for the same person, change over time. Thus we see the main difference between the Confucian treatment of self (person, or human being) and the abstract Western concept of self elucidated in the first part of this chapter.[21] *Li* must be directed toward someone or something else—one's ancestors, the gods, one's parents or siblings, one's superiors or one's friends. And *li* defines the person.[22] Clearly, then, the Confucian concept of self is antithetical to the contemporary Western concept, which conceives of the moral person independently from the details of personal life.

This discussion of *li* must not be permitted to understate the magic that Confucius saw in the distinctive human ability to form harmonious and meaningful relationships. For Confucius, "moral" action could never be just a matter of habit. Rather, it involves a sincere and dedicated orientation toward the person or (more rarely) the thing being engaged. Confucius saw the ability to act appropriately toward one's co-humans in a respectful and dignified way as the essence of all good relationships, and he saw relationships as the essence of self—of being a person. We simply take *li* for granted in so many social contexts, because it has become "second nature," or because we no longer have to be painfully and self-consciously aware of what we are doing in those contexts.

To state the matter even more strongly, if we take for granted the magical quality that Confucius saw to be the essence of *li,* ritual would no longer be proper ritual. It would merely be the rote behavior that an automaton could perform if programmed to do so—not the personally significant, even sacred, gesture of one human being who stands in relation to another. In other words, the conventions of *li* must *mean* something. Yet this outcome requires something much more mysterious than behavior—something that cannot be measured as systematically. I refer here to the proper *spirit* or conscious orientation with which the ritual act must be performed—in short, to *jen.*

The following are some themes of *jen* found in the *Analects* (Book:Section). (a) *Jen* is hard, a burden, difficult: (6:20), (8:7), (14:2). (b) We have the strength to be *jen;* it would be at our side if we wanted it: (4:6), (7:29). (c) *Jen* requires that we care for it: (9:30). (d) The good person speaks little of *jen;* it is difficult to capture in words: (9:1), (12:3). (e) The person of *jen* rests content and is never unsettled or disquieted: (6:21), (9:2), (9:28). (f) The person of *jen* is always *jen; jen* is a "trait of character": (4:5), (9:2). (g) Nothing should be done at the expense of *jen; jen* is central to one's life, essential, all pervasive: (15:8). And (h) *jen* requires the ability to take one's feelings as a guide or, more literally, "to take the analogy from what is near": (6:28).

Jen is a benevolent orientation toward another that is reflected in how a person lives his or her life. Now it is easier to understand why *jen* is more mysterious than *li*—because it is the *conscious aim* that one adopts toward another; it is the "spirit" of openness and decency with which one interacts. We in the West would be inclined to say that one is *jen* if it is characteristic of that person to act toward others in a genuine and respectful way, or in a way that demonstrates moral virtue and personal integrity. This characterization is fine as long as one realizes that, for Confucius, "integrity" was *not* an "internal" psychological trait but, rather, something that must be *expressed through li. Jen* is a feature of *li;* it is a part of the actions or rituals themselves. *Jen* is reflected in the ready and masterful way in which one who is cultivated in social grace can effectively relate to others. *Li* and *jen* are therefore inseparable concepts.[23] Moreover, the person who is *jen* will consistently act benevolently, nobly, or humanely. To put it in Western terms, *jen* must become a part of that person's character.

From the themes and passages referred to above, we can surmise that two central principles apply to *jen*. First, *jen* requires a formal dimension of acting according to *li*. Second, *jen* requires a conscious or imaginative dimension of "analogizing" with others, of being empathetic and respectful toward them. The essential relation between *li* and *jen* was first introduced to Western readers by Herbert Fingarette in his book *Confucius—The Secular as Sacred*.[24] As Fingarette explained this relation, *li* refers to forms of conduct imbued with the right spirit, and *jen* tells us what that spirit is—namely, a matter of approaching others with civility and of treating them with the dignity they deserve.[25] This requires a proper regard not only for their roles as persons but also for their humanity. As Fingarette puts it:

> Thus *li* and *jen* are two aspects of the same thing. Each points to an aspect of the action of man in his distinctively human role. *Li* directs our attention to the traditional social pattern of conduct and relationships; *jen* directs our attention to the person as the one who pursues that pattern of conduct and thus maintains those relationships. *Li* also refers to the particular act in its status as exemplification of invariant norm; *jen* refers to the act as expressive of an orientation of the person, as expressing his commitment to act as prescribed by *li*. *Li* refers to the act as overt and distinguishable pattern of sequential behavior; *jen* refers to the act as the single, indivisible gesture of an actor.[26]

Again, this is precisely how Confucius thought we are established as persons: as wives or husbands, professionals, parents, friends, lovers. Acting appropriately toward others depends on their relation to us; it also requires acting with the proper spirit. Indeed, what Confucius saw to be the essence of a peaceful and civilized society was established by harmonious human interaction.[27]

As noted, Confucius did not employ an abstract concept of self, for the very reason that morality in his day was explicitly understood in terms of social rituals and roles. The closest Confucius came to an "abstract" concept is *jen,* but even this concept—though mysterious—is not truly abstract. *Jen* is not a theoretical property of a conceptually isolated ego or self; it is an "outer-directed" orientation expressed in the specific interactions one has with others. Confucius conceived of morality in just this way: as living a life of *li* and *jen.* Although his philosophy was not concerned with the pursuit of Moral Truth (a pursuit the West has been carrying out for millennia), Confucius provided a profound account of morality that focused instead on what I have been calling "harmonious human interaction"—an event that occurs in a specific human context as people conscientiously carry out their various roles and responsibilities. The point is this: The roles that make us who we are *cannot* be abstracted from who we are. What defines the "self" is precisely what defines us as persons—namely, the various roles and relationships that link us to others. This is also what it means to live a "human" life for Confucius: living a "moral" life of *li* and *jen.*

Confucian Ethics, Aristotelian Ethics, and the Problem of Ethical Indeterminacy

Notwithstanding this difference between Confucian philosophy and Western ethics, specifically, that the former lacks theoretical abstraction,[28] there are several key similarities between Confucian ethics and Aristotelian ethics that this section will examine. With respect to the absence of theory, though, PEI was not a problem of pursuing Moral Truth for Confucius. There was a sure element of *practical* indeterminacy in Confucius's approach to ethics nonetheless, as we can see in his treatment of *jen.* In particular, when Confucius was questioned about whether a living person was *jen* or not, he either said he did not know or simply declined to answer.

Confucius spoke of *jen* in a very paradoxical way because of the indeterminacy that emerges from his moral teachings. I account for this in much the same way as I account for the *paradox of ethics* endemic to Western ethics—or to any rationally acceptable ethical system, for that matter—since all ethical systems must contend with PEI in one form or another. The paradox in Confucian ethics can be explained as follows: The moral person—or the person who is *jen*—must follow a *tao,* or path, that *entails the pursuit of jen.* For even strictly practical aims can embody a kind of "ideal," and the case of *jen* presents as much of an "ideal" as any theoretical moral standard, including the various versions of Moral Truth that we have embraced in the West. Why? Because, from a reasonable point of view, none can finally and completely be reached.

The paradox produced by indeterminacy is a function of ethics itself. Location makes no difference. We have considered examples from the West and from the Orient; in all cases, the moral person must live in a way that reflects commitment to the view she embraces, while being open (within reason) to the personal and moral differences of others. This is the logical result of acknowledging—on a theoretical *or* practical level—that an ideal is embraced that can never fully be realized. Although Aristotle and Confucius did not define "morality" in the same terms, they both grasped this point. Indeed, it is for this reason that both described morality as an ongoing process for the moral person—as a *way of life.* For Aristotle, morality was the deliberate activity of pursuing goodness for its own sake; and for Confucius, it was the activity of skillfully and humanely relating to others. For both, then, morality was considered a personal characteristic that one does, or does not, strive to develop. For this reason, the systems of "universal" ethics that Aristotle and Confucius articulated were socially oriented, since morality was understood as an undertaking for real (nonabstract) people as they live out their lives. The difference is that for Aristotle, this characteristic was elucidated on a theoretical or intrapersonal level—where morality was understood as an activity of the human soul. By contrast, Confucius conceived of morality in an *exclusively* interpersonal way—in terms of nonabstract rituals, roles, and the social harmony they generate. Despite this difference, morality was understood as a *feature of specific persons* in both cases, which is why an abstract concept of self has no place in either ethical system. And in both cases morality overtly receives a paradoxical treatment, because one must continue to strive to be moral *in order to be moral*—by striving for eudaemonia and *jen*, respectively.

So when did Confucius feel safe in saying that a person was *jen?* The answer is that he felt safe when describing the character of the ancient (i.e., dead) "Divine Sages," primarily of the Chou dynasty. For Confucius, *jen* was such an "ideal" personal accomplishment that it required a lifetime of pursuit. Only after one's life was complete could the content of one's character be determined (and in this case also become a matter of historical fact). Consider passage 8:7 in the *Analects:* "Master Tseng said, The true Knight of the Way must perforce be both broad-shouldered and stout of heart; his burden is heavy and he has far to go. For *jen* is the burden he has taken upon himself; and must we not grant that it is a heavy one to bear? Only with death does his journey end; then must we not grant that he has far to go?"

Similarly, Aristotle asked, "Should no man be called 'happy' while he lives?"[29] His answer to this question was that no man should be called "happy," and in the West we may know his reason: Eudaemonia is an activity of the soul that is the *most final end* of all human activity. For Aristotle, what was the essence of such practical indeterminacy? Was it the kind that applies to real, nonabstract persons? Like Confucius's *jen,* Aristotle's eudae-monia is an end we may fail to see, even after death.

Notes

1. It follows that the only kind of criticism that one system could reasonably direct at another with which it conflicts is that its claims are internally logically inconsistent.

2. John Stuart Mill, *Utilitarianism* (Indianapolis, Ind.: Hackett Publishing Co., 1979; originally published in 1861), p. 4.

3. Like Kant, the Utilitarians beg the question of whether happiness *alone* has inherent moral value. More specifically, both ethical theories assume that the thing they take to have the greatest moral value (free will and happiness, respectively) is the *only* thing that has intrinsic moral value. Presumably, this assumption is an implication of a moral precept having *universal* force; one runs the risk of logical inconsistency when allowing for more than one universal imperative.

4. Bernard Williams, "The Truth in Relativism," in *Relativism: Cognitive and Moral,* ed. Michael Krausz and Jack Meiland (Notre Dame, Ind.: University of Notre Dame Press, 1982), pp. 175–185.

5. Notice that the confrontations between the various ethical systems could continue indefinitely for the same reason, since the content of Moral Truth is not something to which any of us can appeal.

6. This claim, that moral relativism entails not just moral skepticism but a denial that Moral Truth exists, is not just stipulative. This distinction is essential, given that different conclusions follow from these positions. Again, one can consistently believe that a universal ethic is possible—even that there *is* Moral Truth—and also believe that the substance or content of this Truth cannot be rationally determined. In fact, it is essential to any universal ethic that its first principle is "unprovable" in just this way. Thus we see why the first principles of ethics are allegedly self-evident or self-justifying. In short, it is precisely the "self-justifying" nature of such principles that leads to the stronger positions held by those who believe in a particular universal ethic. Indeed, a main point of this discussion is that it is also the strong kind of claim that a moral relativist must hold to consistently conclude that a universal ethic is *impossible.* In this way, the moral relativist is distinguished from the moral agnostic who at least believes in the possibility of Moral Truth.

7. Nor does PEI follow from the truth of relativism; for if it did, true moral claims would amount to *logically consistent* claims.

8. Notice that the moral agnostic's view—that Moral Truth may (or may not) exist—is trivially true. For this reason, it is more easily taken for granted than either the relativist's view or one committed to some version of Moral Truth.

9. I am suggesting not that Western ethics is completely accounted for by these two theories but, rather, that they have set the stage for what has happened in the discipline. Thus the abstract concept of self that has emerged in the West since Descartes can be made sufficiently clear in light of their explication alone.

10. Kant also made it clear that his reasoning was not merely circular or analytic; he provided a "transcendental, synthetic" proof that should persuade us that reason does not entail freedom, and that both are necessary for morality to be possible.

11. Since this Truth is indeterminate, valid confrontations between Western ethical theories will continue to legitimately criticize rival theories only on the grounds of logical consistency, practical applicability, intuitive and/or conceptual plausibility, and the like. There is just no way to finally resolve PEI, for it ultimately depends on the first principle that is validated by one's moral intuitions.

12. After Descartes, virtually every branch of philosophy adopted an abstract concept of self; ethics was not alone in doing so.

13. James Rachels claims that such an "impartial" point of view is fundamental to any good ethical theory. Calling it the "impartiality requirement" of moral reason, he states that "almost every important theory of morality includes the idea of impartiality. The basic idea is that each individual's interests are equally important: from within the moral point of view, there are no 'privileged' persons; every life has equal value." (See *The Elements of Moral Philosophy*, 2nd ed. [New York: McGraw-Hill, 1993], p. 12.) I agree with Rachels, but I would qualify his statement by saying that it applies specifically to Western ethics after Descartes.

14. The morally agnostic view will seem the most reasonable, however, to the person whose intuitions are not swayed strongly enough, one way or the other.

15. The paradox is resolved because indeterminacy of Moral Truth does not make it false but only unprovable.

16. The same point can be made to explain why the "paradox of ethics" is a paradox and not a contradiction.

17. This is not to say that we in the West are unable to value what Confucius was trying to say. In "The Truth in Relativism" (in *Relativism: Cognitive and Moral*, ed. Michael Krausz and Jack Meiland), Williams mentions a problem that he terms "incommensurable exclusivity," a kind of "limiting case" of exclusivity between conflicting ethical systems. In this case, S1 and S2 do not just produce different conclusions to the same question; their consequences are *incomparable*. Hence a holder of S1 is theoretically precluded from "going over" to S2 in any sensible fashion, and vice versa. Presumably, the difference between ethical systems would be so extreme that one could not even begin to identify with the values, consequences, and so on reflected in the other system. There would still have to be a "locus of incommensurability" in order for one to identify that C1 and C2 are indeed incomparable. And the question remains as to whether such incommensurability is possible, since it seems to depend on a kind of cognitive relativism that moral relativism *simpliciter* does not entail. Important for our purposes, however, is the fact that, even though Confucius offered a very different kind of ethic, we can identify with what he said and can value it precisely for offering a different way of thinking about human interaction. In essence, then, we are not "going over" to Confucian ethics so much as "bringing it over" to our own way of thinking. We are therefore enriching Western ethics by appreciating— and perhaps even applying—a different (but not incommensurable) ethical system.

18. There are other morally relevant concepts that could be discussed in connection with Confucian philosophy—for example, *te*, or "moral" power, and *yi*, or appropriate conduct. For the purposes of this chapter, however, *li* and *jen* are sufficient to

show how Confucius viewed morality, especially with respect to his not employing the subjective/objective distinction.

19. Strictly speaking, there is no term for "moral" in ancient Chinese, yet the concept as we know it applies quite well. Indeed, the present section should make that apparent.

20. *Li* is therefore learned. It requires guidance from tradition and cannot exist without a foundation of proper social values. With time and continual practice, however, *li* becomes *wu-wei*, or actionless activity. In other words, with perseverance and dedication, ritual becomes effortless; we become masters at behaving in ways that initially were not easy to perform. This is true of any activity performed well. An activity can become "actionless" only when it is learned and perfected. We may take for granted that the language and gestures we use for greeting others, for expressing emotion in any number of contexts, for properly sharing a meal, and so on, were always part of the repertoire of our daily activities. But indeed they were not, as we clearly see upon observing the difficulty experienced by small children who are just learning these skills. In short, we learn about ways of getting along with others only by learning the appropriate conduct; we acquire the skills of personal interaction only by learning *li.*

21. It is interesting to note that the Confucian concept of self, in being essentially personal (like Aristotle's), is completely different from other Eastern concepts of self such as that of Atman/Brahman (in the Hindu tradition) or the Buddhist concept that there is "no self" or nothing personal that maintains identity over time. The latter two Eastern concepts of self are utterly impersonal.

22. For Confucius, then, there is no difference between the self and the person.

23. It was probably the inseparability of these concepts that led Confucius to be so "chary" of speaking of those who are, or are not, *jen.* Together, the two concepts constitute a way of life, a path or *tao* that one must always follow in the proper spirit. This way of life is not a quality that can be attributed to someone easily or lightly. Nor is it something that comes to one easily. Rather, such a "moral" way of life must be nurtured, developed, and practiced consistently and with dedication.

24. Herbert Fingarette, *Confucius—The Secular as Sacred* (New York: Harper Torchbooks, 1972).

25. I am not trying to suggest that Confucius was espousing an egalitarian philosophy where all humans were considered worthy of respect. To the contrary, this would depend on the person—that is, on how one carries out one's various roles and responsibilities. Regardless, the person who is *jen* can tell what conduct would be appropriate, taking such differences into account. And surely, people who are not worthy of respect will be treated differently from those who are, by a person who is *jen* and who can ascertain the difference.

26. Fingarette, *Confucius—The Secular as Sacred*, p. 42.

27. Confucian philosophy is actually very applicable today. The concepts of *li* and *jen* can help us to establish meaningful—and even peaceful—relations with human beings who are "strange" or "alien" to us. For starters, we must learn about them, which means we must learn about the *li* that, although different from our own in form, is not necessarily different in spirit. In any case, learning about the humanity of

the other diffuses the sense of otherness that we so often experience in dealing with people who are different.

28. Henry Rosemont has argued this point in a variety of publications. See Rosemont, ed., *Chinese Texts and Philosophical Contexts: Essays Dedicated to Angus C. Graham* (La Salle, Ill.: Open Court, 1991).

29. See Book 1, chapters 9 and 10, of the *Nicomachean Ethics.*

Chapter Four

Classical Confucian and Contemporary Feminist Perspectives on the Self: Some Parallels and Their Implications

HENRY ROSEMONT, JR.

The topic of this chapter may initially appear overly general, or bizarre, or overly general *and* bizarre. General, because of the growing multiplicity of historical, sociological, and philosophical perspectives that all come under the heading of contemporary feminism—perspectives that, at this stage of scholarship, are sometimes incompatible, rendering the term no longer univocal. There are Marxist, socialist, liberal, lesbian, and other patterns of feminist thought. Some equate gender and sex, most do not; some ignore race and class, most do not; most argue for the primacy of culture over nature (biology), a few do not; and the social, political, and moral prescriptions that flow from these perspectives are equally varied, ranging from gender dualism (but with equality) to androgyny, to traditionally defined feminine virtues over the masculine.[1]

The topic may also appear bizarre given the commonplace that the classical Confucians advocated a rigidly hierarchical society rooted in patriarchy and were paradigmatically sexist. Ab initio, then, at least a rough definition of feminism must be proffered, along with a promissory note that reading Confucius and his followers against a feminist background can tell us some things about them and even more things about ourselves, women and men alike.

Feminism I take to be a set of theories and practices for pointing up, explaining, and overcoming the subjugation, exploitation, and oppression of women that have been characteristic of most of the world's cultures, certainly including Western culture, for most of recorded history. Though few would question this generalization about women's places in cultures, the definition can nevertheless generate uneasiness about feminism, because it seems to run together distinct disciplines—history, sociology, political science, and ethics at the least—as well as to blur the distinction between the impartial scholar and the committed activist, or between objectivity and subjectivity.

Many feminist thinkers, however, would characterize such uneasiness as a symptom of the disease they have been attempting to cure. Although she is speaking specifically about the natural sciences, Sandra Harding makes this point well:

> [T]he concern to define and maintain a series of rigid dichotomies in science and epistemology no longer appears to be a reflection of the progressive character of scientific inquiry; rather, it is inextricably connected with specifically masculine—and perhaps uniquely Western and bourgeois—needs and desires. Objectivity vs. subjectivity, . . . reason vs. emotions, mind vs. body—in each case the former has been associated with masculinity and the latter with femininity. In each case it has been claimed that human progress requires the former to achieve domination of the latter.[2]

Already we have a parallel between contemporary feminist writings and classical Confucian texts, and a hint of why those latter texts have not been considered truly philosophical by the overwhelming majority of Western practitioners of the discipline. Kant properly did his metaphysics and epistemology in the first *Critique*, his ethical theory in the second, and his aesthetics in the third. Aristotle wrote as distinct texts the *Politics*, the *Nicomachean Ethics*, and the *Poetics*. True philosophical writings all of them. Confucius, Mencius, Xun Zi, and other Confucians, by contrast, seem to run together the social, political, the moral, even the economic—seemingly oblivious to needed analytic distinctions. But as the Harding quote suggests, it does not follow from this observation that the early Confucians weren't philosophers, nor that their way of proceeding conceptually was (is) inferior to the style of their European counterparts. Masculine Westerners they were not, but not much else can be inferred from the comparison; although the ethical is indeed not consistently distinct from the sociopolitical or the economic in the *Analects*, this fact can be seen as a strength rather than a conceptual weakness, for such an orientation must expand rather than contract our vision, and it obliges us to confront more directly the social, political, and economic implications of our ethical views.

Moreover, the proper Confucian did not dwell in the ivory tower. As the *Lun Yu* says: "The scholar who only sits at ease is not a proper scholar" (14:3). Or more strongly: "The Master said, Just as to sacrifice to ancestors other than one's own is presumption, so to see what is right and not do it is cowardice" (2:24).

Among the several feminist perspectives currently in force, the one I wish to focus on clusters around the work of Carol Gilligan, Nancy Chodorow, Nell Noddings, and others and is centered on the concepts of care and nurturance.[3] And I want to defend both this feminist perspective and what, I shall argue, are its Confucian counterparts. My arguments must be general, because I wish to suggest an overall picture of compatibility between these two seemingly antagonistic philosophical orientations. If the arguments are to hold up, of course, each of them must be spelled out in greater detail than can be provided in an early study of this kind.

But before turning directly to these arguments, let us briefly consider two related questions of gender: Were men and women in China seen by the Chinese to have the same respective characteristics they were seen to have in the West? And did Chinese thinkers favor the masculine qualities over the feminine?

I answer the first question affirmatively, albeit tentatively and with a number of important caveats. Surely the history of China is replete with instances of the exploitation and oppression of women, and it would be odd indeed if these social and psychocultural practices could endure for millennia without any intellectual support. Women's sphere was the home, not the community; it was the inner (private) sphere as opposed to the outer (public) sphere occupied by men. Wives were to be obedient to their husbands, and to their sons when widowed; descent was patrilineal, not even argued for but simply presupposed in the Confucian texts. The "inferiority" of women was described at least as early as the ninth century B.C.E., as the following stanza from the *Shi Jing*[a] (Mao 264) makes painfully clear:

> A clever man builds a city wall, a clever woman
> overthrows it; beautiful is the clever woman,
> but she is an owl, a hooting owl; a woman with
> a long tongue, she is a promoter of evil;
> disorder is not sent down from Heaven, it is
> produced by women; those who cannot be taught
> or instructed are women and eunuchs.[4]

Similar misogynous quotes could be given at length, just as they are common in Western writings and sayings ("A woman, a dog, a hickory tree; the more you beat them the better they be," an old English proverb instructs us.) Prima facie, therefore, men and women were compared and contrasted similarly in China and the West.

What complicates an analysis of the Chinese perspective(s), however, is the fact that there is also a good deal of prima facie evidence in support of answering the second gender question negatively. Chinese thinkers do not seem to have favored Western stereotypical masculine qualities over their feminine counterparts. This point will be obvious to anyone who has read the *Dao De Jing*[b], wherein qualities associated with the feminine are not only championed but championed explicitly as feminine (though not necessarily female) qualities. In all cultures, issues of gender contribute significantly to the ways in which concepts of personal identity are established and maintained, social relations and divisions of labor are organized, and natural and social phenomena are symbolized or described metaphorically. Yet China seems to be a strong exception to the general rule that in all three spheres, masculine gender qualities are more highly valued than feminine ones.

I could go further than the *Dao De Jing* (and parts of the *Zhuang Zi*[c] and *Lie Zi*[d]) to maintain that the early Confucian writings also conform, in many interesting respects, to this exceptional situation. In the first place, Chinese bipolar terms tend to place the seemingly more highly valued of the two first, as in *Fu/Mu*[e], *Tian/Di*[f], *Shang/Xia*[g], *Chian/Kun*[h], *Ren/Yi*[i], and so on. But there is an exception, the most basic of all—*Yin/Yang*[j]—which is more or less rendered as feminine/masculine. At the social level, the *yin* type of stance is inferior to the *yang* but, it can be argued, not significantly so. As Alison Black has pointed out,[5] the *Li Ji*[k] tells us that the mother's partiality in loving all of her offspring despite their occasional misdeeds is to be expected, and is good, just as it is good for the father to be impartial in giving them credit only when and where credit is due. In the same text, as well as in the *Mencius*[l] and *Xun Zi*[m], it is the man who seeks (public) office (in the public sphere) and the woman who stays home (in the private one); he is outer (*wai*)[n], and she is inner (*nei*)[o]. And above all, the Chinese male, like his Western counterpart, is rational and seeks order, whereas his female counterpart is intuitive, seeking harmony.[6]

However, when we move from the social to the metaphysical and symbolic, the gender distinctions seem to change significantly. Heaven is partial, punishing the wicked; earth (i.e., the feminine) is impartial: Sometimes there are floods, other times not. Heaven is immaterial, Earth concrete, with *kun* much more the public sphere than *chian*. *Ren*, the highest virtue for the Confucians, is associated with Heaven, and *yi* (righteousness) with Earth. But *ren* signifies love, benevolence, and kindness—"inner" intuitive qualities—whereas *yi* denotes order, rational order. Music, again according to the *Li Ji*, comes from within, and ritual, from without. By the same token, music would be equated with *yin* and ritual with *yang*, but in the *Li Ji* music is linked to Heaven, ritual to Earth. Patricia Ebrey, though her focus is somewhat different, makes an observation altogether appropriate in this regard: "Conceptualizing the difference between men and women in terms of *yin* and *yang* stressed that these differences are part of the natural order, not part of the social institutions artificially created by men. . . . Moreover, the natural basis of these distinctions is not limited to the differences in men's and women's bodies."[7] *Yin* and *yang*, in other words, are fully relational terms. Nothing is either *yin* or *yang* in and of itself, but only as it stands relative to something else. An elderly man is *yang* with respect to an elderly women, but *yin* with respect to a young man. This relationality can equally be seen in the *Huang Di Nei Jing*[p] and in other texts from the Chinese *Materia Medica*;[8] according to the latter, the chest is *yin* with respect to the back but *yang* with respect to the abdomen.

This relationality clearly militates against the view that the early Chinese thinkers were essentialistic in their accounts of women and men. Further evidence for this point comes from a recent study by Lisa Raphals, in which she compares and contrasts two Han Dynasty treatises on women, the *Lienu Zhuan* and the *Nujie qian shi*. She says:

> In summary [the *Lienu Zhuan* chapters] all point to a tacit (and non-essentialistic) premise, that the intellectual virtues of men and women were not fundamentally different, insofar as sagely men and sagely women did much the same things.
>
> In the fullness of time, the *Lienu Zhuan* and the *Nujie* became the two most influential texts on female virtue. . . . Yet the essentialistic *yin/yang* paradigm of the *Nujie* seems to have carried the day. . . . In the wide-scale transformation of the *Lienu Zhuan*, its original arguments for the importance of women in statecraft, and its rich account of female intellectual virtue have all but disappeared from view. . . .
>
> By Ming times if not earlier, this intellectual, as well as social and political, separation of women and men was widely accepted as an eternal and essential feature of Chinese civilization.[9]

Now, it is not clear what we ought to make of these examples and many others that could be given; the question of Chinese gender symbolism deserves a much closer and lengthier examination, especially as it appears to be at variance with the historical traditions of Greece and the Middle East. But I am at least initially inclined to accept Alison Black's generalization on the matter: "At the metaphysical level, concepts that Westerners, and sometimes Chinese themselves, would identify as feminine in an ordinary social or psychocultural context are either given masculine affinity or transcend the distinction altogether—and it is not always easy to determine which is the case."[10] If this view is warranted, its implications can be instructive, not least in suggesting alternative gender theories for analyzing the history of women (and hence men) in the West. Following on the work of Joseph Needham, Nathan Sivin, and others, we seldom ask anymore why China did not develop modern science.[11] In just the same way, instead of asking why the Chinese didn't conceptualize the feminine as it was conceptualized in the West, it might be more useful to turn the question around; perhaps it is the West—especially the modern West—that is more in need of explanation.

The implication that I wish to draw attention to, however, is the following: If the sexism revealed in classical Confucian writings was characteristic only of gender structure (patterns of social organization), not of gender symbolism or gender identity, then it is at least possible that Confucian philosophy can be reconstructed to be relevant today, in ways that a great many feminist thinkers might endorse.

As noted earlier, Western philosophy has traditionally distinguished the political from the social, both from the moral, and all three from the aesthetic. What these ostensibly disparate endeavors have shared is a striving for universalism, a search for principles to be applied impersonally—principles grounded in pure reason, logic. Because "universal" implies "for all human beings," and because "impersonal" suggests that gender differences are not being taken into account, we find it difficult to appreciate that the tendency to universalize and impersonalize may not be universal or impersonal tendencies but, on the contrary, tendencies peculiar to the masculine gender in modern Western civilization.[12]

Let us focus on a specific issue. In modern Western philosophy the concept of rights has dominated moral and political discourse for over two hundred years. Elsewhere I have criticized this concept and the view of human beings on which it rests,[13] and I will not rehearse those criticisms now. But I do want to speak briefly about rights in our cultural context and then contrast the Western rights-bearing individual with the Confucian (and feminist, I will argue) role-carrying person.[14]

As citizens of the Western capitalist democracies we have been strongly inclined to insist that certain basic rights obtain independently of sex, color, age, ethnicity, religion, abilities, time or place. Which rights are fundamental may be a matter of dispute, but rights we have, and we have them solely in virtue of being human.

This basic assumption—for some, a presupposition—is embedded in a larger conceptual framework in which the essence of human beings lies in their individuality, their autonomy, their freedom, their rationality, and, however differentially defined, their self-interest. To be sure, within this larger conceptual framework a wide variety of moral, social, economic, and political theories have been put forward, not all of them compatible with each or any of the others. Further, not all of these theories give the concept of rights pride of place. Nevertheless, I think it is fair to say that the view of human beings as rational, autonomous, rights-holding individuals continues to occupy center stage in our moral, social, economic, and political considerations, in domestic as well as foreign issues and policies.

Clearly the view of human beings reflected in this conceptual framework is identified with one culture—namely, modern Western civilization. Some scholars have attempted to tease out parts of this view, especially the concepts of rights and the individual, from the writings of the ancient Greeks or

St. Augustine, from the Magna Carta or the *Leviathan*. But the view as we have inherited and expanded on it today had its philosophical genesis in Locke's *Second Treatise on Civil Government* and found early political expression in the Virginia Declaration of Rights, the Declaration of Independence, and the French Declaration of the Rights of Man.

Historically this view is the ideological child of the Age of Enlightenment, conceived and nurtured in reaction to the preceding era, correctly called the Age of Absolutism. Human rights became a conceptual counter to the notion of the divine right of kings, the latter right seeming to justify arbitrary, despotic rule.

These historical circumstances can be more fully appreciated in light of developments in modern Western philosophy, especially as they relate to political and moral theorizing. A number of moral and political issues, such as the importance of promise-keeping, or truth-telling, are discussed in terms of the importance of social cohesion, the good of the collectivity. But moral and political issues surrounding rights, freedom, or autonomy are discussed against a very different background—namely, in terms of the potentially coercive and/or oppressive qualities of the collectivity, generally seen as the state, or society.

Thus seen as a strong conceptual bulwark against absolutism or totalitarianism, the worth, the power, the scope—indeed the glory—of the concept of human rights would be denied only by a fool. I would venture to say that no other single idea, or set of actions, has contributed as much to the cause of human dignity in Europe and North America during the rise of industrial capitalism as the idea that all human beings have rights. But the modern history of Europe and North America is identical with the history of the rise of industrial capitalism, and hence to the extent that this history is unique, the concept of human rights needs to be seen as culture-specific. (And unless current assessments of the earth's environments are altogether mistaken, that history will remain unique; consequently, the concept of human rights will remain culture-specific. I will return to this point later.)

Given the unspeakable horrors that have been visited on uncountable numbers of people by absolutist or totalitarian governments—from the distant past to the present—it may at first appear that a charge of cultural specificity against the Enlightenment view of human beings carries no force. One can also make the conceptual argument that culture-specific though this view might be, it is not constraining: Within it, there is philosophical room to either endorse or oppose issues as varied as capital punishment, abortion, the free market, euthanasia, animal rights, and the foreign policies of the United States government, not to mention the policies, foreign and domestic, of other governments. Moreover, a major effort to universalize the concept of human rights was undertaken by the victorious allies at the close of World War II, as seen in the United Nations Declaration of Human Rights, subscribed to in principle by all member nations.

A close reading of that Declaration, however, especially the Preamble thereto, shows that the framers were fully aware that they were proposing a particular moral and political perspective as an ideal not yet extant, as a standard toward which all nations, and all peoples, should measure themselves. Five decades have now passed since the UN Declaration was first promulgated, but the ideal is still not extant. Although in one sense we humans can be seen as sharing a global village, it remains the case that over three-quarters of the world's peoples have had no intimate acquaintance with the cultures of the Western capitalist democracies. They never have lived and do not now live in a postmodern, postindustrial cultural context; and because of population, economic, environmental, and other circumstances (including the absence of capitalist industrialization), they almost surely never will. And as most of these people live in cultures that do not have philosophical and/or religious traditions that incorporate something like the concept of human rights, or as the same cultures have concepts incompatible with the concept of human rights, then how could, or should, the members of those cultures come to see what it would be like to have rights or, more generally, to see that conceiving human beings as rational, rights-holding, autonomous individuals was morally, politically, or in any other way superior to their traditional views of what it is to be a human being?

Eschewing coercion, we might attempt to persuade other peoples of the superiority of the view of human beings as rights-holding, autonomous individuals. The task would be a difficult one, however, because I suspect that for most of the world's peoples such a view of human beings would be seen as simply false. For these peoples, social cohesion remains central, and human relationships govern and structure their lives, such that unless there are at least two human beings, there can be no human beings. Hence, on this different view of being human, at the very least humans are neither individuals nor autonomous; and it is difficult to identify us as rights-holders if we are not autonomous individuals.

It might be tempting here to object that the modern Western view of human beings as rights-holding, autonomous individuals was never intended to be taken as literally true. Should it instead be construed as part of a very general "gendanke experiment" useful for theorizing about basic philosophical issues, akin in large measure to Hobbesian capitalists in a state of nature, Rawlsian statesmen behind a veil of ignorance, or Quinean linguists struggling to define "gavagai"? But I believe we should resist this temptation, because it continues to beg all of the cultural questions in favor of certain theories of economics, politics, and morality. For example, absent the view of human beings as rights-holding, autonomous, and self-interested individuals, the ostensible economic virtues of free market forces are as difficult to appreciate as are the political virtues of capitalist representative "democracy." And without such a vocabulary for describing human beings, Kant's Kingdom of Ends principle can't even be formulated clearly.

I do not believe that these culturally specific philosophical questions about rights-bearing individuals can be answered satisfactorily; they can only be begged, as I have argued elsewhere. For now, however, I want to sketch the Confucian alternative briefly and then discuss it within a feminist conceptual framework.

If I could ask the shade of Confucius "Who am I?" his reply, I believe, would run roughly as follows: "Given that you are Henry Rosemont, Jr., you are obviously the son of Henry Sr. and Sally Rosemont. You are thus first, foremost, and most basically a *son;* you stand in a relationship to your parents that began at birth, that has had a profound effect on their later lives as well, and that will be diminished only in part at their death."

Of course, now I am many other things besides a son. I am husband to my wife, father to our children, grandfather to their children; I am a brother, my friend's friend, my neighbor's neighbor; I am a teacher of my students, student of my teachers, colleague of my colleagues.

Now all of this is obvious, but note how different it is from focusing on me as a purely rational, rights-holding, autonomous individual. For the early Confucians there would not have been much of me to be seen in isolation, to be considered abstractly: I am the totality of roles I live in relation to specific others. Moreover, these roles are interconnected in that the relations in which I stand to some people affect directly the relations in which I stand to others, such that it would be misleading to say that I *play* or *perform* these roles; on the contrary, for Confucius I *am* my roles. Taken collectively, these roles weave, for each of us, a unique pattern of personal identity, such that if some of my roles change, others will of necessity change also, literally making me a different person. Marriage made me a different person, as did becoming a father and then a grandfather; and divorce would make me a different person also.

Further, my role as father, for example, is not merely a one–one relation with my daughters. In the first place, it has a significant bearing on my role as husband, just as the role of mother bears significantly on my wife's role as wife. Second, I am "Samantha's father" not only to Samantha but to her friends, her teachers, and, someday, her husband and her husband's parents as well. And Samantha's role as sister is determined in part by my role as father.

Going beyond the family, if I should become a widower, both my male and female friends would see me, respond to me, interact with me, somewhat differently than they do now. A bachelor friend of mine, for instance, might invite me as a widower to accompany him on a three-month cruise, but he would not invite me so long as I was a husband.

It is in this epistemologically and ethically extended meaning of the term *roles* that the early Confucians would have insisted that I do not play or perform but, rather, carry and become the roles I live in consonance with others, so that when all the roles have been specified, and their interconnections made manifest, then I have been specified fully as a unique person, with few discernible loose threads from which to piece together a purely rational, autonomous, rights-holding individual self.

Here it is tempting to paraphrase one of the most famous passages in David Hume's *A Treatise on Human Nature:*

> For my part, when I enter most intimately into what I call *myself*, I always stumble on some particular role or other, of son or father, lover or friend, student, or teacher, brother or neighbor. I never can catch *myself*, at any time apart from a role, and never can observe anything except from the viewpoint of a role. . . . If anyone upon serious and unprejudiced reflection, thinks he has a different notion of *himself*, I must confess that I can no longer reason with him. All that I can allow him is, that he may be in the right as well as I, and that we are essentially different in this particular. He may perhaps, perceive something simple and continued, which he calls *himself;* tho' I am certain there is no such principle in me.[15]

To suggest such a notion of the self is not to deny our strong sense of being *continuous* selves. But as Catherine Keller has argued,[16] we can have a concept of "personal self-identity"—as *persons*—without the philosophically more common (and paradox-generating) concept of strict self-identity. According to Keller, we can thus achieve at least "a light and loose sense of the unity of the person."[17] (I will have more to say on the concept of strict self-identity below.)

Moreover, seen in this socially contextualized way, my own identity is, in an important sense, not achieved by me; I am not solely responsible for becoming who I am. Of course, a great deal of personal effort is required to become a good person. But nevertheless, much of who and what I am is determined by the others with whom I interact, just as my efforts determine in part who and what they are. If I am *yang* to my children and students, I am *yin* to my parents and teachers. Personhood or identity, in this sense, is basically conferred on us, just as we basically contribute to conferring it on others. Again, the point is obvious, but the Confucian perspective requires us to state it in another tone of voice: My life as a teacher can be made significant only by my students; in order to *be* a friend, a lover, or a neighbor, I must *have* a friend, a lover, or a neighbor; my life as a husband is made meaningful only by my wife, my life as a scholar only by other scholars.

The Confucian ideal must of course be modified significantly if it is to have any contemporary purchase in China or elsewhere, for the earlier charge of patriarchy is well taken. Confucius and his followers were indeed sexist as we use the term today, and all efforts at reconstructing the Confucian persuasion must excise those elements of the tradition that assign women inferior roles. This excision—or perhaps, in some cases, exorcism— must in the first instance be evidenced in the socioeconomic realm, because good reasons can no longer be given for restricting freedom to develop one's own capacities to the fullest on the basis of biologically or otherwise constructed sex differences.

The task of modifying the Confucian persuasion to accord with contemporary feminist moral sensibilities may not, however, be an altogether Herculean effort conceptually. Admitting the pervasive downplaying of the abilities and accomplishments of women in classical Confucianism, I nevertheless hold that the thrust of that tradition was not competitive individualism—associated in the West with the masculine—but rather other-directed nurturing, associated throughout Western history with the feminine. And when we come to appreciate that the Western tradition only negatively celebrates qualities and attributes associated with the feminine, we might cautiously opine that the demand for gender equality could well be brought into Confucianism without doing violence to its basic insights and precepts.

We might go even further in this regard, revising, but keeping the central role of the family that dominates the tradition. We can certainly have not only the concept of the family with the concept of sexual equality; we can also expand, yet still keep the concept of the family by allowing for two and perhaps more parents or nurturers of the same sex. Homophobia was, and still is, as characteristic of the Chinese tradition as sexism was, but gays and lesbians, too, are the sum of the roles they live within and outside of the family, and the conceptual framework of Confucianism would surely be as impoverished by their exclusion as it would be enriched by their inclusion.

To see these points in another way, consider a related criticism against Confucianism, that it is hierarchical and, consequently, elitist. I believe the charge is misplaced, for two reasons. First, although elitism does directly entail a hierarchy, the converse does not hold, and hence the two concepts are not logically equivalent. What comes to mind, for example, is a happy, nurturing family, a well-run and productive classroom, a scientist supervising the research of her graduate students, or a family doctor working with the patients he or she has come to know well. All of these and many other social situations are in a sense hierarchical, but to label them "elitist" guarantees that we will not understand them.

Second, the charge against the hierarchical ordering of Confucianism is usually couched in terms of human relationships based on roles that are described as holding between "superiors" and "inferiors," or between "superordinates" and "subordinates." But when we look closely at the Confucian texts for guidance in how to properly fulfill our roles as parents and children, teachers and students, an so on, and when we keep in mind the central role of reciprocity in early Confucianism, we might want to change the descriptive terms of the relationships as holding between *benefactors* and *beneficiaries*. And if we keep equally in mind that all of us are some of the time benefactors and some of the time beneficiaries in our relations, then much of the sting of the accusation of hierarchy or elitism goes away. Again, I would maintain that this account is a fairly realistic one: I am *yin* or *yang* depending on who I am interacting with, and when: I am largely a beneficiary of my parents, benefactor to my children; the same holds as between my teachers and my students; and I would also argue that upon close inspection, even the relationships between friends, neighbors, and colleagues can be cogently analyzed in this way. And is there not a deep satisfaction that comes from having the opportunity to be a benefactor to one who has been a benefactor to you? Again from the *Lun Yu:* "The Master said, In dealing with the elderly, comfort them; in dealing with friends, be sincere; in dealing with the young, cherish them" (5:25). The point deserves further consideration, because any defense of hierarchy will almost surely continue to be seen, especially by rights theorists, as an argument against equality. But to raise the issue of equality in this way begs the question against the Confucian perspective, in which the person is to be seen less as a matter of strict self-identity through time than as the locus of a series of overlapping relationships that change over time.

As Nathan Sivin has observed:

> Scientific thought began, in China as elsewhere, with attempts to comprehend how it is that although individual things are constantly changing, always coming to be and perishing, nature as a coherent order not only endures but remains conformable to itself. In the West the earliest such attempts identified the unchanging reality with some basic stuff out of which all the things around us, despite their apparent diversity, are formed.
>
> In China the earliest and in the long run the most influential scientific explanations were in terms of time. They made sense of the momentary event by fitting it into the cyclical rhythms of natural process.[18]

I would extend Sivin's observation to include not only scientific but Chinese *ethical* explanations (and evaluations) as well. The "basic stuff" of the scientific West resembles the enduring self, or soul ("strict self-identity"), of the moral West, whereas the Chinese made sense of personal self-identity "by fitting it into the cyclical rhythms of natural process." Many factors enter into the analysis of benefactor-beneficiary roles, but time is essential. A common lament among the elderly in the West, especially men, is that "I'm not the person I used to be." For the Chinese, the statement is quite literally true.

Much more, of course, needs to be said about all of these matters, but for now they can be somewhat clarified if we focus attention on what is often seen as the greatest weakness of classical Confucianism (and much feminist moral philosophy): its particularism.

What is supposedly wrong with particularism is that, by definition, appropriate rules of conduct in specific situations cannot be generalized; they cannot become universal. These rules, varying as they do from situation to situation, apply only to the *personal* realm. Genuine moral theory, however, requires the impersonal stance, that of the impartial judge or ideal observer, as noted earlier. Epistemologically, the implication is that we become more competent moral agents as our moral understanding more nearly approaches systematic universality.

A sympathetic reading of the Confucian texts, however, suggests a rather different epistemological view: that our moral understanding decreases as its form approaches universality, and we become increasingly incompetent moral agents. Free, autonomous, rights-holding individuals are indeed impersonal: They have no faces, no abilities, no histories, personalities, hopes, fears, or anything else. Unfortunately, I have never met anyone of this kind. Virtually without exception, the others I need to understand in order to consider my moral obligations to them are always concrete individuals, or groups of them, all with specific histories, hopes, fears, needs, and so on. To the extent that I am encouraged to see them merely as replaceable occupants of a universal status, therefore, to that same extent will I *not* be required to attempt to understand their specific histories, cares, or needs.

Put another way, the Confucian persuasion rejects the distinction between the personal and the impersonal in moral theorizing, in favor of the interpersonal: What I should do is largely determined not by some universal principle but by the unique characteristics of the person or persons with whom I am concretely interacting. This Confucian view is by no means out of date: Consider the following quote from the feminist philosopher Margaret Walker.

Universalism presses me to view you, for instance, as a holder of a certain right, or a satisfaction-function, or a focus of some specifiable set of obligatory responses. I am pressed to structure my response or appeal to you in terms which I can think of as applying repeatably to any number of other cases. We thus see universalist morality as "curbing our imaginations" by enforcing communicative and reflective strategies which are interpersonally evasive. Worse, it legitimates uniformly assuming the quasi-administrative or juridical posture of "the" (i.e., universal) moral point of view. Yet in many cases assuming that viewpoint may foreclose the more revealing, if sometimes painful, path of expression, acknowledgement, and collaboration that could otherwise lead to genuinely responsive solutions.

Feminists have special and acute needs to fend off this systematic de-personalizing of the moral and de-moralizing of the personal. For on a practical level what feminists aspire to depends as much on restructuring our senses of moral responsibility in intimate partnerships, sexual relations, communities of personal loyalty, and day-to-day work relations as it clearly does on replacing in-stitutional, legal, and political arrangements.[19]

Some concrete instances of de-personalizing the moral: The homeless man with outstretched hand does not have a *right* to my spare change, no claim against me, so I need not feel a moral obligation to him. You and I get on the subway; you are eight and a half months pregnant, or carrying heavy packages, or using crutches; I nevertheless take the last seat in the car, be-cause your burden does not give you a right to that seat. Note also that, for all the rights you do indeed have, 99 percent of the time I can fully respect those rights simply by ignoring you.

Similarly for de-moralizing the personal. In contemporary Western uni-versalist moral theories, it is entirely possible for us to be obtuse, uncaring, insensitive, clumsy, even disgusting in much of our behavior, and yet escape moral censure, because the behavior is seen as private. If at those times when an appropriate moral situation arises (how we are to recognize such moments is never made clear) we take account of the situation, invoke our favorite theory, turn on our moral computer for a decision procedure, and then act on the decision, we will all of us be moral agents, no matter how boorish, aimless, repulsive, or empty our "private" lives may otherwise be.

You might be tempted here to object that what I see as civil and sensitive behavior on my part may be interpreted by others as rude and uncaring; after all, wasn't it a great human step forward when tolerance for diversity of manners and private tastes and behaviors accompanied the rise of the bourgeoisie in late seventeenth-century Holland, then spread throughout Europe? In reply, I would suggest that the tolerance gained at the expense of de-moralizing the personal may not be worth the price demanded, be-cause the tolerance all too easily begets moral astigmatism.

If you eschew any real judgments about how I live my life when I am not making moral choices—that is, about 98 percent of the time—you are de-priving yourself of judgments of your own possibilities. Indeed, when any of us adapts an altogether nonjudgmental stance about the ostensibly pri-vate (nonmoral) conduct of others, we run a serious risk of living an aimless life. If *de gustibus non est disputandum* is literally true, where could we pos-sibly look for human guidelines to establish human goals worth striving for? My respect and affection for Chinese culture is great; does tolerance also oblige me to be sympathetic to foot-binding?

There is an even more basic question to ask of modern moral philosophy along these lines: Namely, if a person is indeed obtuse, insensitive, boorish, and so on, how or why can we have any confidence that she or he will even perceive correctly those exceptional circumstances supposedly calling for moral choice when they arise? Any set of circumstances can be seen in a variety of ways; can a highly insensitive person perceive accurately what the categorical imperative requires, or what will truly bring the greatest happiness to the greatest number, or what it means to genuinely respect the rights of others?

In all probability the answer to these questions is "no," thus underlining Annette Baier's claim that without presupposing the concept of *trust*, universalist moral theory will ensure only that human

> life will be nasty, emotionally poor, and worse than brutish (even if longer), if that is all morality is, or even if that coercive structure of morality is regarded as the backbone, rather than as an available crutch, should the main support fail. For the main support has to come from those we entrust with the job of rearing and training persons so that they can be trusted in various ways.... A very complex network of a great variety of sorts of trust structures our moral relationships with our fellows, and if there is a main support to this network it is the trust we place in those who respond to the trust of new members of the moral community, namely to children, and prepare them for new forms of trust.[20]

A final remark on particularism, linking it to the religious: Can the moral lead to the spiritual, and the secular to the sacred?[21] I do not believe that Confucius worried only about one's obligations toward specific others. On the contrary, I believe he had a strong sense of empathy with, and a concept of, humanity writ large.

All of the specific human relations of which we are a part, interacting with the dead as well as the living, will be mediated by the courtesy, customs, rituals, and traditions we come to share as our inextricably linked histories (the *li*) unfold; and by fulfilling the obligations defined by these relationships we are, as the early Confucians would have seen us, following the human way. It is a comprehensive way. By the manner in which we interact with others our lives will clearly have a moral dimension infusing *all*, not just some, of our conduct. By the ways in which this ethical interpersonal conduct is effected, with reciprocity, and governed by civility, respect, affection, custom, ritual, and tradition, our lives will also have an aesthetic dimension for ourselves and for others. And, again, as the early Confucians would have seen us, by specifically meeting our defining traditional obligations to our elder and ancestors on the one hand, and to our contemporaries and descendants on the other, we undergo an uncommon yet spiritually authentic form of transcendence, a human capacity to go beyond the specific spatiotemporal circumstances in which we exist, giving our personhood a sense of humanity shared in common, and thereby a sense of strong continuity with what was gone before and what will come later, and a concomitant commitment to leave this earth in a better condition than we found it. There being no question for the early Confucians of the meaning *of* life, we may nevertheless see that their view of what it is to be a human being provided for every person to find meaning *in* life.[22]

All of these issues, I submit, and many more like them, cannot be addressed properly without making a consideration of values explicit, seeing human beings as role and value-carrying persons, and seeing them as value carriers all of the time, both ethically and epistemologically; which is the thrust of early Confucian interpersonal particularism and much contemporary feminism. It is a humanistic thrust, but it does not require the concept of rights or of universal principles ostensibly binding on all autonomous, self-interested individuals.

I have pressed these views of what it is to be a human being, and the moral particularism that flows from them, for a number of reasons. In the first place, as noted earlier, I believe they much more nearly resemble the views of three-quarters of the human race than does the Enlightenment view. If this is so, then they should command, if not conviction, then at least our careful attention, for otherwise there is little hope for a United Nations being united in anything but fear of those who have the most powerful armies.

Second, Confucianism is a moral tradition of great longevity, and simply in terms of the sheer numbers of people directly influenced by it in China itself—people who lived and died in accordance with its vision—it is arguably the most significant philosophy ever put forward; it should surely not be dismissed merely on the grounds of its antiquity.

Further, it must be remembered that Confucianism was attacked at its inception by Daoists, Mohists, Legalists, and proponents of others of the "Hundred Schools" of early Chinese thought. Later, and for several centuries, it was almost totally eclipsed by Buddhism. Later still, it was challenged by Christianity, first by the Jesuits and Franciscans of the late sixteenth and seventeenth centuries, and then by both Catholic and Protestant missionaries of the nineteenth and twentieth, these latter having been buttressed by the gunboat diplomacy attendant on the imperialistic "coming of the West" to China. And of course democratic/capitalistic thought, as well as Marxist thought, has contributed much to onslaughts on the Confucian philosophical tradition. From all of these challenges Confucianism recovered, was re-visioned, endured. This historical perspective should lead us to consider not that Confucianism must be irrelevant to contemporary ethical issues, nor that it should be put to rest, but, rather, that there might be much in that tradition that speaks not merely to East Asians but perhaps to everyone. Not only in the past, but perhaps for all time.

I chose to sketch the ancient Confucian view of what it is to be a human being for another reason as well: Over and above some feminist perspectives, this view is not altogether foreign even to the great majority of the inhabitants of the Western capitalist democracies; Confucian though it sounds, it was, after all, an Englishman who wrote "No man is an island entire of itself . . . Any man's death diminishes me, because I am involved in mankind, and therefore never send to know for whom the bell tolls, it tolls for thee."[23]

To those who believe that totalitarian governments will continue to pose the greatest threat to human well-being, these sentiments expressed by Donne may be seen as elegantly phrased, perhaps, but condemned to the dead past. Yet Donne continues to live on in the midst of those who believe that among the Western capitalist democracies, as well as in the developing world, the greater threat to human well-being now lies in the increasing atomization of human life, the loss of community and of common purpose, and the increasing rending of the social fabric.

Perhaps Confucius can teach us, then, among other things, that to abandon our roles, communal rituals, customs, and traditions altogether is madness, because they can only be replaced by the ethical, psychological, social, and spiritual void into which far too many autonomous, rights-bearing, individual-oriented, capitalist Americans are already gazing. And perhaps he can teach us as well that it is time to rethink the wisdom of exporting and imposing our ethical conceptual framework on the four-plus billion people for whom it is certainly alien, probably inappropriate, and possibly immoral.

It may seem presumptuous to call into question almost the whole literature of modern Western political and moral theory in the space of a single chapter. But because so much of that literature presumes and elaborates the Enlightenment model of human beings as purely rational, self-seeking, autonomous individuals, the many arguments and views in that literature cannot have more plausibility than the basic assumptions on which they rest. To be sure, this model—especially as it has been taken to imply human rights—has significantly advanced the cause of human dignity, especially among the Western democracies, as noted earlier; but it also has a strong self-fulfilling prophetic nature, which is strengthened further by the demands of capitalist economies that can never be the norm for most of the world's peoples, nor can they continue to be the norm for ourselves much longer. Thus I suggest that this model is rapidly becoming more of a conceptual liability than an asset as we approach the twenty-first century, continuing our search for how to live, and how best to live together on this increasingly fragile planet. And I suspect most feminist philosophers would agree.[24]

Glossary of Chinese Terms

a	詩經	i	仁義
b	道德經	j	陰陽
c	莊子	k	禮記
d	列子	l	孟子
e	父母	m	荀子
f	天地	n	黃帝內經
g	上下	o	烈女傳
h	乾坤	p	女誡淺釋

Notes

1. An excellent survey of these positions, with analysis, is Alison M. Jaggar's *Feminist Politics and Human Nature* (Totowa, N.J.: Rowman and Allenheld, 1983).

2. Sandra Harding, *The Science Question in Feminism* (Ithaca: Cornell University Press, 1986), p. 23.

3. See especially Nancy Chodorow, *The Reproduction of Mothering* (Berkeley: University of California Press, 1979); Nell Noddings, *Caring: A Feminine Approach to Ethics and Moral Education* (Berkeley: University of California Press, 1984); Carol Gilligan, *In a Different Voice: Psychological Theory and Women's Development* (Cambridge, Mass.: Harvard University Press, 1982).

4. This translation, modified from Bernhard Karlgren's *The Book of Odes* (Stockholm, 1950), was originally quoted in Alison Black, "Gender and Cosmology in Chinese Correlative Thinking," in *Gender and Religion: On the Complexity of Symbols*, ed. Caroline W. Bynum, Steven Harrell, and Paula Richman (Boston: Beacon Press, 1986), p. 171. I am deeply indebted to Black's article, as the text and citations below show, although I do not know how much or how little she might appreciate the way I have used her insights in developing my arguments.

5. Black, "Gender and Cosmology in Chinese Correlative Thinking," pp. 179ff.

6. Ibid.

7. Patricia Ebrey, "Women, Marriage, and the Family in Chinese History," in *Heritage of China*, ed. Paul Ropp (Berkeley: University of California Press, 1990), p. 204.

8. The *Huang Di Nei Jing* has been translated by Ilza Veith as *The Yellow Emperor's Classic of Internal Medicine* (Berkeley: University of California Press, 1972). Regarding the problem of correctly interpreting China's *Materia Medica* more gen-

erally, see Manfred Porkert, "The Difficult Task of Blending Chinese and Western Science: The Case of Modern Interpretations of Traditional Chinese Medicine," in *Explorations in the History of Science and Technology in China*, ed. Li Guohao et al. (Shanghai: Shanghai Chinese Classics Publishing House, 1982), pp. 553–572.

9. Lisa Raphals, "The Mind Has No Sex?: Essentializing Gendered Intelligence," paper read at the annual meeting of the Association of Asian Studies (1995), and cited with the kind permission of the author.

10. Black, "Gender and Cosmology in Chinese Correlative Thinking," p. 167.

11. Nathan Sivin, "Why the Scientific Revolution Did Not Take Place in China— Or Didn't It?" in *Explorations in the History of Science and Technology in China*, ed. Li Guohao et al. (Shanghai: Shanghai Chinese Classics Publishing House, 1982), pp. 89–106.

12. This point is elaborated in Genevieve Lloyd, "The Man of Reason," in *Women, Knowledge, and Reality*, ed. Ann Garry and Marilyn Pearsall (Boston: Unwin Hyman, 1989). See also Harding, *The Science Question in Feminism*.

13. Henry Rosemont, Jr., "Rights-Bearing Individuals and Role-Bearing Persons," in *Rules, Rituals, and Responsibility: Essays Dedicated to Herbert Fingarette*, ed. Mary I. Bockover (LaSalle, Ill.: Open Court, 1991), pp. 71–101.

14. What follows for the next several pages is modified from my *A Chinese Mirror: Moral Reflections on Political Economy and Society* (La Salle, Ill.: Open Court, 1991), chapter 3.

15. I first constructed this paraphrase in "Who Chooses?" in a *Festschrift* I edited for Angus Graham: *Chinese Texts and Philosophical Contexts* (La Salle, Ill.: Open Court,1991).

16. Catherine Keller, *From A Broken Web: Separation, Sexism, and Self* (Boston: Beacon Press, 1986), pp. 197–198.

17. Ibid., p. 198.

18. "Chinese Alchemy and the Manipulation of Time," in *Science and Technology in East Asia*, ed. N. Sivin (New York, 1977), p. 110.

19. Margaret Walker, "Moral Understandings: Alternative 'Epistemology' for a Feminist Ethics," *Hypatia* 4/2 (1989): 22.

20. Annette Baier, "What Do Women Want in a Moral Theory?" *Novs* 19 (1985): 60; quoted in Jim Cheney, "Eco-Feminism and Deep Ecology," *Environmental Ethics* 9 (Summer 1987): 129. I have profited much from Cheney's article and believe that my arguments here are fully compatible with those he advanced for a new morality; but I cannot take up the ecological issues in this chapter.

21. The title of a splendid work by Herbert Fingarette: *Confucius—The Secular as Sacred* (New York: Harper Torchbooks, 1972). For discussion, see my review in *Philosophy East and West* 26/4 (1976) and his response and my reply in *Philosophy East and West* 28/4 (1978).

22. Kurt Baier, "The Meaning of Life," in *Twentieth Century Philosophy: The Analytic Tradition*, ed. Morris Weitz (New York: Free Press, 1966). Moreover, Margery Wolf has argued well and cogently that, in my terms, the ability to feel oneself linked to ancestors as well as to descendants was much easier for men than women throughout the history of China, owing to patrilineal succession; a woman could achieve this feeling only in descending order, through her uterine family. See Wolf's "Beyond the Patriarchal Self: Constructing Gender in China," in *Self as Person in Asian Theory and Practice*, ed. Roger T. Ames et al. (Albany, N.Y.: SUNY Press, 1994). Accepting

her basic claim, I would maintain that insisting on gender equality in reconstructing classical Confucianism is a necessary, and perhaps sufficient, condition for reconfiguring both gender roles and family responsibilities so that women and men could equally learn and practice the regimen of self-cultivation, which lies at the heart of the religious dimension of the Confucian tradition.

23. John Donne, Meditation XVII.

24. Earlier drafts of this chapter were read at the Center for the Study of Cultural Values at the University of Illinois, the East Asian Studies Center at Stanford University, the Department of Religious Studies at Brown University, and the Center for Chinese Studies at the University of California–Berkeley. I am grateful to the audiences for their comments and criticisms, especially to David Nivison, David Keightley, P. J. Ivanhoe, Hal Roth, Jock Reeder, and Barney Twiss. The middle third of the chapter has appeared in several earlier forms in the works I have cited in Notes 13 and 14; these works include additional references and further discussion of the topics treated herein.

Chapter Five

Buddho-Taoist and Western Metaphysics of the Self

KENNETH K. INADA

Cultural exchanges have little to do with surface contacts but much to do with the understanding of the nature of the self behind those contacts. Although a self might seem similar to other selves in its involvement in identical activities, still, the results are significantly different from others owing to certain traits germane to the individual. In a sense, what counts most is not the finished product per se but the means by which the product came into being. This aspect of human traits has been ignored for the most part and, furthermore, has been smothered by the apparent success of science and technology and the various gadgets that have inundated our lives. But it is time to reflect and focus on the nature of the self in order to get at the heart of the matter in understanding any culture or engaging in cultural exchanges. To amplify on this point, I would like to relate an interesting anecdote concerning the Queen's Bridge in Cambridge, England.

In the 1870s the Ching Government, as a friendship gesture, dispatched to Cambridge a team of engineers and carpenters to build a simple arched wooden bridge. The bridge was built in a relatively short time and immediately attracted visitors from all over England because of its novel construction: Here was a simple dovetailed wooden bridge that carried the normal load and traffic just like one built with nails, nuts, and bolts!

The most curious spectators were a group of scientists at Cambridge University. They studied the structure of the bridge meticulously, analyzing the stresses and strains of the dovetailed pieces, but they could not fathom the basis for the overall strength of the bridge nor how it was put together. Someone had a brilliant idea: Why not dismantle the bridge, piece by piece, taking photos and notes in the process. After consultation with the authorities, the scientists received permission to dismantle the bridge in the hope of advancing scientific knowledge. And so they engaged themselves in the dismantling task with relish and utmost confidence that the so-called secrets of the dovetailed wooden bridge would soon be aired. The task was completed in no time.

Now came the time to assemble the bridge in reverse order. As the scientists began to fasten the larger pieces and sections together, they were stymied by the fact that the sections would not hold up in and of themselves, much less when weight was applied. They tried countless times and from different angles and perspectives, but to no avail. The assemblage of the bridge, spanning about fifty feet, threatened to end in failure. Indeed, short of any breakthrough, the scientists admitted as much. In time, having exhausted all resources, they finally decided to conjoin the pieces and sections with the standby material of nuts and bolts.

That is the story behind the Queen's Bridge as it stands there today, straining very unnaturally to transport students across the narrow bend of the Cams River. Apparently the great minds of Cambridge, the home of such luminaries as Sir Isaac Newton and Earl Bertrand Russell, could not unravel this particular Chinese puzzle. But the story does not end here, for it is a poignant symbol for further East-West dialogues. The implications of the story are legion.

First of all, why didn't the Cambridge scientists consult with the original Chinese builders? That would have been the easiest solution. Was it hubris, stubbornness, shame, or plain ignorance that prevented such an inquiry?

Obviously, the scientists did not go beyond the realm of science and technology. In defeat and dejection, they simply closed the doors that, if opened, would have let them peer into the remarkable Chinese cultural tradition. Perhaps we who are not directly involved in the field of hard sciences may have a meaningful role to play here in expanding on the Chinese tradition as well as other Asiatic traditions. The solution to the problem actually lies in the simple philosophy of life based on a thoroughgoing form of naturalism, Taoism. Among its basic ideas or doctrines are nonbeing (*wu*), vacuity (*hsu*), change (*hua*), reversal (*fan*), nonaction (*wu-wei*), correlative dynamics (*yin-yang*), uncarved block (*p'u*) and, in sum, simply the way of nature, or Tao.

What the Cambridge scientists overlooked was the role and function of the Tao in terms of its dynamics as displayed in the harmonious triadic relationship of human-earth-heaven. This dynamics, as we shall soon see, is actually the unique function of *being in nonbeing,* which I refer to as "Oriental dynamics." Oriental dynamics is novel in the sense that it does not negate or limit anything but instead brings into play everything within the comprehensive scheme of things. It depicts the triadic relationship as a comprehensive harmony, the classic Chinese way of life as expressed by the late Thome H. Fang.[1]

How do we come to grips with and realize this comprehensive harmony? This is the crucial challenge, an experiential challenge, that we must encounter; but it can be a success only if we are open and flexible enough to bring into play dimensions of being that touch the very structure of our experiences, though unrecognized in ordinary perception. This calls for a novel metaphysics that might be forbidding for the westerner; but at any rate, the difference here between the East and West is shown especially in terms of the crucial concept of the self as the pivot of all experiences.

The concepts of being and becoming, in the East as well as the West, are basic to our perception and understanding. They are in short the pillar metaphysical concepts in which our modes of perception are framed. Yet, interestingly enough, many in the West are unaware that these concepts do not exhaust the categories in which we structure the basis of our epistemology. One of the basic reasons for the limited metaphysical orientation in being and becoming may be traced back to the Greek tradition whereby Plato argued cogently for the absolute status of things in epistemology. In so doing, Plato, by design, separated being and becoming and made the former more real than the latter. His argumentation was quite cogent and persuasive; indeed, anyone would be enthralled by the characteristics of permanence and absolutism over impermanence and relativism. So, from the outset, a metaphysics based on the concept of being became the guide and support of all empirical, rational, and logical understanding. Meanwhile, the concept of becoming or change (impermanence) was relegated to a secondary position because of its relative and dependent nature. In consequence, the bifurcation of nature in terms of being and becoming or, more precisely, *being over becoming,* began early in the Western tradition and has continued to the present without arousing serious questions concerning its function and value.[2] Along the way, thinkers were given free rein to concentrate on the permanent and enduring entities with which the empirico-rational modes of perception function most effectively. The results have been dramatic in all disciplines, but especially so in the scientific and related fields.

It is interesting to note that, on the whole, we still think and act Platonically owing to the fact that Plato's metaphysics lends itself readily to the empirical and rational scheme of things. But time moves on. The modern period began with the great cosmological shift from Ptolemaic theory to Copernican theory and the subsequent development of Newtonian physics, which, in turn, opened up further doors. And at the turn of this century, another momentous development occurred in the form of Einsteinian physics. The movement from Newtonian to Einsteinian physics is not only remarkable but dramatic in the sense that it now required a real shift in our perceptual orientation, from the nature of being to becoming or from absolutism to relativity. Although Einsteinian physics opened the way to a truly dynamic world, cosmologically as well as experientially, the public, ironically, was ill-prepared to accept it, much less to accommodate its nature of things. Indeed, paradoxically and anachronistically, most of our ordinary perception of things is still anchored in a Newtonian world. That is to say, we still perceive and understand things on the basis of absolute, permanent, and enduring entities within a set spatiotemporal context. We do so because the Newtonian world is far easier to grasp and accommodate than the Einsteinian framework of relativity, which is far too abstract and dynamic for the average mind to cope with. Simply put, relativity does not blend well with the ordinary perception of things, despite its universal appeal and acceptance by the scientific community. We are burdened, then, by a historical lag in terms of our mode of perception steeped in the Platonic legacy of being or substance-orientation. We thus find ourselves in a bind or quandary and continue to face a dilemma so long as we maintain the strict dichotomy of being and becoming or *being over becoming.* How can we resolve this dilemma?

A shift to the Eastern sector would reveal a refreshingly new and different realm of existence to the westerner. The Buddhists and Taoists had anticipated an Einsteinian world for centuries by incorporating the realm of becoming in ordinary perception. The basic principles relative to the nature of becoming were spawned simultaneously in the Indian and Chinese civilizations. Although in recent centuries these civilizations have fallen behind the West in terms of science and technology, their traditional cultural achievements and consequent impact on the Asiatic continent and beyond are inestimable. In many respects, the globalization of politics and economy has engendered interest in and implementation of alien culture and thought. So what is the metaphysical grounding for the rise of the special Asiatic mode of perception? In answering this question, I shall facilitate matters by treating Buddhist and Taoist metaphysics together, although no scholar would treat them as identical in the strictest sense.

At the outset, it should be noted that Buddho-Taoist metaphysics is not confined to the concepts of being and becoming as is ordinarily done in the West. What is unconfined is the fact that this metaphysics involves an important third member, nonbeing, a concept that is not taken seriously in the West and perhaps has been summarily dismissed as a nonentity. To the easterner, this stand is unfortunate for he or she perceives nonbeing as a pivotal element of existence, the true underpinning of all experiences. As stated earlier, all experiences are located in the becoming process and never in static permanent nature of being. Thus, becoming is the locus of existence, and being and nonbeing are the two dynamic rubrics or components. Generally speaking, whereas the West expanded on becoming in terms of the nature of being, the East took becoming to function primarily in terms of the dynamics of being and nonbeing. The difference is indeed great, but its consequences have yet to be fully understood and appreciated in the West. It certainly calls for a radical interpretation of our ordinary apparatus of perception.[3]

Ordinary perception of things has contents far fuller, deeper, and richer than are normally attributed to it; and these contents, moreover, are not only glossed over but also denied their rightful due because of the so-called ill-habit of perception formed from a remote past. One may refer to this ill-habit as an ontological misperception since only the tangible elements are focused on and taken to be important. Indeed, the real problem is that we hardly question the very nature and function of perception itself. In the West, the Platonic legacy of *being over becoming*, for example, has fostered from the beginning a dichotomy in the very structure of perception. This implicit dichotomy was then carried over into the modern period, at which time British empiricism solidified it in terms of the perceiver (subject) and perceived (object). Even the brilliant David Hume got himself into trouble by neatly separating things into "matters of fact" (empirical elements) and "relations of ideas" (rational entities). He hoped to bridge them later but couldn't do it because of the basic structural flaw in perception itself.

Clearly, the onus of bridging them would lie with the one who split them initially into independent categories. The easterner, on this point, has fared better and is not burdened at all because there is simply nothing to split up but instead there is everything to accommodate and incorporate in every perceptual instance. In this respect, Eastern nature of perception is always coherent, holistic, or total, but in a uniquely dynamic sense.

Returning to Buddho-Taoist metaphysics, we find that it begins and ends in the realm of becoming. For the Buddhist, life is always on the go, impermanent (*anitya*) and momentary (*kshanika*). For the Taoist, likewise, the vitality of life is captured in change (*yi*) or transformation (*hua*), which constitutes the central thrust of the *Book of Changes* (*Yi Ching*). Before going any further, we would do well to consider the Buddhist doctrine of nonself (*anatta, anatman*) within the context of becoming.

The Buddhist nonself doctrine, in a word, defies exact definition or description owing to the fact that Buddhist thought is process oriented. This is not to say, however, that all thought play is impossible and should thereby be abandoned. Far from it. The Buddhist, seeing that our lives are nothing but a series of paradoxical situations, spoke and wrote in terms of the twofold nature of the truth of existence (*Dharma*): (a) defiled or covered nature of truth (*samvriti-sat*) and (b) undefiled or absolute nature of truth (*paramartha-sat*). Because of these two aspects, there are, respectively, the ordinary conventional or provisional type of knowledge and the absolute type of knowledge. The former refers to our normal empirico-rational forms of knowledge, and the latter, to the inordinate trans-empirical, trans-rational forms of knowledge. More specifically, the former refers to the realm of samsara, the wave-like arising and subsiding nature of existential cyclic phenomena, graphically depicted by the turning of the wheel of life in virtue of the attachment (*upadana*) to passions and desires (*trishna*), whereas the latter refers to the pure realm of nirvana signified by the cessation of passions and desires and the consequent undefiled turning of the wheel of life.[4]

Now with the proviso that this discussion hereafter will proceed in the conventional or provisional realm, I can assert that the Buddhist nonself doctrine may be expanded by utilizing three action-oriented concepts—namely, aggregating phenomena (the five *skandhas*), conditioned or relational origination (*pratitya-samutpada*), and intentional action (*karma*). In turn, the five *skandhas* are corporeality (*rupa*), feeling (*vedana*), primary perception or imagery (*samjna*), mental objects or play of imagery (*samskara*), and conscious play or consciousness of mental objects (*vijnana*).

The *skandhas* are referred to as aggregates because they describe, in totality, the constant organic conditioning process. This process, also known as conditioned or relational origination, spells out the turning of the wheel of life mentioned above. The wheel is normally depicted with twelve links—ranging, for example, from ignorance (*avidya*) to old age and death (*jaramarana*)—and it exhibits essentially a magnified picture of what is occurring in the aggregating phenomena. Finally, the turning of the wheel itself is based on or prompted by the presence of an organic force called *karma*, the intentional act laden with elements of passion-attachment (*trishna-upadana*). In other words, the wheel begins to turn when there is a hint of the rise of passion, such that the organic nature is activated in ways that reach out to satisfy the alleged passion; but then the satiated state does not expend itself but becomes fodder for further grasping in order to continue the satiation, and so forth. More specifically, the satiated state becomes an element of attachment and thereby feeds on itself, thus turning the samsaric wheel incessantly.

In consequence, the total dynamic phenomena, involving the aggregates, relational origination, and karmic force, are mere designations for what we normally call the self. Strictly speaking, however, this empirical self cannot be located anywhere in the becomingness of things, as it is part and parcel of the whole process. In brief, by reference to the doctrine of nonself, the Buddhist has advanced a unique organic or functional theory of the empirical self.[5]

In *The Questions of King Milinda*, the classic analysis of the nonself doctrine is presented in the very first dialogue between the king and the venerable monk, Nagasena.[6] Nagasena instructs the king through similes suggesting that a person cannot be identified or located in terms of any descriptive parts, such as the face, head, hair, body, hands, or legs; and, likewise, the chariot on which the king rode cannot be identified in terms of, say, the wheels, carriage, axle, reins, driver, or whip. Thus the person and the chariot are mere designations for the conventionalized way in which we communicate.[7]

Returning to Chinese dynamics, recall that the Taoists focused on change or transformation as the locus of existence—indeed, as the grounds for the Tao manifestation. Since the Tao is inexpressible in the strictest sense of the word,[8] the Taoists also accepted two levels of understanding: the realm of the nameable and the realm of the unnameable. The nameable is the mother of all things; and the unnameable, the origin of heaven and earth.[9] The former refers to the realm of manifestation, a realm that is relative to the empirico-rational function and is thus in the nature of being; and the latter, as the origin of heaven and earth, refers to the primordial nature of things—in other words, to the realm that is prior to human perception of things and is thus in the nature of nonbeing. Still, as Chinese metaphysics is grounded in the triadic relationship of human-earth-heaven, the total relationship spells out the Tao activity; moreover, each element in the triad involves the other two and thus they define as well as inform one another. Yet, the defining-informing action is what was referred to earlier as Oriental dynamics, the dynamics of *being in becoming.* The activity is one or unity, but we refer to it conventionally in terms of the nameable aspect of things. So, whereas the nameable or being is the visible and empirical side, the unnameable or nonbeing is the invisible and nonempirical side; but, still, we rely on the former to exhibit the outcome of the dynamics, though not the full dynamics, which is beyond visibility.

Here we might pause to consider the nature and function of words. Chuang Tzu, the great Taoist thinker of the fourth century B.C.E., spoke of three types of words—namely, imputed, repeated, and goblet words.[10] In speaking of our communication, he asserted that imputed words make up nine-tenths of it and repeated words for the sake of argumentation make up seven-tenths of it, and that goblet words come forth day after day to harmonize things in terms of heavenly equality. To emphasize the use and nature of goblet words, he further asserted:

> With these goblet words that come forth day after day, I harmonize all things in the Heavenly Equality, leave them to their endless changes, and so live out my years. As long as I do not say anything about them, they are a unity. But the unity and what I say about it have ceased to be a unity; what I say and the unity have ceased to be a unity. Therefore I say, we must have no-words! With words that are no-words, you may speak all your life long and you will never have said anything. Or you may go through your whole life *without* speaking them, in which case you will never have stopped speaking.[11]

Certainly we need language to communicate, but in the final analysis we do not need it for the sustenance of life. Imputed and repeated words are fine on the conventional level, but life could go on without depending on them, especially as we would want to have insight into the unity and harmony of things. This is where goblet words come into play, to have us understand the dynamic flow of life and not get entangled in the process of affirming or denying anything. This, in Taoist terms, is the so-called secret of survival.

The relationship between being and nonbeing is unique and subtle. From a purely metaphysical standpoint, one can assert that being has a disparate character that cannot remain as it is for long and that in order to sustain itself it must reside in nonbeing, like an island in the seas; but nonbeing, contrariwise, has a nondisparate nature that enables it to absorb and incorporate all beings. Thus the dynamics is strictly *being in nonbeing* and never the other way around, nonbeing in being. Moreover, whereas being thrives in finitude and conditionality, nonbeing merely inheres in infinitude at all times. Finally, on a purely ontological level, being exhibits limitations but nonbeing does not; put another way, beings interact in relational ways but nonbeing is a steady receptacle in which all actions take place. To expand on these points, let us examine one of the most intriguing verses in the *Tao Te Ching:*

> Tao produced the One.
> The One produced the two.
> The two produced the three.
> And the three produced the ten thousand things.
> The ten thousand things carry the yin and embrace the
> yang, and through the blending of the material force
> (*ch'i*) they achieve harmony.[12]

Normally, this verse is taken to describe the sequential creation of the world, from the Tao to the whole run of things. In this respect, the creation is presumably marked by a temporal flow from the original source of being. But though common, this interpretation is naive and misleading, for, according to the Taoist, the creative nature from the primordial to the complex manifestation is atemporal.[13] The reason for this is that the creative dynamics is not merely peripheral in terms of spatiotemporal characteristics but deeper and greater with the involvement of nonbeing, as when one views the total scene of trees and other vegetation nestled in the valley. The Neo-Taoist Wang Pi affirms this condition by stating succinctly that beings originate from nonbeing.[14] Here he is asserting the cosmological priority of nonbeing over being within the atemporal nature of things.

Can the mind capture this unique form of dynamics? No. Do we then abandon everything? Of course not. This is where the Taoist persevered in reaching for the fullness and depth of cosmological existence despite one's finite nature and limitations. In other words, the fullness and depth persist regardless of the macrocosmic or microcosmic nature of things.

Individual existence, then, is never severed from the larger cosmological scheme of things. We are part and parcel of the world, not a mere puff of existence. Hence the intriguing verse I quoted from *Tao Te Ching* is not off the mark; indeed, it is both an illustration of the Tao-based nature of things and a challenge for all to assimilate with the all-consuming Tao.

The uniqueness of *being in nonbeing* can be further explicated by reference to two familiar terms, symmetry and asymmetry. These are respectively analogous to being and nonbeing, with the proviso that the concept of asymmetry has now taken on a peculiar turn to the Oriental character of nonbeing—that is, as a dynamic component complementing being in every moment.

The symmetric is what we normally take to be in the nature of ordinary perceptual data. It can be characterized as, for example, dimensional, spatial, temporal, quantifiable, ordinary, finite, particular, limitable, causal, unitary, and measurable. It refers to all that is relatable in the oft-framed subject-object perception of things, which focuses wholly within the context of empirical and rational construction. In this sense, it has all to do with our normal epistemic functions, but these are limited to surface or peripheral perceptions. However, the Orientals saw perception to be holistic in visible as well as invisible ways—hence the play of nonbeing or the asymmetric aspect of things.

The asymmetric, contrary to the symmetric, is "characterized" as nondimensional, aspatial, atemporal, nonquantifiable, inordinate, infinite, universal, illimitable, noncausal, holistic, and immeasurable. It is the unseen, intangible component in the dynamics; but due to our accustomed empirical and rational orientation, we can only speculate or infer its presence within the visible dynamics of things. Yet it must be noted that ordinary perception requires the asymmetric nature in order to sustain itself. Or, more precisely, the asymmetric complements the symmetric in two vital ways: (1) It provides the basis for the continuity of ordinary perception; if this were not so, then each perceptual act in momentariness would be independent and separated from subsequent perceptions. And (2) it firms up the substance or content of perception; if this were not so, then each perception would be hollow of content, but upon which the mind would be quick to "entify" and provide fodder for the epistemic mill. Thus we note the importance of the asymmetric nature vitally involved in the nature of ordinary perception. And, furthermore, both symmetric and asymmetric components are so intimately locked together, interpenetrating and mutually identifying each other, that we cannot dichotomize the dynamics at all. Finally, like *being in nonbeing,* the symmetric-asymmetric dynamics runs throughout the micro-macro realm of existence.

In the context of the dynamics just discussed, nowhere could there be the possibility of locating or establishing a self as we know it. But this does not mean that we cannot refer to the function of a conventional self in our daily activities. It goes without saying that we live by conventions for the most part, but we are not thereby prevented from seeking true reality in the dynamic flow of things. Seeking true reality is precisely what the Orientals did when they reached beyond the ordinary nature of the self to realize the state of buddhahood and sagehood. As a model, the Chinese sage has thrived in perceiving things (beings) under the aegis of nothingness (nonbeing). Once a disciple asked, "Does nonbeing contain all phenomena?" To which the master simply replied, "Nonbeing."[15] This dialogue reminds us of the primordial silence (i.e., nonbeing or asymmetry) of the deep forest only to be broken by the bird's song (i.e., being or symmetry) or by the sounds of the woodcutter hewing a tree. Or, listen to Basho's famous haiku:

> The old pond, ah!
> A frog jumps in:
> The water's sound.[16]

The old pond depicts the nature of permanent nonbeing or asymmetry, which is instantly disturbed by the splash of the leaping frog. But in the next moment all has returned to the stillness of nonbeing.

Oriental dynamics has naturally wielded great influence in molding a unique culture. In paradoxical ways, all cultural forms are really formless or what the art masters call formless form. And true to this formless context, the masters refer to themselves as personalities without rank, position, or self; it is a context in which finite forms are incorporated harmoniously within formless nonbeing. As forms are properly housed in the formless, they in turn become more prominent in being what they are. This is the natural inviolable state of existence in which nothing is added or detracted; everything is simply what it is.

It should be clear by now that, on the one hand, the Queen's Bridge fiasco caused by the Cambridge scientists amounted to a violation of the innermost dynamics of nature. On the other hand, the Chinese builders were versed in the art of dovetailing the pieces of the bridge based on *being in nonbeing.* Each piece supported another piece or multiple pieces in mutual ways, but all pieces worked in unison to create the total bridge with its marvelous strength. If there is a principle to be educed from this dynamics it is that the more mutual pressure applied by the pieces, the stronger the collective pieces would be. This principle reminds us of the uncommon strength displayed by the tetrahedral structure of Buckminster Fuller's huge domes. Nature certainly acts in unknown ways but harbors no secrets. It is humankind in its quest for and systematic polarization of selfhood that has vitiated against the simplicity, softness, and resiliency of nature. Should there ever be a quest for Asian wisdom, however, the hope is that it will be intimately based on Oriental dynamics.

Notes

1. See Thome H. Fang, *The Chinese View of Life* (Hong Kong: Union Press, 1956).

2. Those of us living in the twentieth century, imbued as it is with Einsteinian spirit and other scientific advances, have begun to understand the dynamics of relativity and no longer retain a strict Cartesian concept of the self. Indeed, we have witnessed the denial of the Cartesian self, especially among contemporary European

thinkers belonging to the postmodern and poststructuralist schools of thought. I often wonder how much influence, directly or indirectly, Eastern thought has had on these thinkers. American pragmatic thinkers, especially George H. Mead and John Dewey, have always worked within the framework of problematics relative to the dynamic self and contributed greatly to the openness and resiliency of the self.

3. Paradoxical as it may seem, modern physics has led the way in closing the gap in our perceptual-conceptual view of things. Particle physics, in particular, has expanded Einsteinian physics in such a way that the dynamic behavior of subatomic particles seems to coincide with the Asiatic mode of perception.

4. The twofold nature of the truth of existence should not be confused with Plato's concepts of appearance and reality, despite the great temptation to draw a parallel. His division into appearance and reality is an extension of the metaphysical bifurcation of nature into the realms of becoming and being, respectively. In contrast, Buddhist and Taoist metaphysics do not bifurcate anything into distinct categories.

5. For a succinct and clear analysis of the nonself doctrine, see Walpola Rahula, *What the Buddha Taught* (New York: Grove Press, 1959), especially chapter 6, "The Doctrine of No-Soul: Anatta," pp. 51–66.

6. *The Questions of King Milinda*, trans. I. B. Horner; in the series entitled *Sacred Books of the Buddhists*, Vols. 22 and 23, Part 1, Section 1 (London: Luzac & Co., 1963–1964).

7. Ibid., Part 3, Section 6. The venerable Nagasena instructs that there is no experiencer in any experience but, rather, only experiencing. Later on, the great Theravadin, Buddhaghosa (c. the fifth century C.E.), would sound the same theme by asserting poignantly that there is no sufferer but only suffering.

8. Wing-tsit Chan, *A Source Book in Chinese Philosophy* (Princeton: Princeton University Press, 1963), p. 139.

9. Ibid.

10. The term *goblet* (*chih*) refers to its action of tipping when water fills it up and immediately righting itself when empty, thus expressing graphically the phenomena of continuity, flexibility, and dynamicity. This should be the way life flows without being caught up in words, whether expressed or intended. See Chuang Tzu, *The Complete Works of Chuang Tzu*, trans. Burton Watson (New York: Columbia University Press, 1968), p. 303. Also, for an excellent discussion on the use and function of goblet words, see Kuang-ming Wu, *Chuang Tzu: World Philosopher at Play* (New York: Crossroad Publishing Co., 1982), pp. 31–36.

11. Chuang Tzu, *The Complete Works of Chuang Tzu*, p. 304.

12. Chan, *A Source Book in Chinese Philosophy*, p. 160.

13. Ibid., p. 161.

14. Ibid., pp. 321–323.

15. Chung-yuan Chang, *Original Teachings of Ch'an Buddhism* (New York: Vintage Books, 1971), pp. 230–231. I have taken the liberty of changing "six phenomena" to "phenomena" and "Void" to "Nonbeing."

16. Daisetz T. Suzuki, *Zen and Japanese Culture* (Princeton: Princeton University Press, 1959, 1970), p. 227.

Part Three

Indian and Western Perspectives

Chapter Six

Reducing Concern with Self: Parfit and the Ancient Buddhist Schools

ANANYO BASU

Derek Parfit, in his book *Reasons and Persons,*[1] makes the claim that the Buddha would have agreed with the reductionist ontology of self that he proposes. The present chapter is both an examination of that claim and an exploration of some topics in Buddhist self-theory. I begin with an exegesis of the fundamentals of Parfit's views regarding personal identity and self. Thereafter, I discuss an attempt by David Bastow to expand this reductionist view along Buddhist lines, and I provide some background information regarding Buddhist psychology to help contextualize Bastow's work. Following this, I indicate some problems with the methods and conclusions of these two scholars. I end the chapter with an examination of some competing Buddhist schools and suggest the most promising line of further investigation.

Derek Parfit describes his work as a reductionist theory of the self. As we shall see, he is self-consciously in the Humean tradition and argues against any transcendental subject of consciousness. Indeed, Parfit's aim is to unsettle and problematize some of our most unquestioned and commonplace assumptions about ourselves. Thus in an early article, a precursor of the popular text mentioned above, he says: "My targets are two beliefs: one about the nature of personal identity, the other about its importance. The first is that in these cases [where we cannot answer a question regarding personal identity] the question about identity must have an answer. . . . [T]he belief which is my second target . . . is that unless the question about identity has an answer, we cannot answer certain important questions."[2] Parfit also

shares Hume's hopes and fears about the consequences of such a view. At the
end of the same article he quotes Hume to express the hope that though such
a reduction may necessarily entail the loss of some positive passions (love toward other humans for one),[3] in the end false beliefs lead to more bad consequences than good.

Parfit begins the section of *Reasons and Persons* dealing with self and
identity (pp. 203 ff.) by reminding us of the shortcomings of the standard
view that sees identity as the spatiotemporal physical continuity of an object
over time. This criterion would not give us a good account of cases where an
object changes dramatically (as when a caterpillar metamorphoses into a
butterfly) or an object does not exist for some time (as when a watch is dis-
assembled for repairs and put back together later). Parfit, always the pragmatist, would suggest that decisions in such cases should be based on utilitarian and contingent considerations. In the case of personal identity the
physical criterion appears even less persuasive: So much of what we value
about a person is psychological. Thus most of us can easily conceive of a person changing so dramatically that she just cannot be considered the same individual.[4] Indeed, many people would argue that what matters is the psychological. They would argue that we could, after all, imagine the same person
in a different body. This view of identity, then, is characterized by psychological and not physical continuity.

On Parfit's view, this *psychological continuity* may be understood in terms
of another relationship, one that he dubs *psychological connectedness* (pp.
205–206). The latter is said to exist between two psychological states at different times if they are causally related in the right way. For example, I could
remember an earlier event because I experienced it, or I could carry out an
action now because I had intended it before, or I could just continue to hold
the same belief I had twenty years ago about something or other simply because I did not change my mind. Anticipating the obvious objection that
such conceptions of memory and so on presuppose one's identity across
time, Parfit suggests the possibility of impersonal descriptions of memories
that could belong to anyone.[5] These he terms *quasi-memories* (pp. 219 ff.)
following the coinage, and borrowing the essential concept, of Sydney Shoemaker.[6] The idea is that if someone else's memories were to be transplanted
into my brain (e.g., by some future technology), then I would have psychological connectedness with that person's earlier experiences. If there are a
sufficient number of strong connections between a person X today and a
person Y tomorrow (the exact number is left a little vague, though on p. 206
Parfit suggests that he means half of what an average person has), then these
persons may be said to be psychologically continuous. Thus *strong chains of
overlapping connectedness* guarantee continuity even where there are no direct connections left. Similarly, if what I experienced at the age of two was
connected to what I experienced at five and this is connected to me today,

then I am continuous with myself at two even if I have no direct memories of my experiences at that time. What matters, according to Parfit, is not some sense of personal identity but, rather, what he calls "Relation R": psychological connectedness and/or continuity with the right cause.

The question remains as to what Parfit's view of reductionism is. He believes that both the physical and the psychological criteria are reductionist views. Why? Because they both claim that a person's identity over time *consists simply in the holding of certain more particular facts* and that these facts can be given *impersonal* descriptions (e.g., through the use of quasi-memory). Nonreductionists would have a different idea of what might make psychological connectedness possible. Thus, for instance, a Cartesian dualist might believe in an immaterial soul that is the true subject of consciousness and identity. Even nondualists might believe that a psychological subject continues to exist because of some "deep further fact." In either case we cannot *reduce* the continuing subject to some set of more particular or fundamental facts or elements. It is this fact that makes such views nonreductionist. All reductionists, Parfit elucidates, would endorse the following: "A person's existence just consists in the existence of a brain and a body, and the occurrence of a series of interrelated physical and mental events" (p. 211). Add to this the fact that Relation R is what matters (not the physical criterion) and it becomes the true source of identity—such as it is.

The persistence of one's actual physical constituents, on Parfit's view, is of no crucial significance. In this regard he is something of a functionalist—it is the psychological and social functions of an individual that constitute what matters in her identity, not her specific physical embodiment. Consider Parfit's use of various science-fiction examples to prime our intuitions in favor of holding onto identity in the face of replication, cloning, multiple brain-transplantation, and so on. Two clones might have equal claim to being the same person as the original, and what we should say about their competing claims may be contingent or pragmatic. There may be cases where questions of identity remain recalcitrantly indeterminate. In short, given that Relation R is what matters, there may be cases where we know all there is to know about the matter but we cannot make any absolute judgment with respect to identity.

One implication of this view is that uniqueness or individuality is not of any importance—continuity is what matters. Indeed, Parfit feels that his reductionism also entails a reduced level of concern for the self. This reduction he regards as entirely positive and, for that matter, as being allied to the reductionism of Buddha, Hume, and Wittgenstein. In particular, he feels that certain utilitarianist consequences follow from his reductionism in the domain of ethical theory. In short, if what matters are the experiences and continuities as such and not individual interests, then acting out of concern for the well-being of the anonymous majority is no violation of rational self-interest. Certainly egoism in particular, and self-interest generally, makes lit-tle sense on such a view.

This utilitarianist altruism does resemble the undifferentiating and univer-sal compassion enjoined in most schools of Mahayana Buddhism, largely as a consequence of their recognition that self-ascription and egoism is a perni-cious delusion. So Parfit may indeed share with the Buddha the same ethical impulse in developing his theory. It is for this reason above all that I believe Parfit merits serious consideration from Buddhists. Norman Daniels, how-ever, has raised an interesting problem with the particular ethical conse-quence that Parfit alleges. Parfit says: "When some morally important fact is seen to be less deep, it can be plausibly claimed to be less important." In other words, when we recognize that the concept of personal identity is not as deep as we had supposed, we may act in less selfish ways. Daniels retorts: "I am worried that there is not a single argument that reducing the (meta-physical?) depth of the fact is sufficient reason to warrant reducing the (moral) weight ascribed to a relevant principle." Indeed, Daniels suspects that we consider facts to be deep because they already play a central role in our moral and social theories.[7]

I think this is a reasonable objection, but perhaps not a decisive one—it could be argued both ways in most instances. Thus, for example, in various times and places honor has been deemed deep or romantic love unimportant. One could say that people's perception of their depth led to their centrality or vice versa, and I see no sure way of settling such a dispute. However, it seems fairly safe to assume that perceptions of the depth and centrality in our ethical schemas of various concepts are mutually determining. And this may be all that Parfit requires. It seems eminently plausible that a society in which the notion of identity is weakened will also exhibit reduced levels of egoistic and sociopathic behavior.

Parfit's Humean approach has, not unexpectedly, gained him some oppo-sition from Kantians. The best Kantian objection to Parfit comes from Christine Korsgaard.[8] Reasoning from the standpoint of moral agency, which for the Kantian is always the realm of practical reason, Korsgaard ar-gues that on purely pragmatic grounds we cannot avoid regarding ourselves as the same rational agent as the one who will occupy our body in the future. She begins with two arguments for synchronic unity: first, that we are in-deed able to act in a way that synthesizes the manifold of conflicting desires and emotions that well up in us, and, second, that we seem to deliberate from a unified stance—from the perspective of a subject who possesses these sundry desires and chooses among the outcomes. That is, we feel and act as *agents*. It is this possession of agency that Korsgaard believes is ignored by Parfit: We do not just passively await the outcome of conflict among com-peting impersonal desires—we *choose* among them. Turning next to di-achronic unity, she uses the same kind of argument to point out that we do in fact have projects that extend across years, decades, and indeed lifetimes. And, indeed, the very act of deliberating about future courses of action and their consequences indicates the assumption of some continuing subject. Parfit could argue that this is still pragmatic and does not reflect a deep view of self, but she says instead that there may be nothing shallow about practical necessity. With respect to understanding identity, she feels that a focus on agency is more rewarding than a Humean focus on experience. Interestingly enough, although she rejects the utilitarian consequences that Parfit supposes, Korsgaard is willing to accept that there is a sense in which people are not deeply or metaphysically separated from one another. For instance, if what defines our unity is unified agency, then we could include in our identity any and all members of a group who share our interests and intentions. Thus she can accept some of the anti-egoist implications that Parfit derives.

I find Korsgaard's argument quite compelling, but would offer the following suggestion. Parfit could escape her critique by being perhaps more Buddhist than he is. On the Buddhist view it is our intentions and desires that give rise to the very construction of this thing we call a self or a person. So it clearly makes sense to infer subjecthood from agency. The trick for the Buddhist, then, is to *get rid of the desires* and hence the *affliction of selfhood!*

Another crucial implication of Parfit's view is the rejection of an all-or-nothing conception of existence. This implication has great significance for his own work and also, as I will argue below, for the perspective and program of the Buddhist. Parfit is very explicit about his commitment to a scaleable notion of personhood and existence whereby one could imagine a whole spectrum of cases of survival within the clichéd disjunction of "dead or alive." In Parfit's view we can, in all seriousness, discuss comparably greater or lesser degrees of survival or survivorhood. Existence on this account becomes contingent, dependent, and inessential. That is, a full and inherent attribute of essential existence can no longer be considered to be in the very nature of all beings—not even of humans. This is a point of considerable consequence and I will return to an investigation of some of its important implications in a Buddhist context later in the chapter.

For now, however, I want to work out, at least in part, an answer to the question that I first asked myself when I encountered Parfit's claim that "Buddha would have agreed"—namely, Is there truly a school or view in Buddhism that would be compatible with Parfit's form of reductionism?

David Bastow is the only scholar, to the best of my knowledge, who has previously examined this question about Parfit's compatibility with Buddhism—specifically, in his excellent article "Self-Construction in Buddhism."[9] Here, Bastow argues that Buddhist views of self actually serve to fill certain lacunae in the Humean and Parfitian model of reductionism about self. In particular, he believes that Hume and Parfit do not provide any mechanism for the active construction of the self-concept. Though quite comfortable with a constructivist notion of self, Bastow seeks a more sophisticated exposition whereby it is possible to generate a range of differing constructions such that there may be a variety of answers to questions like "Is x the same person as y?" He also wants to be able to say more about the relationship between the person qua constructor and the person qua construct. Bastow's critique (not unlike Korsgaard's above) is largely argued along traditional Kantian lines and is, I think, quite reasonable. It is for his positive program that he turns to Buddhism, and here I do have some queries regarding his Buddhist hermeneutics. However, before discussing Bastow's exposition of Buddhist forms of self-construction, I want to lay out some of the basic elements of Buddhist self-theory that he appears to be assuming.[10]

First, let us consider the views that are common to almost all the schools (see especially Conze,[11] da Silva,[12] and Venkat Ramanan[13]). The basic analysis of the self as a composite (called *namarupa*) of five psychological and physical elements, or *khandas,* is widely accepted and may be broadly characterized as follows. The first *khanda* is *rupa,* which refers to the physical form, or really the matter, of the composite. Schools differ regarding the specifics of this issue, but for the most part *rupa* can be understood as the physical or enmattered aspect of a hylomorphic composite whose remaining factors are all psychological.[14]

These in turn may be conceptualized as follows, beginning with the second *khanda,* which is *vedana.* This is the emotive or feeling part of our experiences. These experiences fall into three categories: pleasant feelings engendering greed and attachment, unpleasant ones arousing anger and repulsion, and neutral feelings breeding indifference and ignorance. The goal for the sage is to be rid of all three classes of feelings along with their outcomes and to become altogether detached from the world. Such detachment is different in quality from the mere apathy that would result from cultivating neutrality.[15] The third *khanda* is *sanna,* or perception. Perception is seen as a series of flights and perchings. If we ignore the flights and focus on the perchings, we may generate the illusion of discrete objects and experiences out of the continual process of cognitive flux.[16] The fourth *khanda* is *vinnana,* or consciousness. Consciousness is attached to each sense-perception, and a stream of consciousness is the chief agent in transmigration. Finally, the fifth *khanda* is *sankhara,* or dispositions. This is the vehicle for the transmission of habits, attitudes, and the like, which in turn are the main characters passed from one birth to another.

The mode of origination of the being of things in the world is given in all Buddhist schools by some form of *pratityasamutpada,* or dependent co-origination. On this view, events depend on other events, wholes on their parts, and so on. In the case of the human person it is the coming together of the five *khandas* upon which the notion of person depends. This process is commonly described in terms of the uprising of a particular form of thinking that leads to a temporary and co-dependent union of the aggregates to which we falsely attach the idea of a permanent or continuing self. But there are very serious disagreements among the various schools with respect to the nature of this dependence, and as we shall see, Bastow's analysis suffers from a lack of attention to such heterogeneity in Buddhist thought.

Bastow describes three different forms of self-creation through the arising of thought and the coming together of *khandas*. His description, which is based on the Pali canon, can be paraphrased as follows.

The first and most common form is motivated by *tanha,* or craving. Construction of a personal unity involves both seeing the existing aggregate of *khandas* as a continuant unity and organizing the future so that it will fit the individual's self-conception. Thoughts may, but need not, give rise to persons. Ignorant people do not realize that these thoughts have the potential of rising to a better construction. They identify with the present and illusory self-consciousness based on *tanha.*

The second form of self-creation is the possibility that the arising thought does not extend in time, calling in past and future elements. The thought is entirely reflexive in its intention and wishes to take cognizance only of itself. Even the specific temporal reference provided by the present disappears, as there remain no times to contrast it with. The only true reality is the here and now.[17] There are two further possibilities within this introspective option. The first is to reach a kind of extinction by a progressive dissolution of all dualities. One moves in stages from concentration upon boundless space to boundless consciousness and, finally, to neither perception nor nonperception. The second approach is a more positive treatment of the arising thought itself. The thought becomes an alert vision of how things are—a kind of deep mindfulness of all that appears. These approaches should seem familiar to anyone who has experienced Buddhist meditation techniques.

The third form described by Bastow is the possibility of extending the Buddhist vision to provide a whole way of life. The implication is that self-creation is best avoided as we strive to avoid illusory desire and the suffering consequent upon it. Thus this third form is that of the Buddha nature itself, whereby a person has a unified understanding of past, present, and future, but without reference to her or his personal perspective. Bastow sees this option as a kind of universalist, objectivist, rational, scientific view.

I find this last description a somewhat problematic reading. In fact, a Buddha may be better understood as a selectionist and, like the rest of us, can grasp only one aspect of reality at a time.[18] She can shift perspectives but does not possess a divine omniscience. It is as though she is the ultimate hermeneut.

Overall, Bastow's is an interesting analysis in many ways, and certainly not all self-constructs share the same nature. Also, his view gives a certain agency to the self as constructor and indicates different ways in which the

aggregates may combine. I have two somewhat related concerns about Bastow's view, however. First, I do not see how the form of constructivism he
describes can truly claim to explain the nature of dependent co-origination.
Bastow describes the Buddha-nature as an impersonal and desire-free life in
the world. But he is never clear about the precise nature of the relationship
between the *khandas* and the various self-constructions or about the ontological status of the *khandas* themselves. He does state his intention to develop an explanation for "a theory which analyses a long-lived person into
short-lived constituents."[19] But he never delivers the details of the relationship—probably because (and this brings me to my second point of contention) he never indicates which school of thought he has in mind.

Indeed, I am hard-pressed to imagine which school could accept even his
premise here. For the substantialist schools are more committed to the reality of the elements than to that of the self and the nihilist schools would dismiss both, whereas Madhyamika—which I will discuss shortly—would ask
a very different set of questions altogether.

So in the end I do not think that Bastow will be able to use Buddhism to
extend and complete the reductionist view of self professed by Parfit.

I now return to my original question about the compatibility of Buddhist
conceptions of the self with Parfit's reductionist view as well as to the issue
of anti-essentialism with respect to all entities and specifically selves. My
analysis is restricted to a survey of some of the positions articulated in the
first few centuries after the death of Buddha, both because these are closest
in time to Buddha himself and because they already provide almost the full
range of relevant internal diversity. Specifically, I am discussing views that
might have been encountered during the period between 500 B.C.E. and
around 200 C.E.

The Sarvastivadins, or realists, asserted the ultimate existence of fundamental elements that have their own unique, unvarying essences. The
essences themselves do not arise or cease; rather, only their functions may
alter over time. Thus the Sarvastivadin metaphysics entailed an atomic and
objectivist analysis of the world into fundamental eternal essences or *dhar-
mas*. However, they did not count the individual self as being among the real
entities.[20] The phenomenal self as we know it is merely a complex of the
functions of elements that emerge and end over time. It is perhaps this kind
of view that is realist about fundamental elements and components but anti-
realist with regard to the individual self that Parfit has in mind when he invokes the approval of Buddha.

But there is an important point of difference between the Sarvastivadin
view and Parfit's style of reductionism: The Sarvastivadin denial of self does
not brook any half-measures—the self is totally denied and the elements are
asserted *simpliciter*.

Some of the ancient schools wanted to distance themselves from the Sarvastivadins' excessive realism and eternalism, which seemed to run counter

to the basic Buddhist teaching of the three *lakshanas,* or marks of all being. The *lakshanas* assert that all being is impermanent, ill, and not-self. The Sarvastivadin view does violence to the first two of these characteristics. Furthermore, the ancient schools deemed as too rigorous the Sarvastivadin view of not-self with regard to human self-construction. It left no room for any kind of phenomenology, which is at the heart of the Buddhist tradition.

The Sautrantikas comprised one of the principal dissenting schools. They emphasized subjectivity and the unity of the person and viewed the elements of the world as themselves changing and evolving over time. By contrast, the essentialism of the Sarvastivadins could not allow for any genuine change since alteration cannot preserve identity or essence. It is not clear, however, that Parfitian reductionism sits any better with the Sautrantika view. The problem here is that the Sautrantikas were effectively nihilists. They denied the reality of both the elements and the composites, whereas Parfit, who gives every indication of being a materialist, appears to be committed to the existence of at least the brain and the body as well as the psychological components of the Relation R.

The most extreme and influential opposition to the Sarvastivadins came from the Mahasanghika school. It provides a diametrical opposition to the Sarvastivadins, with the Sautrantikas being roughly in the middle.[21] On the Mahasanghika view, a distinction must be made between the conventional reality that arises in the world of human concepts, language, and so on, and the ultimate reality that is free of all categories, essences, and individuals. Thus the phenomenal self may have a conventional reality, but the ultimate reality is that of the universal Buddha-nature, which in turn may be referred to as the ultimate truth or dharma-substance. The Mahayana schools of Buddhism predominant among Buddhists today are in the main descended from the Mahasanghikas. Now, as the Mahasanghikas' dichotomy between the ultimate and conventional was considerably closer to the split between the noumenal and the phenomenal in Kant than to the empiricist materialism of Hume, Parfit can hardly find their interpretation very congenial.

In fact, it is possible to demonstrate for the extant schools what I have attempted to demonstrate for the ancient ones of more than two thousand years ago: that there is no obvious niche in the logical space of Buddhism for a reductionism of the form that Hume or Parfit would uphold. So Bastow's hope of using Buddhist self-psychology to complete what Parfit leaves undone may turn out to be infeasible.

But then what is to be done? After all, Parfit is motivated by desires that many of us share. He is hoping that the adoption or realization of a view that reduces or denies the individual ego could lead to a more altruistic and less narcissistic attitude. As I do not want to end this chapter without a more positive offering, I shall now adumbrate the chief contours of what I think is the most promising strand of Buddhist person theory from the perspective of the modern philosopher of mind—in particular, that of the cognitive scientist. The school I have in mind is one that in India is called Madhyamika (which refers to its espousal of Buddha's middle way) and whose offshoots are called San-lun and San-ron in China and Japan, respectively. I am also thinking specifically of the work of Nagarjuna, who lived during the first and second centuries C.E. and was arguably the greatest ancient Buddhist philosopher.

In most of its characteristics Madhyamika is a Mahayanistic school and provides perhaps the most workable brand of anti-essentialism of all the Buddhist schools. To an extent, Nagarjuna accepts the traditional Ma-hasanghika dichotomy between the conventional and the ultimate reality.[22] On his view, no individual thing is possessed of an essential nature. Every-thing must be seen as mutually dependent, mutually enacting and dynamic. Nagarjuna extends this critique of elements and substances even to the ulti-mate reality. For this higher emptiness is also to be characterized by empti-ness. The intellectual regimen that Nagarjuna preaches is the *anupalambha-yoga,* or the skillfulness of nonclinging. Only the foolish, in his view, grasp at particular philosophical positions or creeds. Like the Pyrrhonian or aca-demic skeptics he preaches the avoidance of all dogma. The truth of all being is emptiness. This emptiness, however, is to be construed not as the nihilistic void but merely as the lack of any inherently existent essences. Thus it is a form of relativism rather than of nihilism. In the conventional realm it is per-fectly acceptable to refer to a table or a room or a person, but there is no ul-timate essence to be found. And when we look toward what underlies all this (i.e., the ultimate reality), the answer is still emptiness. There are no sub-stances or essences to be found anywhere.

The same approach is enjoined in pedagogy: When preaching to Hindus or Buddhist substantialists, one is well advised to speak of not-self or the emptiness of self. But when preaching to the nihilist or the vulgar materialist, one should assert the conventional sense of self so that they do not deny all karmic effect and moral responsibility.

The same analysis is true for causality, perception, consciousness, and their objects. Again we see that there are no inherently existent essences with unalterable properties, and no individual causes with separate and isolable effects. Similarly, our consciousness is affected by, and indeed orig-inates in, a web of dependence; and we construct our objects even as they shape our phenomenology. Furthermore, perceptions are contextual and co-dependent on a host of accompanying factors. This paradigm is quite compatible with our contemporary understanding of cognition, as many scholars of cognitive science today are beginning to acknowledge.[23]

Madhyamika, in its holistic interconnectedness and its emphasis on de-pendence and contextuality, is also much better attuned to both the new physics and the new philosophy of our times. Indeed, from quantum me-chanics we are learning that there is no observer-independent or context-free truth about the world, and from the contemporary critiques of objectivist metaphysics we are relearning a new relativist and pragmatist way of being in the world.

Before I end, let me return to Parfit and the specific issue of reductionism with respect to the human person. What we give up, on Nagarjuna's account, is not these familiar aggregates bound by mutual and co-dependent ties. Nor do we surrender our normal and conventional ability to act and operate in this world. Rather, we renounce only the grasping and the desire to call it "me" or "mine." This realization engenders all the salutory ethical implications that Parfit desires, for as the Mahayanists like to say: The nondifference between self and not-self cannot be understood by those who place their self-interest above and against the interests of others. Madhyamika is also more compatible with Parfit's attempt to move away from an all-or-nothing view of identity and survival. Given the thoroughgoing mutual interdependence and enactment of all entities on the Madhyamika view, conventional identity can change as often as we switch context, perspective, or purpose. There is no longer some sort of ineluctable facticity about things—no single right description of the world.

Indeed, this Madhyamika interpretation is also closer to the words of the Buddha himself as recorded in the *Kaccayana-gotta sutta,* which is recognized as authoritative by almost every school of Buddhism. For there the Buddha says:

> This world Kaccayana is generally inclined towards two: existence and non-existence.
>
> To him who perceives with right wisdom the uprising of the world as it has come to be, the notion of non-existence in the world does not occur. Kaccayana, to him who perceives with right wisdom the ceasing of the world as it has come to be, the notion of existence in the world does not occur.
>
> The world for the most part, Kaccayana, is bound by approach, grasping and inclination. And he who does not follow that approach and grasping, that determination of mind, that inclination and disposition, who does not adhere to a view: "This is my self," who thinks: "suffering that is subject to arising arises; suffering that is subject to ceasing ceases," such a person does not doubt, is not perplexed. Herein his knowledge is not other-dependent. Thus far, Kaccayana, there is "right view."
>
> "Everything exists,"—this, Kaccayana, is one extreme.
>
> "Everything does not exist,"—this, Kaccayana, is the second extreme.
>
> Kaccayana, without approaching either extreme, the Tathagata teaches you a doctrine by the middle.

So on this reading Parfit and Buddha do agree, at least about existence not being an all-or-nothing issue. However, Madhyamika may represent too thoroughgoing an anti-essentialism and relativism for Parfit's taste—and indeed for that of most contemporary philosophers of mind. But then perhaps we have just not yet learned the skillfulness of nonclinging.

By way of conclusion let me briefly recapitulate the main points of this chapter. I have provided an exegesis of Parfit's view of self along with some responses to his critics. I have also indicated some weaknesses in Bastow's attempt to extend Parfit's work by way of Buddhism. In the latter part of the chapter I have compared Parfit's view with those of the early Buddhist schools and shown that there is no perfect fit. And at the very end I have advocated relying on the Madhyamika school to provide a viable reductionist, anti-essentialism about self. It is this form of Buddhism that I believe will provide the most insights for the philosophers and indeed the scientists of today.

Notes

1. Derek Parfit, *Reasons and Persons* (Oxford: Oxford University Press, 1984).

2. Derek Parfit, "Personal Identity," in *Philosophy of Mind*, ed. Jonathan Glover (Oxford: Oxford University Press, 1976).

3. Even positive self-love does not find much support from the Buddha and Parfit, neither of whom makes Rousseau's distinction between positive and perverse forms of self-love.

4. In this connection I would suggest the canonical Buddhist example of the great emperor Ashoka who, after the conquest of Kalinga, becomes a Buddhist and abandons all his lustful, belligerent ways to adopt the life of a Bhikku. In the history books he is often referred to as Chandashoka in the first phase of life and as Dharmashoka in the second.

5. The same analysis could also apply mutatis mutandis to intentions, beliefs, and the like.

6. Sydney Shoemaker, "Persons and Their Pasts," *American Philosophical Quarterly* 7 (1970).

7. The foregoing passages are quoted in Norman Daniels, "Moral Theory and the Plasticity of Persons," *The Monist* 62/3 (July 1979).

8. Christine Korsgaard, "Personal Identity and the Unity of Agency: A Kantian Response to Parfit," *Philosophy and Public Affairs* (1989).

9. David Bastow, "Self-Construction in Buddhism," *Ratio* (December 1986).

10. I should mention, as a brief aside, that Bastow and Parfit, like many other Western philosophers, do not appear to be very concerned about internal debates within the Buddhist tradition—a disregard that has led in general to a certain monolithic image of Buddhism that can sometimes have unfortunate exegetical consequences. Bastow's analysis does not specifically suffer from this tendency, since he assumes what nearly all the major schools agree upon. Still, this monolithic image does give rise to some problems, as I point out later. At the end of this chapter, where I make some positive suggestions of my own, I will indicate a few specific and traditional affiliations of different Buddhist schools of thought on the self and situate them with respect to the views of Parfit.

11. Edward Conze, *Buddhist Thought in India* (Ann Arbor: University of Michigan Press, 1962).

12. Padmasiri da Silva, *An Introduction to Buddhist Psychology* (New York: Barnes and Noble, 1979).

13. K. Venkat Ramanan, *Nagarjuna's Philosophy: As Presented in the Maha-Prajnaparamita-Sastra* (Delhi, India: Motilal Banarsidass, 1966).

14. I adopt the Aristotelian terminology as a quick approximation but not too much should be construed on this basis, for the similarities between the Buddhist and Aristotelian views are limited at best.

15. Indeed, such detachment may be closer to the *epoche* of the early academic skeptics in Greece as far as psychological attitudes go, but in this case there is an underlying metaphysics of radically questioning the very ontology of the cognizing subject.

16. The error here is precisely the reverse of the one that gives rise to a false notion of identity on Hume's view. According to Hume, we falsely ascribe identity to a series of similar and contiguous phenomena. Here we falsely consider as discrete objects what are in fact aspects or segments of a continuing flux.

17. This Buddhist phenomenology has some affinities with the Husserlian phenomenology in its focus on the here and now. Its relationship with the objects of thought is similarly affective and functional rather than reflective of a clear dualism of observing subject and independently existing object.

18. David Kalupahana extends this selectionist idea through a comparison with the work of William James. (See his *Nagarjuna: The Philosophy of the Middle Way* [Albany: State University of New York Press, 1986].) Thus the mind is always selecting between different stimuli, some of which rise to consciousness while others are retained in memory. Universal awareness is always only a potential never a simultaneous panoptikon. Consciousness is always local and dependent, but the Buddha nature can move uninhibitedly from one realm to another.

19. Bastow, "Self-Construction in Buddhism," p. 103.

20. For background on the discussion here and immediately following, see, in particular, Ramanan, *Nagarjuna's Philosophy: As Presented in the Maha-Prajnaparamita-Sastra*, pp. 57ff.

21. Thus the Sarvastivadins are realist pluralists, the Mahasanghikas are absolutists and anti-essentialists, and the Sautrantikas are anti-essentialists but not absolutists.

22. Jay Garfield, *The Fundamental Wisdom of the Middle Way* (New York: Oxford University Press, 1995).

23. See, for example, *The Embodied Mind,* by F. J. Varela, E. Thomson, and E. Rosch (Cambridge, Mass.: MIT Press).

Chapter Seven

Sartre and Samkhya-Yoga on Self

ASHOK K. MALHOTRA

In this chapter I delineate six perspectives on the self as presented by Jean-Paul Sartre in his work *Being and Nothingness*. Sartre views the self as a prereflective consciousness, an ego, a body, a social entity, a value, and an egoless being. I compare and contrast Sartre's position with that of Samkhya-Yoga, which describes the self in terms of *purusha* (consciousness), *buddhi* (intelligence), *ahamkara* (ego-sense), *manas* (mind), *indriyas* (the sense-motor organ complex), and an egoless reality. Though the two views pose major differences, they are similar in spirit.

This chapter is divided into three parts: Sartre's perspective on the self, the Samkhya-Yoga view described in terms of the transcendental and the empirical selves, and, finally, a comparative analysis of the two positions.

Each person's understanding of the word *self* is influenced by training in a particular discipline as well as by upbringing in a specific culture. For a philosopher or a theologian, *self* could mean the immutable, unchanging, eternal, substantial essence of a person; for a psychologist, it could mean the mental and physical capacities with which one is endowed; for a sociologist or an anthropologist, it might mean the construction of a person in conformity with the prevailing norms and ideals of the society; and for a poet or an artist, it could mean "something" that is in the process of being created during every instant of one's life and is complete only when one is dead. Though all of these views could be present within a culture, one or another view tends to be given more importance than the others. For instance, Sartre's perspective on the self was influenced by the French culture as well as by his training in the history of Western philosophy, whereas that of Samkhya-Yoga was influenced by the Hindu culture and the history of Indian philosophy. Despite these diverse influences on Sartre and Samkhya-Yoga, which in turn led to the development of substantially different positions on the self, the two views, as noted, exhibit similarity in spirit.

Sartre's Perspective on the Self

A commonplace criticism of Sartre is that since he discusses a human being in terms of a nonsubstantial nothingness, he adopts a nihilistic position on the self. This criticism appears to be valid given that Sartre, in describing the self, uses such phrases as "a human being is a nothingness," "in human beings existence comes before essence," "human being is a non-substantial being," "a human being is a transcendence of being," and "a human being is an openness." These descriptions, which highlight the difficulty of grasping the true nature of the self, might sidetrack the reader into thinking that Sartre has nothing of significance to say about the subject. However, a close reading of the text of *Being and Nothingness* reveals that Sartre's investigation of the self is much richer than has been believed by some critics.

Before presenting his own position, Sartre evaluated the traditional view of the self. In the West, when the word *self* is used, it has been understood either as an essence or as a common nature possessed by all human beings. Those who believe that human beings are born with an essence are guided by the artistic model of the universe. According to this view, God creates the universe the way an artist creates a painting. Before the world and human beings come to be, they are already conceived by God. And like an artist, God utilizes a preconceived notion and a technique to bring the world and human beings into existence. Thus a human being who is created by God has a preordained purpose and a definition. The goal of life consists in bringing this divine seed to its fruition. Therefore, self equals the actualization of this potential divine essence.

In the West, a second view identifies self with human nature. According to this view, every person is born with a human nature. Irrespective of one's cultural upbringing, educational training, and intellectual or social status, each human being is a particular instance of a universal concept. The primitive man, the slave, the serf, the worker, the capitalist, the bourgeois, the king, the pauper, the artist, the genius, the highly cultured person, and the ordinary human being—all share the same definition and fundamental qualities. Thus, every human being is made from the same mold and substance called the human nature.

But Sartre rejects both of these positions by asserting that, since there is no God, a human being is born with no essence or nature. The self that is identified with either of these is then reduced to a nothingness.

Sartre draws the following inferences from this position. First, a human being at birth possesses no substantial self; second, one's life has no preordained purpose or direction; third, one's future is an open book on which one's life will make its marks; fourth, what a human being should or should not become cannot be stated in general terms; and last, one's acts during one's life will determine how one's self is to be defined.

At the core of Sartre's position is the notion that the self is a nonsubstantial nothingness. In *Being and Nothingness*, while presenting a phenomenological analysis of this nothingness, he reveals the following six semantic and ontological layers of meanings: the self as a prereflective consciousness, an ego, a body, a social being, a value, and an egoless person.

Prereflective Consciousness as Self

According to Sartre, since a human being possesses no essence or nature at birth, he or she can be described as a mere consciousness (being-for-itself).[1] Moreover, this consciousness that lacks any substantial content is nothingness. In radical contrast to this consciousness, the world of objects (being-in-itself), which has a substantial essence, is nonconscious. Sartre describes this consciousness as prereflective. The unique feature of prereflective consciousness is that it reveals itself by being conscious of something; it is an awareness of being not an object. By combining the two statements in the previous sentence, we can obtain a view of the self of the prereflective consciousness. This self is the consciousness's realization that it is nothing more than an awareness of an object and that, at the same time, it is not that object. To put it differently, the consciousness apprehends itself as distinct from the object of which it is aware. Consciousness is other than the object, yet through awareness of the object, consciousness is revealed. It is never identical with the object except at death. According to Sartre, the freedom of the prereflective consciousness lies in apprehending itself as different from the object.

Sartre's phenomenological analysis provides the following descriptions of the prereflective consciousness as the self. First, it is nonpersonal and yet uniquely individual; second, it is an egoless consciousness; third, all emotions, motives, desires, passions, or psychic qualities reside outside it; fourth, it is the basis for all acts of consciousness; fifth, it exists as a revelation of an object; sixth, it is something other than an object; and seventh, it is a nonpersonal self-consciousness identical with freedom.

Ego as Self

The prereflective consciousness is the basic intentional awareness of the object. Through intentional acts, it reveals the world, which is other than itself. While performing these conscious acts, it becomes aware of them. The conglomeration of these acts, attitudes, and experiences through which consciousness relates to the external world constitutes one's ego. The self as ego is the psychic unity imposed by consciousness on its own acts, through which it personalizes the universe. The ego-self is a person's point of view on the world—that is, the crystallization of the totality of attitudes taken by consciousness. It is consciousness's attempt at objectification of itself in relation to the world. The ego-self is a stance one takes toward objects, things, and people. It is one's choice of being, through which one relates to the world.

Furthermore, ego may be regarded as one's attempt at creating oneself as a work of art. If one is humble, aggressive, heroic, cowardly, creative, submissive, fearful, angry, frustrated, anguished, or depressed, one has created oneself this way through intentional acts. Though the ultimate responsibility for constructing the ego falls on one's shoulders, this construction may also be influenced by one's upbringing (family, society, culture, books one has read, art one has been exposed to, etc.). During one's developmental years, one may accept these external influences, yet might challenge them later on. The levels of acceptance, rejection, and modification of these influences are ultimately chosen by the individual. When taken together, these intentional acts constitute one's ego. The ego-self so constructed, through which one perceives, apprehends, and appropriates the world, is one's unique approach to reality.

The ego-self can be defined through the following essential points. First, it is a product of consciousness and not something one is born with; second, it is a combination of all one's mental or psychic acts; third, it is a unified response of one's psyche through which one relates to the world and to other people; fourth, it expresses itself through such words as *I, me, my,* and *mine;* fifth, it is one's unique individual self that is more or less permanent; sixth, it is a combination of all of one's past acts that make up one's script of life; and seventh, it is the solidification of one's freedom.

Body as Self

Sartre's phenomenological analysis further reveals the connection between the self and the ontological dimensions of the body. A human being is not just a consciousness or an ego but also a body. It is through the body that one becomes aware of other people and oneself. According to Sartre, the body is grasped at three levels: as being-for-itself, as being-for-other, and as being-known-by-other.

In the first dimension, the body is a being for itself. Here one exists as one's body. Consciousness and body are inseparable at this level. A person is one's body, and one's body is the person. Furthermore, the world of objects and people exists in relationship to one's body. The body is the center, whereas everything else becomes the locus. Every item in the world is measured with reference to one's body. The body constitutes one's unique point of view on the world. In fact, there is no difference between one's body and one's self.

One's body has a being for oneself but also a being for the other. The other's body is understood either as a being-for-itself for which one's body is an object or as an object confronting the gaze of one's body, which is incarnated by one's consciousness. In all human relations, these two modes of the body are revealed.

Sartre gives the example of a person A who is sitting on a bench in a park looking at the trees, the flowers, the park gate, and the sky. Everything in the park is measured by reference to this person A, who constitutes the center. But if at any moment another person B enters the park and looks at person A, not only is the latter's world snatched away but he or she is also reduced into a body. In this situation, B's body is perceived as consciousness incarnate looking at A's body as an object. This situation could be reversed such that person A looks back at B's body by transforming it into an object. When one person gazes at another, the second person feels the other's consciousness through bodily awareness and is transformed into an object among other objects. And when the second person looks back on the first, the first one's body is transformed into an object. Through these modes Sartre reveals two ways in which a person's self could be identified with one's body.

One's perspective on the other's body is not limited to regarding it as an object among other objects. The other's body is made of flesh and blood. When one sees another person momentarily, the other's body is revealed as a flesh-and-blood object. But as one's acquaintance with this person increases and continues over time, one is able to see the other's body as constituting one's past, where freedom is fixed and objectified. This objectification of the other's freedom in the body gives unity to one's various acts. This unity may be regarded as the unique character of the other person. And this other person may be regarded as possessing a moral, immoral, amiable, or unhappy character that is the sum total of various behavior patterns.

There is also a third dimension of the body, a dimension intimately connected to the other two. In the first case, one exists as one's body as it is lived by oneself, and in the second, one exists as one's body as it is used by the other; but in the third, one exists as one's body as it is known by the other. In the first dimension, one's consciousness and the body are so intimately connected that there are no inner or outer aspects of a person. However, in the second dimension, the other's look can transform a person into an object and thus can create an outer aspect of him or her; and in the third dimension, the other knows a person by creating an outwardness for him or her that escapes the person's freedom. This exteriority of a person's body for the other is unknown to the person and discloses one's alienation from one's own body.

The first, second, and third dimensions can best be illustrated in terms of the distinctions among pain, illness, and disease. When one experiences pain in the stomach, one is this painful stomach and nothing else. One is not an object-pain but a person-suffering. When experienced at a nonreflective level, this pain and one's body are the same. However, one's reflective awareness of the pain will reveal it as a psychic object—that is, as an illness. A suffered illness is a strange bodily sensation that incapacitates one's body and prevents it from functioning at its optimum level. But when a physician views this pain through the theories and concepts of medical science, the pain is revealed as a disease harbored by a patient's body. The physician knows the patient's body only as an object that needs to be treated through medicine and surgery. This knowledge of one's body by the other escapes one's grasp. Thus the bodily self could be revealed in all the three dimensions: body as lived by one, as used by the other, and as known by the other.

Social or Community Self

Besides the bodily self, Sartre discusses a dimension of the self that can be called the social or community self. This self, which develops only in the context of a concrete situation, reveals itself as "we-subjects" or as "us-objects." Though conflict underlies most of human relations, the possibility of a community experience does exist. Sartre identifies situations that bring about a shared experience among people. This community with others occurs in various concrete situations: "We" watch a play or a sports event, "we" listen to a concert or a political speech, "we" use the subway or public parks, "we" elect the president or governor. Here, "we" refers to the experience of being as "subjects in common."

However, there is another aspect of this community self that Sartre designates as "us." In this case we experience our being as objects in common or our common being as it is revealed to the other. The other constitutes a class or a group that oppresses or controls us. For instance, we may experience ourselves as part of a working class that is suppressed by the upper class or the capitalist hierarchy. The class consciousness of any oppressed group such as factory workers, prisoners, patients, disgruntled consumers, alienated young people, the silent majority, and so on brings about the "us" experience. Common to this experience is the feeling that we are trapped in a network of external factors influencing our destiny over which we have no control. The feeling of collective alienation, of being reduced to mere object or a replaceable number, is an example of the "us" experience.

Though the community self revealed through the "we-subject" or the "us-object" arises through an intense shared experience, it has an unstable existence. Its transiency is due to the fluidity of human consciousness. The "we-subject" feeling can be wiped out by the other's glance, which in turn can reduce the former into the experience of the "us-object." Similarly, the "us-object" feeling can be transformed into the "we-subject" experience if the suppressed group glances back at the oppressor. Both aspects of the community self are unstable and result from the concrete situation confronting the group.

Self as Value

Sartre offers yet another unique perspective on the self. I refer here not to the social self, the bodily self, or the ego-self but to the self that a person is not yet but would like to be. Sartre calls this self "value." It is that which one lacks at present and wants to bring into being in the future. This desired self is not an actual entity but a pursuit or a project. When we observe our desires carefully, we discover a fundamental underlying desire that is the wish to create a self that is its own justification. In all our projects, this aspiration is implicit. The pursuit of this kind of self is the desire to be God (the highest value).

But why does a human being desire to be God? Sartre asserts that it is the peculiar predicament of human beings that they lack self as well as the justification for their existence. This experience of meaninglessness is the cause of human uneasiness and suffering. To get rid of this feeling, a human being aspires to be a self that is substantial and its own justification. This desire for a justified existence is the yearning for the fusion of the being-for-itself (consciousness) and the being-in-itself (materiality), which is equivalent to the desire to be God. Since this fusion is of mutually contradictory states, it can never be actualized. Thus the self as value is never an actual self but a self-making process. Though each of us strives for this kind of self, no one can ever achieve it.

Egoless Being as Self

As we have seen, the prereflective consciousness is able to project itself through such masks as the ego, the body, and the social self as well as through value. Yet in spite of these projections, the prereflective consciousness is always beyond these masks and is at no time identical with any of them. A careful reading of *Being and Nothingness* reveals that Sartre makes no distinction between the prereflective consciousness and the egoless self. For him, they are one and the same. A further question can be raised here. Is the Sartrean authentic person an egoless self? For Sartre, an authentic person is one who performs existential acts originating from the spontaneity of his or her freedom. These acts are chosen and performed by the individual with the full awareness of this freedom and with the understanding that they do not curb another person's freedom. Furthermore, one who performs such acts accepts the responsibility entailed by them. Because the existential acts involve regard as well as responsibility toward other people, they cannot be egoless. Thus an ideal existential person has a two-tiered task. First, the person must accept having an ego that is held responsible for the performance of existential acts. Second, the person must acknowledge that he or she is truly the prereflective consciousness, which is nothing more than an awareness of an object. As the prereflective consciousness directs itself toward the world through sensation, feeling, emotion, thinking, and valuing, it is an egoless flow toward objects or events. Since an existentialist has to keep a balance between the ego-self and the prereflective consciousness in order to be authentic, the ideal existential person cannot be egoless. Thus, in Sartre's view, the only self that can be egoless is the prereflective consciousness.

The Samkhya-Yoga Perspective on the Self

The Samkhya-Yoga perspective on the self is intimately connected with its ontological view, which understands the universe in terms of two ultimate realities: *Purusha* and *Prakriti. Purusha* is pure consciousness, whereas *Prakriti* is the unconscious psychophysical substantiality. *Purusha,* which is devoid of any substantiality, is revealed when it witnesses or intends the psychophysical reality; *Prakriti,* which is unconscious, is disclosed when it is observed or intended by *Purusha. Purusha* is the pure subject, whereas *Prakriti* is the pure object. Though the two realities can exist independently of each other, only through their interaction is the entire universe, including human beings, created.

According to Samkhya-Yoga, a human being is a unique combination of both the conscious *Purusha* and the unconscious *Prakriti.* Though the *prakritic* components of *buddhi* (intelligence), *ahamkara* (ego-sense), *manas* (mind), and *indriyas* (the sense-motor organ complex) are intrinsically unconscious, they display the borrowed consciousness of *Purusha.*

Samkhya-Yoga compares the *Purusha's* consciousness to the sun's light. When the light of the sun touches the moon, the moon glows; when the moon's light is reflected in the water, it brightens up the entire pond; and when the rays of the reflected moon splash on a building, the walls become luminous. A child who looks at the building might say that the luminosity belongs to it, whereas an adult knows that the building is radiant because of the light of the moon. However, a scientist would say that even the light of the moon is not its own but, instead, is borrowed from the sun.

By utilizing the above metaphor, Samkhya-Yoga shows that like the sun, consciousness that belongs to *Purusha* is reflected through different layers of *Prakriti.* Since *buddhi* (intelligence) lies in close proximity to *Purusha,* it is the first product of *Prakriti* to be lit up. Similarly, as consciousness reflects itself through *ahamkara* (ego-sense), *manas* (mind), and *indriyas* (the sense-motor organ complex), they too become conscious. As each displays *purusic* consciousness, it assumes that consciousness is its sole property rather than a borrowed entity.

Buddhi as Self

The first in the line of *purusic* consciousness is *buddhi* (intelligence). According to the Samkhya-Yoga system, *buddhi* is the finest product of *Prakriti*. As the purest psychophysical substantiality, it is the link between *Purusha* and the other components of *Prakriti* (i.e., those constituting the mind-body complex). When *Purusha's* consciousness comes in contact with *buddhi*, *buddhi* becomes *Purusha-incarnate* or the living spirit. As a corporeal manifestation of the *purusic* consciousness, it plays the role of the knower and inner controller. *Buddhi* has the dual responsibility of injecting harmony into the mind-body complex and making the knowledge of truth or *Purusha* possible.

At an *individual* level *buddhi* is the source of all inspiration, whereas at the *cosmic* level all creative endeavors flow from it. It is the conscience in each person that counsels and guides the individual. When it is untainted by desires, needs, or wishes, it offers uninterrupted intuitive knowledge of *Purusha*. It is the place where enlightenment or illumination takes place. A person might identify his or her self with *buddhi*.

Manas and Ahamkara as Self

Though *buddhi* (intelligence) is the controller and harmonizer of the mind-body complex, it leaves all basic managerial functions to the *ahamkara* (ego-sense) and *manas* (mind), the two other psychophysical aspects of *Prakriti*. The *ahamkara* and *manas* are the hub of ceaseless activity and constitute the most restless part of the human personality. Since they initiate and direct mental and physical action, all distractions and agitations take place in this center.

The commotion within the heart of *ahamkara* and *manas* is propelled by desire. The goal of desire is to appropriate and control the world. *Manas* (mind) utilizes desire to accomplish this goal in the following way: While displaying *purusic* consciousness, it directs itself toward *indriyas* (the sense-motor organ complex), which in turn becomes conscious. As the senses become activated, they provide us with the experience of objects. And once these perceptions are gathered in the mind, the latter sorts them out under different categories. Furthermore, as this conceptualized information is modified by memory, imagination, and emotions, *ahamkara* (ego-sense) appropriates it by declaring itself to be their owner. Moreover, *ahamkara* personalizes the contents of the mind by imposing on it the sense of *I, my, me,* and *mine.* Since these experiences, ideas, images, feelings, and emotions have happened to *me, ahamkara* dubs them as *mine.* Furthermore, *ahamkara* unifies all the mental possessions by stamping on them the word *me* or *I*. Through the constant desiring and appropriating of the world, *ahamkara* is involved in an endless quest for broadening its own domain. Thus, *ahamkara* confuses the person into believing that the ego is his or her true self.

Chitta as Self

In the Samkhya-Yoga terminology, *buddhi, ahamkara,* and *manas* make up the *chitta,* or the ordinary consciousness of an individual. *Chitta* is the most dynamic arena because the drama of a person's life is enacted here. Since all desires, wants, aspirations, and intentions as well as all sensations, feelings, emotions, images, thoughts, and values reside in it, an individual might identify his or her self with the *chitta* and its contents.

For example, suppose a man has just bought a new Oak Green Toyota Camry equipped with a six-cylinder engine, leather seats, a sunroof, two air bags, air conditioning, and a six-speakers stereo. As the owner observes the interior and exterior of the car, he might ascribe to it the properties of beauty, grace, prestige, and power. Though these properties originate in his mind, he might assume that they belong to the automobile. The more he observes these qualities in the car, the more he becomes attached to it. The owner might tell himself that the car belongs to him or that it is his car. If someone else admires it, the owner feels happy; and if someone scratches or dents it, the owner feels unhappy. This car then becomes an extension of the owner's body, of his self.

One relates to other objects in a similar fashion. When one observes anything in the world, one assigns to it a certain value. As the objects are perceived through the five sense organs, they leave an impression in the mind. If this experience is gratifying, as in the case of the new car, one believes that one is happy, and if it is unpleasant, one believes that one is unhappy. Similarly, all one's knowledge of the external world (things or people) is nothing more than the profusion of impressions in the mind. As the ego asserts its ownership of these experiences, a person believes that he or she is nothing more than the *chitta,* or the ordinary consciousness. In other words, the person takes the *chitta* or the *buddhi-ahamkara-manas* complex to be his or her real self.

Body as Self

The process of identifying one's self with *buddhi, ahamkara, manas,* or *chitta* does not stop here but moves on to incorporate the five perceptual and the five motor organs of the body. As consciousness of *Purusha* is reflected through the eyes, ears, nose, tongue, skin, arms, legs, mouth, and organs of generation and excretion, each of these organs starts to believe that consciousness is its unique property. While perceiving, a person thinks that his or her eyes see, ears hear, tongue tastes, nose smells, and skin touches. At no time does a person believe that each of the senses operates on consciousness that is borrowed from *Purusha*.

One distinctive feature of these ten senses is that they are oriented toward the external world. Through perception and action they offer the person experiences of the outside reality. When these perceptual experiences are presented to the mind, the latter sorts them out under various categories and asserts its ownership of the information by calling it "mine." Since one's body, consisting of five sense and five motor organs, works in such close cooperation with the psychological and conscious parts of one's being, it becomes a mirror of the inner world. This indissoluble connection of the two leads to the confusion that there is no difference between one's body and one's real self.

In the Samkhya-Yoga system, though *Purusha* is the sole owner of consciousness, its reflection through the *prakritic* components of intelligence, ego-sense, mind, and sense-motor organs bestows upon them consciousness. All of these parts of the psychophysical reality work together, but each might regard itself as independent of the others. Since in our various personal and social encounters, we confront our mind-body complex and not *Purusha*, it is easier to identify ourselves with the mind or the body. This confusion, when repeated on a regular basis, leads an individual to believe that he or she is nothing more than a psychophysical entity. When a person takes the real self to be *Prakriti* rather than *Purusha*, this false identity results in suffering.

But why and how does a person mistake one for the other? The why is answered in terms of one's ignorance about the nature of reality. This ignorance lies in taking the unreal for the real—that is, the carnal condition for the spiritual condition or the *prakritic self* for the *purusic self*. It is a matter of mistaking the flesh for the spirit, of confusing the cage with the encaged bird. How does this happen?

Since each one of us is brought up in a culture that through its language and logic, and its social, political, ethical, and religious values conditions us to view the world and ourselves in a unique way, we hold this cultural view of ourselves to be real. Our upbringing teaches us to believe that we are nothing more than the mind-body complex. There is no spiritual bird (*Purusha*) in the mind-body cage (*Prakriti*). The *prakritic self* is regarded by us as real, and the presence of the *purusic self* is totally ignored. What, then, is the *purusic self* or *Purusha*?

Purusha as Self

There is a stark contrast between the natures of *Purusha* and *Prakriti*. *Purusha* is the pure conscious self that is immortal, spiritual, and free, whereas *Prakriti* is the unconscious empirical self that is mortal, material, and determined.

As pure consciousness, *Purusha* lacks all substantial content. It is not the intelligence (*buddhi*), the ego-sense (*ahamkara*), the mind (*manas*), or the sense-motor organs (*indriyas*). Though *Purusha* is beyond the *prakritic components,* it reveals them through the activities of witnessing, experiencing, and enjoying. As it witnesses the *prakritic parts,* they become conscious, and as it experiences and enjoys them, they are disclosed as existing. By revealing the world of *Prakriti, Purusha* discloses itself as consciousness. Though both *Purusha* and *Prakriti* are immutable and independent realities, the products of *Prakriti* are mutable. *Purusha* is the inner seer, eternal and totally free, whereas the *prakritic components* have borrowed consciousness, and are mortal and determined. Identifying one's real self with the intelligence, the ego-sense, the mind, or the sense-motor organs leads to suffering. However, when a person realizes that one's real self is the eternal, spiritual, and free *Purusha*, one is enlightened. This enlightenment, which brings an end to all suffering, offers one a great sense of peace or happiness.

Comparative Analysis of the Perspectives of Sartre and Samkhya-Yoga

As noted earlier, the preceding exposition of these perspectives reveals numerous points of agreement and opposition regarding the nature of the self. Though the two systems originated in different cultures, a close examination of their questions, concerns, descriptions, and aims reveals some vital points of connection among them. In spite of the fact that their positions differ significantly on the ontological and religious status of the self, there is an overall compatibility between the two systems.

Both Sartre and Samkhya-Yoga present their views on the self in agreement with their ontological positions. Indeed, both believe in a bifurcated reality consisting of consciousness and materiality. The term for consciousness in Sartre's work is *being-for-itself,* whereas in Samkhya-Yoga it is *Purusha.* Sartre's depiction of the being-for-itself as lacking all psychophysical content is similar to Samkhya-Yoga's description of *Purusha.* Moreover, the being-for-itself and *Purusha* are analogous in that both reveal themselves by disclosing something other than themselves. This revelation is made possible when they witness, observe, intend, desire, sense, or feel the material world. In contrast, the psychophysical reality (*Prakriti*) or materiality (being-in-itself) is disclosed only when it is intended or observed by the consciousness of *Purusha* or the being-for-itself.

Furthermore, both Sartre and Samkhya-Yoga posit that a human being is a blend of the two realities of consciousness and materiality. According to both views, the true self of a person is more akin to consciousness than to the material components. For Sartre this self is the prereflective consciousness, whereas for Samkhya-Yoga it is *Purusha.* Since the prereflective consciousness is deprived of all substantial content, Sartre designates it as nothingness. This consciousness is a lack of being because everything substantial lies outside it. Similarly, for Samkhya-Yoga *Purusha* is the real self of a person. It is the pure consciousness that is deprived of all psychophysical content. According to Samkhya-Yoga, qualities that constitute the essence of the material world of *Prakriti* are totally absent from the nature of *Purusha.* Though *Purusha* lies in close proximity to materiality (*Prakriti*), the latter remains external to it.

Moreover, like the prereflective consciousness of Sartre, *Purusha* is an openness that is directed outside itself toward the world of objects. Though the prereflective and *Purusha* represent consciousness and are responsible for injecting awareness into the psychophysical parts of a human being, they are not identical with any one of them. Similar to the prereflective consciousness, which constructs the ego, the social self, and the self as value and body, *Purusha* by reflecting its consciousness through the intelligence (*buddhi*), the ego-sense (*ahamkara*), the mind (*manas*), and the sense-motor organ complex (*indriyas*) supplies them with awareness. Though both the prereflective consciousness and *Purusha* present themselves through these psychological and bodily masks, they are unlike these disguises.

A further resemblance between the two positions is seen in the case of an individual mistaking the true self with the constructed one. Sartre believes that when one assumes one's ego, social self, or body to be one's authentic self, this false identification leads to unfreedom. Samkhya-Yoga's position is comparable to that of Sartre on this point. It holds that though the genuine self of a person is *Purusha,* he or she might identify this self with the *buddhi, ahamkara, manas,* or *indriyas.* In Samkhya-Yoga's view, this distorted identification leads to unfreedom and suffering.

Moreover, Sartre and Samkhya-Yoga share the belief that the cause of this mistake lies in one's upbringing in a culture that conditions one, through language, logic, values, and personal likes and dislikes, to view oneself as nothing more than a psychological or physical being. This conditioning, which sullies one's genuine view of the self, is hard to change. However, both Sartre and Samkhya-Yoga also believe that one could go beyond this restricted conviction of reality: in the case of Sartre, through the use of the phenomenological method, and in the case of Samkhya-Yoga, through the yogic method. Sartre provides the reader with this kind of understanding through his character Roquentin in the novel *Nausea* and through his philosophical descriptions in *Being and Nothingness,* whereas Samkhya-Yoga describes a step-by-step yogic procedure consisting of physical-meditative exercises as a way of offering the initiate a revelatory experience of *Purusha.*

Sartre's use of the phenomenological method reveals the being-for-itself as consciousness, nothingness, and freedom. Similarly, Samkhya-Yoga's application of the method of physical-meditative exercises helps break the conditioning barriers by disclosing *Purusha* as pure consciousness, no-thing, and unlimited freedom.

For Sartre, the prereflective consciousness is experienced as nothingness because there is nothing at the core of a human being. A person is born with no solid self or substantial human nature. And since a human being is deprived of any essence, he or she is perpetually desiring to fill this emptiness with a concrete self. This constant pursuit for the self explains why one keeps attempting to identify one's self with one's body, one's ego, or one's social role. In Sartre's opinion, all attempts at equating one's self with any of these roles are unsuccessful because, as a human being, one will always remain a deprivation of being. This nothingness will persist as long as one lives and will disappear only when one is dead.

For Samkhya-Yoga, *Purusha* is no-thing. *Purusha* is no-thing because all the physical and psychological ingredients that make up the universe of *Prakriti* lie outside it. Here, the use of the word *no-thing* instead of *nothing* or *nothingness* is more appropriate because the latter words invoke the image of *total nonexistence, total emptiness,* or *total absence;* but for Samkhya-Yoga, though *Purusha* is deprived of all psychophysical content, it is not nothingness or nothing. Unlike the Sartrean prereflective consciousness, *Purusha* has a unique kind of presence. *Purusha*'s distinctiveness consists in its being a pure subject that operates as the inner seer, witness, and observer. It is no-thing because, though it imparts consciousness to the intelligence (*buddhi*), the ego-sense (*ahamkara*), the mind (*manas*), and the sense-motor organ complex (*indriyas*), it has its own separate existence outside them.

Another parallel between Sartre and Samkhya-Yoga is revealed in their perspectives on freedom: Both Sartre and Samkhya-Yoga believe that freedom is the being of the prereflective consciousness as well as that of *Purusha*, that freedom is unrestricted, and that the denial of freedom leads to suffering.

When Sartre regards freedom to be unrestricted and absolute, he means that there are no internal or external restrictions to human freedom. In every situation, a human being is free. Since this existential freedom makes up the very core of the prereflective consciousness, Sartre asserts that this freedom is the source of all creativity. Though human beings are naturally free, they can deny this freedom through their false identification with the ego, the body, or the social role. This false identification leads to unfreedom and suffering.

Similarly, Samkhya-Yoga's method of physical-meditative exercises helps break the conditioning barriers in order to offer the initiate the experience of

Purusha in terms of unlimited freedom. Samkhya-Yoga's view is analogous to Sartre's inasmuch as it is the very nature of *Purusha* to be free. Furthermore, this freedom might appear to be restricted when a person identifies his or her self with any of the *prakritic components*. But when properly used under the supervision of intelligence (*buddhi*), this freedom can express itself as the inner controller of the mind-body complex as well as the creative source of all human endeavors. However, when improperly used by the ego-sense (*ahamkara*), the same freedom could turn out to be the source of false identification of the real self with *prakritic components* and thus becomes the cause of suffering.

Having examined the obvious similarities between these two positions, we now consider their fundamental differences. First, when Sartre designates the prereflective consciousness as nothingness, he is indicating that this consciousness lacks a substantial self. The privation of a solid self is the existential predicament of a human being. Facing this ontological situation, a human being is compelled to seek a substantial self. In Sartre's opinion, human beings spend their lives pursuing the goal of filling this emptiness through some form of self. In contrast, Samkhya-Yoga does not believe that a human being is deprived of a genuine or true self. In its view, instead of feeling the privation of a self, a human being lacks the knowledge that his or her true self is *Purusha*. Because of this ignorance, the person identifies his or her real self with the *prakritic components*. This situation, according to Samkhya-Yoga, is an epistemological problem that leads to the ontological confusion of taking the unreal to be real; for Sartre, however, the same situation displays the ontological-existential predicament of a human being.

A further point of contrast between *Purusha* and the prereflective consciousness is that they are two different kinds of concepts or entities. For Sartre, the prereflective consciousness is unlike physical, mental, or spiritual substance; it is simply not any kind of substance. But *Purusha,* though deprived of all the physical and psychological components of *Prakriti*, is a kind of spiritual substance. Scholars have described *Purusha* as infinite existence, consciousness, and bliss. Furthermore, as infinite existence, *Purusha* is articulated as indestructible, timeless, and immutable; as infinite consciousness, it is grasped as the source of all awareness, knowledge, and wisdom; and as infinite bliss, it is understood as the creative source of all pleasure, joy, and happiness. Finally, since *Purusha* is unrestricted by time and space, it is described as total freedom. In contrast to Sartre's depictions of the being-for-itself as lack, nothingness, nihilation, openness, separation, projection, and desire,[2] these descriptions of *Purusha* clearly point to the latter as a spiritual substance.

The two systems' views on desire are also different, even though their descriptions of consciousness and freedom as constituting the core of a human being are analogous. For Sartre, desire is the basic ontological structure of the being-for-itself. Without desire there will be no being-for-itself. It is through desire that a human being relates to other human beings, and through desire that he or she is able to create a self in the future. For Sartre, the phenomena of love, hate, sadism, masochism, longing to be God, and the like make sense only in the context of desire as a fundamental structure of the being-for-itself. However, in Samkhya-Yoga's view, desire is not the basic ingredient of *Purusha*. All physical and psychic content, including desire, lies outside *Purusha*. In fact, desire belongs to the mind-body complex only. Furthermore, Samkhya-Yoga holds desire to be responsible for confusing the individual regarding the true nature of the self. It is through desire that one identifies one's true self with the *prakritic components* of intelligence (*buddhi*), the ego-sense (*ahamkara*), the mind (*manas*), and the sense-motor organ complex (*indriyas*). According to Samkhya-Yoga, all pain and suffering result from this kind of craving. When the desire for the material world as well as for the ego is eliminated, one comes to the understanding that one's real self is *Purusha* and not the *prakritic components*. Samkhya-Yoga calls this discriminative knowledge *enlightenment*.

Underlying the above discussion is another difference between the two positions. According to Sartre, the fundamental desire of every human being is to become God, a desire that manifests itself through the wish to make one's life meaningful. Since this desire involves the juxtaposition of two contradictory beings of in-itself and for-itself, the ideal is beyond the realm of human possibility. This goal cannot be achieved, then, but aspiration for the goal is essential for human survival. In *Being and Nothingness*, though Sartre shows no interest in discussing the phenomenon of religious consciousness, his admission that the fundamental project of each person is the desire to be God refers to a spiritual quest.

It is significant that Sartre does not recognize the existence of a religious self. He believes that when the body dies, the prereflective consciousness disappears with it; no transcendental self survives the death of the body. Moreover, Sartre attaches no religious significance to death. Since death for him is an incomprehensible event, it is to be regarded as absurd. Death does not give life meaning; instead, it takes away all significance and the future possibilities of a person. After death, whatever one "had-been" becomes one's permanent essence, and the future is closed forever.

In contrast, Samkhya-Yoga describes *Purusha* as a transcendental-religious self that is immortal, immutable, and eternally free. When the body of an enlightened person dies, the *Purusha* of this person frees itself from the entanglements of the world of materiality and lives eternally in a blissful state. But when an unenlightened person dies, his or her *Purusha*, which has been corrupted by bad deeds, remains entangled in the eternal birth-death cycle and will stay that way until the person achieves salvation in the future. In both instances, the person's religious self survives the death of the body as either a free or an unfree *Purusha*.

The above discussion centers on the comparison and contrast of the being-for-itself and *Purusha* because these concepts come very close to conveying the notion of the self in the two systems. Both systems designate the underlying conscious reality in a person in contrast to all other forms of the self such as the ego, the body, and the like, which are nothing more than selves constructed by this consciousness. One could use the aforementioned model of comparison to show similarities and differences between the Sartrean analysis of the self in terms of the ego, the body, the social self, and the self as value, on the one hand, and Samkhya-Yoga's depiction of the self as the intellect (*buddhi*), the ego-sense (*ahamkara*), the mind (*manas*), and the sense-motor organ complex (*indriyas*), on the other.

Sartre describes the ego as something constituted by consciousness; as a combination of various mental acts; as a unified response of the person to the world; as a unique solidified self that reveals itself through such expressions as *I, my, mine*, and *me;* and as the solidification of a person's freedom. Analogous to the Sartrean portrayal of the ego, Samkhya-Yoga uses the word *chitta* to refer to the combination of the acts of the *buddhi* (intellect), *ahamkara* (ego), and *manas* (mind). *Chitta* as *buddhi* acts as an inner controller and knower, as the source of all inspiration and creativity, as a counselor and a guide, and as a place of enlightenment. Furthermore, *chitta* as *ahamkara* and *manas* acts as a manager of the mind-body complex, as a hub of ceaseless activity, as an initiator of all mental action, as a desire to appropriate the world, as the source of the sense of I-am-ness, and as the center that restricts a person's freedom.

The Sartrean concept of the ego appears to be similar to the Samkhya-Yoga view of the *chitta* in three respects. First, since ego is a combination of one's mental acts, it is like the *chitta*, the hub of all mental activity. Second, as both the ego and the *ahamkara* induce in a person the sense of *I, my, mine,* and *me,* they both act as the principle of individuation whereby the person obtains a sense of his or her objective self, which is unique and personal. Third, for Sartre the ego is a product of the being-for-itself, not something one is born with. Since it is a constructed self, it is solid like the world of materiality (being-in-itself). Similarly, Samkhya-Yoga holds that the *chitta* has no consciousness of its own. When *Purusha* injects its awareness into *chitta*, the latter becomes conscious and acts as a person's unique self. Though *chitta* is consciousness-incarnate, it is still a part of the material world of *Prakriti*.

Another similar concern of both Sartre and Samkhya-Yoga is the identification of the self with one's body. Sartre reveals the connection between the self and the three ontological dimensions of the body. And Samkhya-Yoga (though it does not delve into all three aspects) describes the body as self in a way that parallels the first Sartrean dimension. For Sartre, at the first level a person is one's body and one's body is the person. The body is the center, whereas the world and objects exist in relationship to it. Since every item in the universe is measured with reference to one's body, the latter constitutes one's unique point of view on the world. However, though the Samkhya-Yoga position agrees with the Sartrean descriptions pertaining to the body at this level, the former asserts that the identification of the self with the body is an epistemological confusion. When repeated on a regular basis, such perplexity leads one to think that one is nothing more than one's physical self. This false identity is the cause of human suffering.

As we have seen, there are also a few points of contrast between the two systems. For Sartre, the community self and the self as value are so significant that he presents an extensive discussion of the two. His analysis of these concepts provides the reader with a critical understanding of the ontological-existential predicament of the human being. In contrast, the Samkhya-Yoga system does not delve into these two levels of the constructed self because they are not essential to knowing the true self.

I should point out here that in opposition to Sartre's *Being and Nothingness,* which is strictly philosophical, the Samkhya-Yoga texts are both philosophical and religious in nature. They were written to accomplish religious goals by providing the aspirant with important insights as well as salvation knowledge. In contrast, Sartre's major philosophical work, *Being and Nothingness,* was not written to achieve any religious goal. Though it offered the individual an insight into his or her existential predicament, it also served a therapeutic purpose.

As we have also seen, the views of Sartre and Samkhya-Yoga on the self—though developed in two different cultures and times, and influenced by two different philosophical traditions—still clearly reveal an overall compatibility.

Notes

1. Sartre makes a distinction between two aspects of being. For the being of a human being, he uses the phrase *being-for-itself* whereas for the material world he utilizes the phrase *being-in-itself.*

2. For a further discussion of Sartre's view of the being-for-itself, see Ashok Malhotra, *Jean-Paul Sartre's Existentialism in Literature and Philosophy* (Oneonta, N.Y.: Oneonta Philosophy Studies, 1995), chapter 4.

Part Four

Japanese and Western Perspectives

Chapter Eight

Nietzsche and Nishitani on Nihilism and Tradition

GRAHAM PARKES

Since cultures develop always within traditions, problems arise when disruptions take place in this process—and especially when dislocations bring on a phase of nihilism. Some of the most illuminating reflections on human participation in such phenomena come from Friedrich Nietzsche;[1] and some of the best responses to those reflections, from the Japanese philosopher Nishitani Keiji. The present chapter discloses how these thinkers envision our relations to tradition following an eruption of nihilism. To the extent that what Nietzsche called "European nihilism" still appears to be endemic in advanced industrial societies (Asian as well as American), a comparison of his views with Nishitani's on this phenomenon will apply to contemporary cultural conditions.

In view of the bulk of recent Nietzsche scholarship in English (some of it very good), a justification is in order for this chapter's focus on a Japanese text written almost fifty years ago.[2] Indeed, there are two major reasons to expect a reading of Nietzsche from the East-Asian perspective to be instructive.

The first reason concerns the advantages that accrue from a certain hermeneutic *distance*. Nietzsche's interest in the ideas of non-European cultures appears to have been motivated more by a desire to gain perspective on the modern Western condition than by an urge to understand those foreign worlds for their own sake.[3] Nishitani comes to a deeper understanding of his tradition through the intensive study of European philosophy, though he still has a strong drive to understand the latter on its own terms. And by viewing it from the standpoint of a completely alien philosophical tradition he can better discern the larger contours of European nihilism, as well as Nietzsche's role in diagnosing and responding to it, than can thinkers from that same tradition. (Counterparts on this side of the Pacific appear sadly lacking, in that no major figure in Western philosophy has gone to the trouble of learning an East-Asian language well enough to think in it.)

The second reason has to do with differences in *language*, in the context of interpretation. To borrow Nietzsche's language in *Beyond Good and Evil*: The fact that Japanese philosophers grew up under the "unconscious domination and direction" of a set of "grammatical functions" quite different from that of thinkers in the West is likely to afford them an interestingly different perspective on his texts.[4] And just as Nietzsche speculates that "philosophers from the domain of the Ural-Altaic languages (where the concept of the subject is least developed) will most likely look 'into the world' differently and be found on different paths than Indo-Germans," so Japanese philosophers (as a philologist, he presumably knew that Japanese was considered a member of the Ural-Altaic family) will look into the worlds of Nietzsche's texts differently from their Western counterparts.

This circumstance might render Japanese readers blind to certain features of the text (however well they read Western philosophy in the original languages); but, conversely, it might enable them to see features generally overlooked from our side. The above passage from *Beyond Good and Evil* suggests that thinkers who think in languages where "the concept of the subject is least developed" will be less likely to see the world as populated by subjects perceiving and acting upon objects. And indeed whereas the early Western commentators on Nietzsche (and by no means only they) saw rampant egoism and a megalomania of the individual subject, the Japanese interpreters, some coming from the perspective of the Buddhist idea of "not-self" or "no ego" (*muga*), often discerned in Nietzsche a self that gets emptied out in such a way that a greater self (or "Self") can operate through it.

Two early interpretations of Nietzsche in Japan were the influential studies by Watsuji Tetsurô and Abe Jirô that appeared during the second decade of the twentieth century.[5] It has been fashionable to criticize both authors for importing inappropriate conceptions from the Asian tradition into their readings of Nietzsche—and specifically for interpreting the idea of will to power as representing some kind of cosmic self, suggesting that Nietzsche's program involves a transcending of the boundaries of the conscious ego in order to achieve participation in this universal self. Whereas Abe's interpretation may appear suffused with an excess of sweetness and light, Watsuji's understanding of the human self with respect to will to power (as the driving force of all existence) is quite profound—and deeper than most of the Western interpretations developed during the first half of the century. Whatever their shortcomings in the long run, these works highlight some salient features of Nietzsche's thought.[6]

Nietzsche is often regarded as an iconoclast whose philosophy is nihilistic in a negative sense. A consideration of Nishitani's discussion of his ideas on nihilism reveals an aspect of Nietzsche's thinking about the optimal relationship of the self to its cultural tradition that is often overlooked.

The Role of History

Let us begin, as Nishitani does, with a consideration of the role of history in the development of the human individual and culture. In the second of his *Untimely Meditations* Nietzsche presents a vivid "image of the mental processes taking place in the soul of the modern human being," especially in relation to past tradition.

> Historical knowledge streams in unceasingly from inexhaustible wells, things strange and incoherent press in on us . . . and our nature strives to receive and arrange and honor these strange guests, but they are themselves in conflict with each other, and it seems necessary to constrain and master them if we are not ourselves to perish in the struggle.[7]

The ability to accommodate this constant influx from the past depends on what Nietzsche calls one's "plastic strength," upon which in turn the health of the organism hinges. He writes of this capacity as "the *plastic strength* of a human being, or a people, or a culture . . . the strength to grow out of oneself in one's own way, to transform and incorporate what is past and foreign, to heal wounds, to replace what has been lost, to reform out of one's self forms that have been broken."[8] It is a force that would counteract nihilism to some extent. Animal life, for Nietzsche, is naturally conditioned by a constant forgetting, whereas to become fully human one must remember and assimilate the past:

> The stronger the roots of a human being's innermost nature, the more one will appropriate and arrogate to oneself; and for the most powerful and tremendous nature there would be no limit to the historical sense. . . . It would draw to itself and take in the entire past, its own and the most foreign, and transform it as it were into blood.[9]

Maximum openness through the appropriate kind of historical sense is something Nietzsche always considers worth striving for, even though this early essay warns repeatedly of the dangers consequent upon a hypertrophy of history. Indeed, a primary symptom of the sickness of the modern age is its inability to assimilate the past properly: "An excess of history has attacked the plastic power of life, such that it no longer understands how to use the past as strong nourishment."[10] Since the discernment necessary to maintain the balance between admitting the influx of the past and experiencing life in the present is a rare trait, Nietzsche emphasizes that history can be borne "*only by strong personalities.*"[11] And since he maintains this idea all the way through to its apotheosis in the figure of Goethe in *Twilight of the Idols*, it will be appropriate to ask how one's relationship to the tradition is transformed in the encounter with nihilism.[12]

Nishitani begins his discussion of nihilism by insisting that we understand it first and foremost as "a problem of the self," as "an existential problem in which the being of the self is revealed to the self itself as something groundless."[13] This is not to deny that nihilism is also "a historical and social phenomenon"; in fact, Nishitani's first chapter is devoted to showing how these two aspects of the phenomenon are to be integrated. Because history (especially since becoming world-historical) highlights the contingency of the religious and philosophical systems that have given meaning to human life in different places and epochs, the study of history tends to open up a "void" at the ground of existence—which in turn prompts the onset of nihilism. The two aspects can be brought together when a philosopher of history understands the subject existentially: "The great historical problems need to become a problem of the self."[14] Nishitani sees this happening in Nietzsche, for whom "the history of humankind has to be made the history of the self itself, and history has to be understood from the standpoint of Existence."[15] And indeed Nishitani's characterization of the impact of European nihilism in the late nineteenth century applies most pertinently to Nietzsche himself: "The problem of how to live came to be fused with the problem of how to interpret history."[16]

A salient feature of Nietzsche's interpretation of history is his claim that cultural advancement requires occasional phases of *degeneration* (which we can understand as a major factor in nihilism). In an aphorism entitled "Ennoblement through Degeneration," he argues that the point at which "degenerate natures" weaken an otherwise healthy cultural community provides the opportunity for it to be "inoculated with something new" that will contribute to its richer and more robust development.[17] Some of these degenerate natures will turn out to be what Nietzsche calls "free minds" (or "free spirits") that are able to liberate themselves from orthodoxy because of the greater range of possibilities to which they are open.[18] (Indeed, it is precisely the greater multiplicity of motives and viewpoints that renders them *weaker* than the minds that are bound by tradition.)[19] And yet, though the free mind operates in opposition to its cultural heritage and needs to be liberated from tradition in order to be creative, Nietzsche by no means thinks that human flourishing can take place in isolation from the historical past. This he believes would be impossible since he understands history not only as something acculturated from outside, as it were, but also as something ineluctably "in the blood." In *Assorted Opinions and Maxims* he writes: "Direct self-observation is not nearly sufficient for us to know ourselves: we need history, for the past flows on within us in a hundred waves; indeed, we ourselves are nothing but that which at every moment we experience of this continual flowing."[20]

Recent scholars have discussed the importance for Nietzsche's project of the idea of experimentation (Nietzsche's term is *Versuch*, for which there are cognates having to do with testing and seduction); Nishitani's emphasis of its importance in 1949 was somewhat prescient. Nietzsche writes along the lines of Montaigne and Emerson, insofar as he declines to set down truths about the human condition but, instead, offers propositions and hypotheses for the reader to experiment with in direct experience. Nishitani discloses the historical dimension to Nietzsche's experimentalism by pointing out that Nietzsche advocates that one "experiment with history within oneself" and "experiment with the future tendencies and issues of history by making the self one's laboratory."[21] Nietzsche was thus a philosopher of history in the sense that he "lived history within history experimentally and philosophically, and in such a way that the self lives in history and history lives in the self."[22]

The Self-Overcoming of Nihilism

Nishitani goes on to discuss in detail the various forms and phases of nihilism in Nietzsche's thought, but it is with respect to the latter's suggestions for engaging the phenomenon that the discussion becomes most interesting. Nishitani approved of *The Self-Overcoming of Nihilism* for the title of this English translation as expressive of the book's major theme—namely, that if one lets oneself down into it deeply enough, there will come a point at which nihilism *overcomes itself*. He sees Nietzsche as the first thinker to suggest this possibility, though the actual words appear to have occurred only in an unpublished note where Nietzsche refers to the thought of eternal recurrence as "the self-overcoming of nihilism."[23] Nishitani thus helps us understand the sense in which the thought of eternal recurrence is "the highest formula of affirmation" (as characterized in *Ecce Homo*). All too often Nietsche is assumed to have brought our attention to the prevalence of nihilism only to indulge in a cynical wallowing in it thereafter. Or else he is interpreted as saying that if nihilism can be overcome, it is only through the summoning of tremendous willpower on the part of some super-heroic ego.

Nishitani offers a reading of the epilogue to *Nietzsche contra Wagner* in which he links the (self-) overcoming of nihilism to Nietzsche's concern with *amor fati*, or love of fate:

> As my innermost nature teaches me, everything necessary is, when seen from a great height and in the sense of a *great* economy, also useful in itself—one should not only bear it, one should *love* it. *Amor fati*: that is my innermost nature. . . . Only the great pain is the ultimate liberator of the spirit, as the teacher of the *great suspicion*. . . . [And] out of the abyss of the *great suspicion* one returns newly born.[24]

Taking "the abyss of the great suspicion" to refer to nihilism, and interpolating a few phrases from the preface to *The Joyful Science*, Nishitani amplifies this passage with some telling images:

> In this rebirth from the depths with a higher health and with a second and more dangerous innocence one's innermost nature bursts forth like a natural spring from which the covering debris has been removed. At this point the spring proclaims as its liberator the sharp pick-axe of necessity that has pierced down through the debris and brought it pain.[25]

This striking image shows how spontaneous is the overcoming of nihilism. The blow from the "pick-axe of necessity" (a nice variation on Nietzsche's hammer) at first appears not to be willed by the self but, rather, to reach the depths of the abyss from outside, falling as a stroke of fate. The subsequent emergence of one's "innermost nature" is seen as a natural consequence of such an intrusion, like the gushing forth of a spring. Nishitani illuminates Nietzsche's otherwise puzzling assimilation of the self and fate when he says that "ultimately the spring will come to affirm even the debris it burst through and which now floats in it." The idea is that things and persons that have obstructed one's development, that have been rejected as *other* and definitely *not*-self, can ultimately be seen as necessary for one's "becoming what one is," as part of one's fate. In the "great economy" of life, then, "what is not oneself—what has prevented one from being oneself—is appropriated into the self and transformed into something uniquely one's own [*eigen*]."[26]

Nishitani's interpretation provides a helpful perspective on the appropriate relation to tradition in the self-overcoming of nihilism, insofar as the project of appropriation extends back beyond one's personal past to a broader history. The image of the debris covering the self can be related to the "camel stage" in the "Three Transformations" in *Zarathustra*, specifically as the sedimentation of layers of traditional values with which the spirit has burdened itself.[27] After these values have been dissipated by the lion's roaring "No!" in the second transformation, the child of the third phase becomes an image for the possibility of creating new values. The question then arises: *From what* are these new values created? Nishitani's reading suggests that the creation of new values is a *creatio ex nihilo* only in the sense of being a creation from out of the abyss of nihilism—and not in the sense in which the Christian God creates out of nothing, since the creation signaled by the image of the child *reappropriates* certain elements from the tradition that was rejected at the stage of the lion.

Nishitani's image, which apparently derives from a Zen background, suggests that when one's true nature bursts through the overlays of conceptualization and conventional values that have kept it repressed, the resultant condition is not one of pristine purity but, rather, one in which the pool of the psyche is still polluted by debris from the barriers that have been breached. The point would be that such debris need not be rejected but may properly belong to the development of the new self. In Nietzschean terms, one fulfills one's responsibility to previous generations by reconnecting with the appropriate branches of one's tradition.[28]

Love of Fate

One of the major obstacles to affirming life, and doing so with sufficient verve to entertain the prospect of its eternal recurrence, is naturally the phenomenon of suffering—especially in its "fateful" aspect, when one is moved to ask "Why did this have to happen to *me?*" Nishitani offers in this context an interpretation of a pivotal wordplay in *Zarathustra*. The wordplay first occurs (though he doesn't mention this occurrence) in the section entitled "On the Bestowing Virtue," where Zarathustra praises those possessed of a magnanimous selfishness by saying: "You force all things into yourselves, so that they may flow back out of your well as the gifts of your love."[29] The aquatic imagery flows on with Zarathustra's telling his disciples that the primal source (the *Ursprung*) of their virtue is attained "when you are willers of one will, and this turn of all need [*Wende aller Not*] is for you necessity [*Notwendigkeit*]."[30] This virtue of giving, he continues, is "a new deep rushing [*Rausch*] and the voice of a new welling up [*eines neuen Quellens Stimme*]." And in "On the Great Yearning" Zarathustra addresses his soul as "turn of need" (*Wende der Not*) and "fate"—the former phrase again a trope on the word for "necessity."[31]

Nishitani interprets this wordplay on distressful need in the light of his earlier discussion of *amor fati*:

> Under the compulsion of the need or necessity that prevents one from becoming oneself and from becoming free, one is forced to descend into the abyss within. But once one is freed within the abyss, the need is turned into an element of this life of freedom. . . . In this case necessity becomes one with the creative.[32]

He stresses the aspect of *Not* that connotes distress (i.e., suffering *in extremis*), suggesting that it persists through the descent into nihilism and then becomes the axis, as it were, of the turn to creative existence.

This turn within the abyss can also be understood as a transformation of the configuration of will to power that comprises the self. Alluding to his previous discussion of that type of will to power, which manifests as "will to illusion" (*Wille zum Schein*), Nishitani writes: "Absolute affirmation affirms even the deceptions that had blocked it, and which themselves are part of that 'great economy' through their biological usefulness as lies of principle. Even that which negates and obstructs life is affirmed as useful for life."[33] In arguing that *amor fati* has to do with fate's being "made one with the self's creative will," Nishitani makes a further connection through the idea of will to power to the "thought of eternal recurrence."[34]

Since the nature of this connection remains somewhat enigmatic in Nishitani's exposition,[35] it is helpful to adduce the idea of the redemption of the will from "the spirit of revenge" as described in the section "On Redemption" in *Zarathustra*.[36] Affirmation of the recurrence involves teaching the will to power to affirm fate creatively by learning to *will* the past (to will all "it was")—in other words, by learning what Zarathustra calls *Zurück-wollen*, in the dual sense of "willing backwards" and "wanting everything back again."[37]

What now becomes clearer is how the willing of eternal recurrence can constitute "the self-overcoming of nihilism." Nishitani discusses "the nihilistic formulation of [the thought of] eternal recurrence" with reference to an unpublished note by Nietzsche that reads "the most extreme form of nihilism: nothingness ('meaninglessness') eternally!"[38] Adducing two more notes that speak of the thought of recurrence as "the turning point of history," "the consummation and *crisis* of nihilism," and "*the self-overcoming of nihilism*," Nishitani argues that "only those who can bear the thought [of recurrence] with courage and without deception in order to consummate their nihilism will be able to attain the will to . . . absolute affirmation."[39]

If we recall that Nietzsche regards the thought of eternal recurrence as in some sense a principle of *selection*, we can make explicit the connection with tradition, which remains implicit at this point in Nishitani's discussion.[40] Entertaining at every juncture the possibility of the eternal recurrence of one's entire life ("the question with each and every thing: 'Do you want this once again, and innumerable times again?'") helps one to choose those actions and responses to circumstances that will make one truly oneself and to dismiss those possibilities that one might otherwise unthinkingly accept under pressure from society.[41]

The possibility also provides a principle of selection in the process whereby the self "becomes what it is" in relation to the tradition from which it springs, and from which it is distanced through nihilism.[42] This is an important part of the force of Zarathustra's characterization of "redemption": "To redeem what is past and to recreate all 'It was' into a 'Thus I willed it!'" Since it is impossible for a finite being to recreate *all* "It was," whoever thinks the thought of eternal recurrence must be content with redeeming selected elements from the past (both personal and transpersonal) and letting the fact that "all things are firmly knotted together" take care of the rest.[43] Most discussions of Nietzsche fail to appreciate his emphasis on our responsibility (*Verantwortlichkeit*) to the past—to the tradition as well as to our personal past: The thought of eternal recurrence can help one select those features of history that are to be redeemed in the task of becoming what one is to be.

Creative Appropriation

In a later chapter in *The Self-Overcoming of Nihilism* entitled "The Meaning of Nihilism for Japan," Nishitani brings together the "positive" responses to nihilism that he has found in the work of Nietzsche, Max Stirner, and Martin Heidegger under the rubric of "a unity of creative nihilism and finitude," and proceeds to apply them to the case of Japan in the twentieth century.[44] He describes how, with the Europeanization of Japan that began toward the end of the nineteenth century, the Buddhism and Confucianism on which the country's development had been based "lost their power, leaving a total void and vacuum in our spiritual ground."[45] The subsequent emptiness is "the natural result of our having been cut off from our tradition."[46] After dismissing as inappropriate two opposed responses—those of contempt for one's Japaneseness and of an exclusionist patriotism—Nishitani invokes Nietzsche's "sense of responsibility toward the ancestors,"[47] thanks to which one can take on "the accumulation of every possible spiritual nobility of the past." Here he is referring to a passage in *The Joyful Science*, where Nietzsche writes of the historical sense as the peculiar virtue and sickness of contemporary humanity.

> Anyone who knows how to experience the history of humanity as his own history . . . [and could] endure this immense amount of grief of all kinds . . . as a person with a horizon of millennia in front of and behind him, as the heir of all the nobility of all previous spirit and an heir with a sense of obligation . . . : if one could take all of this upon one's soul . . . this would have to produce a happiness that up until now humanity has not known.[48]

Nishitani sees this attitude as a potentially salutary one for the condition of postwar Japan.

> [Nietzsche's] standpoint calls for a returning to the ancestors in order to face the future, or to put it the other way around, a prophesying toward the tradition. Without a will toward the future, the confrontation with the past cannot be properly executed; nor is there a true will toward the future without responsibility toward the ancestors. For us Japanese now, the recovery of this primordial will represents our most fundamental task. It is here that European nihilism will begin to reveal its fundamental significance for us.[49]

When Nishitani considers the task of comparing "the fundamental integration of creative nihilism and finitude" that he finds in Stirner, Nietzsche, and Heidegger with "the standpoint of Buddhism, and in particular to the standpoint of emptiness in the Mahayana tradition" (though he does not actually undertake this task in *The Self-Overcoming of Nihilism*), he finds the three "remarkably close." Yet he still thinks that "there is in Mahayana a standpoint that cannot be reached even by nihilism that overcomes nihilism, even though this latter may tend in that direction."⁵⁰ Though it would be illuminating to consider Nishitani's reasons here, as well as those implied by his discussions of Nietzsche and Heidegger in his later masterwork *Religion and Nothingness*, it must suffice simply to note the important place he assigns these figures in the contemporary elaboration of Mahayana thinking (as practiced, presumably, by the Kyoto School of philosophy).⁵¹

Nevertheless, Nishitani distinguishes among three significant traits in European nihilism that he considers relevant to the situation in postwar Japan—and that seem no less relevant fifty years later. The first is that a consideration of European nihilism can disclose the "hollowness in [the] spiritual foundations" of modern Japan and stimulate reflection on the historical process (extremely complex in the Japanese case) whereby the culture has become dislocated from its tradition.⁵² Second, such analysis can thus prompt a rediscovery of the tradition from the perspective of the new horizons opened up by Japan's westernization—an undertaking that is by no means "a turning back to the way things were," since modernization has rendered the tradition profoundly problematic.⁵³ And third, an engagement with European nihilism can enable contemporary Japanese thinkers "to recover the creativity that mediates the past to the future and the future to the past" in the context of their own philosophical traditions. When set in the context of the "creative nihilism" developed by the German thinkers, "the tradition of oriental culture in general, and the Buddhist standpoints of 'emptiness,' 'nothingness,' and so forth in particular, become a new problem." Nishitani concludes the chapter by exhorting his contemporaries, in light of the examples of Dostoevsky's and Nietzsche's anticipations of nihilism, to find their own means to engage nihilism so that "the spiritual culture of the Orient which has been handed down through the ages [may] be revitalized in a new transformation."⁵⁴

There was surely no expectation on Nishitani's part, when he delivered his talks on nihilism in 1949, that the text would ever be translated into English or be considered a contribution to Nietzsche scholarship in the West. But even if the Eurocentrism of much of that scholarship prevents a general acknowledgment of Nishitani's contribution, we can acknowledge that it highlights an important aspect of Nietzsche's thinking about the self's relation to traditional culture. For while Nietzsche emphasizes the impossibility of a conservative return to earlier cultural conditions, in his abiding concern to raise the level of culture he also advocates a judicious enhancement of the "plastic strength" that incorporates the past—and of "the will to tradition, to authority, to responsibility ranging over centuries, to *solidarity* of chains of generations forwards and backwards *ad infinitum*."⁵⁵ But since Nietzsche also remarks (in the aphorism just cited, which bears the title "Critique of Modernity") that "the whole of the West no longer possesses the instincts from which [true] institutions grow, and out from which a *future* grows," Nishitani's book can help us recognize that in contemporary Western attempts "to recover the creativity that mediates the past to the future and the future to the past" the ideas of thinkers from the Japanese Buddhist tradition may have a significant role to play.

Notes

1. All translations of citations from Nietzsche's works are my own, from the original texts edited by Giorgio Colli and Mazzino Montinari (see *Friedrich Nietzsche: Sämtliche Werke, Kritische Studienausgabe* [Berlin/New York: de Gruyter, 1980]). Each citation is followed by the corresponding aphorism and/or section number so that it can easily be found in any translation.

2. In this connection, see Nishitani Keiji, *The Self-Overcoming of Nihilism*, trans. Graham Parkes with Setsuko Aihara (Albany: State University of New York Press, 1990). And for a fine exposition of the historical antecedents to European nihilism, see Michael Allen Gillespie, *Nihilism Before Nietzsche* (Chicago: University of Chicago Press, 1995). Sadly, the latter ignores Nishitani's treatment of the topic.

3. For an illuminating treatment of this topic, see Eberhard Scheiffele, "Questioning One's 'Own' from the Perspective of the Foreign," in Graham Parkes, *Nietzsche and Asian Thought* (Chicago: University of Chicago Press, 1991), pp. 31–50, as well as the contributions to that volume by Arifuku Kôgaku, Okôchi Ryôgi, and Sonoda Muneto. For an overall view of the topic, see my essay "Nietzsche and East Asian Thought: Influences, Impacts, and Resonances," in Bernd Magnus and Kathleen M. Higgins, eds., *The Cambridge Companion to Nietzsche* (Cambridge/New York: Cambridge University Press, 1996), pp. 356–383.

4. Friedrich Nietzsche, *Beyond Good and Evil* (New York: Vintage Books, 1966; London/New York: Penguin Books, 1990), aphorism 20.

5. Watsuji Tetsurô, *Niichie kenkyû* [A study of Nietzsche] (Tokyo: Iwanami Shoten, 1913); Abe Jirô, *Niichie no Tsuaratsusutora kaishaku narabi ni hihyô* [Nietzsche's *Zarathustra:* Interpretation and critique] (Tokyo: Kadokawa Shoten, 1919). For a sketch of the relevant historical background, see my essay "The Early Reception of Nietzsche's Philosophy in Japan," in *Nietzsche and Asian Thought*, 177–199. There is also a brief discussion of Watsuji's reading of Nietzsche in my "Nietzsche and East Asian Thought" in Magnus and Higgins, eds., *The Cambridge Companion to Nietzsche*.

6. In conversation, Nishitani has acknowledged the importance of Watsuji's study for his own intellectual development. He came upon the book during his high school days in Tokyo and was thereby encouraged to study German so as to be able to read Nietzsche's works in the original. Watsuji's study of Nietzsche prompted him, he writes, to "read *Thus Spoke Zarathustra*—over and over." See Nishitani Keiji, *Nishida Kitarô*, trans. Yamamoto Seisaku and James W. Heisig (Berkeley: University of California Press, 1991), p. 6.

7. Nietzsche, *On the Use and Disadvantage of History for Life*, section 4 (see Colli and Montinari, eds., *Friedrich Nietzsche: Sämtliche Werke, Kritische Studienausgabe*). For a more detailed discussion, see the section "Rootings Through the Past" in

chapter 3 of my *Composing the Soul: Reaches of Nietzsche's Psychology* (Chicago: University of Chicago Press, 1994), pp. 100–105.

8. Nietzsche, *On the Use and Disadvantage of History for Life*, section 1.

9. Ibid.

10. Ibid., section 11.

11. Ibid., section 5; original emphasis.

12. *Twilight of the Idols* (Harmondsworth, England: Penguin Books, 1968), section 9, aphorism 49. For a discussion of the import of this and adjacent passages, see Parkes, *Composing the Soul*, pp. 357–361.

13. Nishitani, *The Self-Overcoming of Nihilism*, pp. 1, 3.

14. Ibid., p. 5.

15. The term *Existence* is a translation of Nishitani's translation of Karl Jaspers's *Existenz* and refers to human life as lived "existentially." The existential attitude toward history is summed up nicely in the dictum from Goethe with which Nietzsche begins his *Untimely Meditation* on history (in *On the Use and Disadvantage of History for Life*): "I hate everything that merely instructs me without enhancing my activity or directly enlivening it."

16. Nishitani, *The Self-Overcoming of Nihilism*, p. 7.

17. Nietzsche, *Human, All Too Human*, aphorism 224 (see Colli and Montinari, eds., *Friedrich Nietzsche: Sämtliche Werke, Kritische Studienausgabe*).

18. Ibid., aphorism 228.

19. Ibid., aphorism 230.

20. Nietzsche, *Assorted Opinions and Maxims*, aphorism 223 (see Colli and Montinari, eds., *Friedrich Nietzsche: Sämtliche Werke, Kritische Studienausgabe*).

21. Nishitani, *The Self-Overcoming of Nihilism*, p. 30.

22. Ibid., p. 31.

23. Nietzsche, *Werke: Grossoktavausgabe*, Vol. 16 (Leipzig: C. G. Naumann, 1901), p. 422; cited in Nishitani, *The Self-Overcoming of Nihilism*, p. 64.

24. *Nietzsche contra Wagner* (see Colli and Montinari, eds., *Friedrich Nietzsche: Sämtliche Werke, Kritische Studienausgabe*, p. 224); cited in Nishitani, *The Self-Overcoming of Nihilism*, p. 51.

25. *The Joyful Science* (see Colli and Montinari, eds., *Friedrich Nietzsche: Sämtliche Werke, Kritische Studienausgabe*, p. 224). Though Nietzsche often employs metaphors of springs, wells, and fountains, the conjunction with the image of the pick-axe appears to be Nishitani's own. There is perhaps a resonance here with a passage in Nietzsche's *Untimely Meditation* on Schopenhauer (*Schopenhauer as Educator*, section 1), where educators are called liberators and culture, *liberation*, "a clearing away of all weeds, rubble, and vermin that would encroach on the delicate buds of the plants, an outpouring of light and warmth, a loving downpour of nocturnal rain."

26. Nishitani, *The Self-Overcoming of Nihilism*, p. 51.

27. Nietzsche, *Thus Spoke Zarathustra*, 1.1.

28. Heidegger's account of the authentic relation to history is couched in strikingly Nietzschean language when he writes of "the fateful repetition [*Wiederholung*— "fetching again"] of possibilities that have already been" (*Being and Time*, section 75; see Colli and Montinari, eds., *Friedrich Nietzsche: Sämtliche Werke, Kritische Studienausgabe*).

29. Nietzsche, *Thus Spoke Zarathustra*, 1.22, section 1. In a later passage, Zarathustra expresses his admiration for the soul "that loves itself most, in which all things have their flow and counterflow, their ebb and flood" (3.12, section 19).

30. The wordplay is impossible to convey in English translation without reference to the German terms. As one sees from Nishitani's reading, both Kaufmann's translation of *Wende aller Not* as "cessation of all need" and Hollingdale's rendering, "dispeller," miss the point of the *turn*.

31. Nietzsche, *Thus Spoke Zarathustra*, 3.14.

32. Nishitani, *The Self-Overcoming of Nihilism*, p. 52.

33. Ibid., p. 51.

34. Ibid., p. 53.

35. Ibid., pp. 53–68.

36. *Thus Spoke Zarathustra*, 2.20. It is surprising that Nishitani doesn't discuss this section, especially in view of his respect for Heidegger, whose interpretation of eternal recurrence puts so much emphasis on overcoming the spirit of revenge.

37. The second sense is lost in the translations by Kaufmann and Hollingdale.

38. Nietzsche, *The Will to Power*, section 55; cited in Nishitani, *The Self-Overcoming of Nihilism*, pp. 62–63. (See also Colli and Montinari, eds., *Friedrich Nietzsche: Sämtliche Werke, Kritische Studienausgabe*, p. 224.)

39. Nietzsche, *Grossoktavausgabe*, Vol. 14, p. 364, and Vol. 16, p. 422 (original emphasis); cited in Nishitani, *The Self-Overcoming of Nihilism*, p. 64.

40. Nietzsche refers to the thought of eternal recurrence as an "auswählendes *Prinzip*" in an unpublished note from the period during which he was working on *Thus Spoke Zarathustra*. (See *The Will to Power*, section 1058.)

41. The parenthetical is taken from the *locus classicus* for the thought of eternal recurrence—namely, *The Joyful Science*, aphorism 341. Note the striking similarity between this idea and the role played by *Angst*, which brings one face-to-face with the nothingness of one's death, in Heidegger's *Being and Time* (section 40): "[Anxiety] liberates one *from* 'nugatory' possibilities and lets one be free *for* authentic [*eigentliche*] ones" (*Being and Time*, section 68b).

42. The issue is actually much more complex than this, insofar as the thought of eternal recurrence helps transform the self into a multiplicity—as Pierre Klossowski was one of the first to realize, in his *Nietzsche et le cercle vicieux* (Paris: Mercure de France, 1969). The nature of this multiplicity is a major topic of my *Composing the Soul:* See especially chapters 3, 8, and 9.

43. *Thus Spoke Zarathustra*, 3.2, section 2. This idea of the interconnection of all things, which is central to the thought of eternal recurrence, bears a striking similarity to the Buddhist idea of "codependent arising" (*pratîtya samutpâda*).

44. Nishitani, *The Self-Overcoming of Nihilism*, p. 174.

45. Ibid., p. 175.

46. Ibid.

47. Ibid., p. 177.

48. Nietzsche, *The Joyful Science*, aphorism 337.

49. Nishitani, *The Self-Overcoming of Nihilism*, p. 177.

50. Ibid., p. 180. Of the three figures mentioned, Nishitani thinks Nietzsche comes closest, especially "in such ideas as *amor fati* and the Dionysian as the overcoming of nihilism."

51. Nishitani Keiji, *Religion and Nothingness*, trans. Jan Van Bragt (Berkeley: University of California Press, 1982).

52. Nishitani, *The Self-Overcoming of Nihilism*, pp. 177–178.

53. Ibid., p. 179.

54. Ibid., pp. 179, 181. Nishitani's book also contains a chapter entitled "Nihilism in Russia" in which there is a lengthy discussion of Dostoevsky in relation to the topic of nihilism.

55. Nietzsche, *Twilight of the Idols*, section 9, aphorisms 43 and 39.

Chapter Nine

Views of Japanese Selfhood: Japanese and Western Perspectives

MARA MILLER

Scholars and lay observers alike largely agree that selfhood in Japan is unlike selfhood in the West—at least the modern West—in fundamental ways. I would argue, however, that it is important to recognize both the similarities and the divergences between (and within) the two types of selfhood, and that in several important respects the Japanese self is closer than we think to our own. If this is true, much of our "common knowledge," both scholarly and popular, is mistaken. I refer most notably to the misperceptions of the Japanese as lacking creativity, originality, independence, and/or moral autonomy.

These misperceptions arise in part from several problems with the ways we customarily think about Japanese selfhood and personal identity. Most disturbing, of course, is the frequently met assumption of universal validity of Western paradigmatic descriptions of selfhood. These descriptions in themselves are highly problematic,[1] given that they are based almost exclusively on the experience and behavior of privileged groups of middle- and upper-class white males. But also contributing to the misunderstanding are simplistic ideas of Japanese selfhood: the ideas that there is only one kind of selfhood in Japan, that this has remained constant over the years, and that the Japanese themselves are in accord regarding the kind of description of the Self that is appropriate, the need for such descriptions, and the ways they can or should be used.

Also very much in evidence in this field of study are the distinctive patterns of Japanese cultural history. One important thing to recognize about the history of selfhood in Japan is that it is very much of a piece with the history of Japanese culture in general—and the characteristic pattern by which

Japanese cultural history progresses differs from the characteristic Western pattern in two respects. First, in Japan new approaches and new solutions to problems often do not displace preexisting ones; the new find a place along-side the old. This phenomenon is particularly salient in both the history of art and the history of selfhood. Second, as in the history of religion, we find in the history of selfhood a high degree of tolerance for mutually exclusive views (not necessarily held by the same parties).

Careful study of Japanese selfhood shows it to be (and to have been from very early times) a congeries of complex and interrelated phenomena—a cat-egory in which I include not only *kinds* of selves but also *views* of what selves are. (Since we may now take it as established fact that selves are shaped and evolve at least partly in response to the views of what selves are and can and should be, these kinds of selves and views of selfhood are very closely interrelated indeed.)[2]

The similarities between Japanese and Western forms and views of self-hood have become easier to perceive over the past fifteen years, and for two reasons. First, students of East Asia have come to recognize the vital roles played by the individual within Confucianism, most notably in the context of "self-cultivation."[3] Second, Western students of selfhood have begun to do historically informed and culture-specific studies[4] guided by the recogni-tion that selfhood is socially constructed rather than a God-given fact or a metaphysical postulate and are starting to recognize the ideological commit-ments that lurk within apparently objective notions of individualism and the Subject.[5]

The information one gleans about Japanese selfhood varies enormously depending on the source(s) studied (e.g., it may be influenced by the disci-pline or nationality of the writer), but also on the type of evidence being ex-amined (whether behavior, written texts, or works of art). Buddhist and Confucianist texts, for example, frequently possessed highly normative agendas that adopted an explicit bias against the Self, albeit in different ways and stemming from different concerns. However, the evidence afforded by the visual and performing arts—including that found in Buddhist and Con-fucianist work—reveals a high degree of self-consciousness and self-reflec-tiveness, an enjoyment of individual difference, and a keen awareness of moral dilemmas of conflicts between individuals and society that are hidden by the more didactic texts.[6] And the evidence from natural language suggests both a systematic destabilization of the Subject or Self (at least prior to the heavy influence wielded by Indo-European languages), yet paradoxically re-quires a degree of autonomy on the part of speakers that most Indo-Euro-pean native speakers find quite unnerving.

This chapter began as a comparative study of selfhood in *Oedipus Rex* and the tenth-century Japanese novel *The Tale of Genji*. I immediately discov-ered, however, that it was impossible to write about Genji without first dispelling some of the myths by which we Americans commonly approach Japanese selfhood and preparing the ground by guaranteeing some recognition of the complexities of the Japanese self. It is in hope of accomplishing these goals that I have written the present chapter, in which I consider some of the theoretical problems, solutions, and critiques regarding the study of Japanese selfhood by social scientists and then examine some of the ways in which autonomy and creativity are in evidence within traditional Japanese religion and language—despite being often hidden from view either by our methodologies or by theoretical assumptions and preferences.

Social Science Views and Critiques

The history of American views of Japanese selfhood is ably summarized—and criticized—by Nancy R. Rosenberger in *Japanese Sense of Self*, and we need not recapitulate it here. The chief difficulty is that the self in Japan is rarely seen as autonomous—either ideally or actually, either by outsiders or by the Japanese themselves, either by observers such as social scientists or by participants. On the one hand, this apparent lack of autonomy—which I would argue is less an absence than a refusal to value autonomy greatly—has led many observers to the conclusion that the Japanese lack a "self" in any Western sense at all. And in so doing, they overlook the distinctively Japanese forms of expression of individuality, such as those that are foreign to Indo-European languages (as discussed below).

Anthropologist Takie Lebra, on the other hand, sees this socially defined self as only one of three "levels" of self:

[T]he social or "interactional" self is at the basic level, where Japanese find themselves most of the time; above this level is the "inner" or reflexive self, which centers around the kokoro (heart/mind) and engages in monologue, with a leave of absence from dialogic involvement; at the highest level, there is the "boundless" or chaotic self, where the boundary disappears between subject and object, self and other, or the inner and outer self, so that both the social and inner self are upgraded into an empty self.[7]

Thomas Kasulis has characterized the difference as being a matter of what is foregrounded and what is backgrounded in Japanese versus the various Western cultures.[8] Such an approach has the advantage of allowing us to recognize that many of the same characteristics of and attitudes toward the self exist (however inconsistently) within both cultures but are given different degrees of attention or "privilege," revealing what I have called in another context the culture's philosophical "preferences" for certain kinds of things and explanations over others.[9] This approach is particularly useful for recognition of types of selfhood that may exist within a culture yet don't fit into its prevailing theoretical paradigms, such as certain female kinds of selfhood in the United States.[10] Indeed, Kasulis's approach allows room for the role of ideology in shaping selfhood, permitting us to perceive that many of the differences in kinds of selves lie largely in the roles or functions (social, political, psychological, exhortatory, constraining, etc.) ascribed to the self by the society in question.

In the introduction to her anthology *Japanese Sense of Self*, Nancy Rosenberger points out that, until recently, the study of Japanese selfhood has been severely hampered by the conceptual apparatus—most conspicuously, dichotomous thinking—with which we (Americans) have approached the subject.

> The dichotomy between individual and society emerged from Galileo's and Copernicus's refiguring of the world on a mathematical and mechanical basis. . . .
>
> A dichotomy of Western ("us") versus non-Western ("them") became embedded in the dichotomy of individual versus society, with the first term superior in each case. Westerners living in industrial, economically "modern" societies idealize themselves as individuals, in control of emotions and social relations, able to think abstractly by cause-and-effect logic. Westerners often affirm this ideal by viewing non-Westerners as swayed by emotion, relation and context—only able to think in the specific case and then only by metaphor. It follows that Western societies can take the "higher" form of democracy because decision making can be entrusted to the hands of rational individuals, whereas non-Western societies require a strong collectivity for cohesion and control of people enmeshed in the immediacy of relationship and superstition.[11]

From Rosenberger's perspective, these attitudes continue to prevail:

> This point of view remains with anthropologists, even those studying complex, industrialized non-Western societies. Whether anthropologists characterize Japanese as disciplined and submissive (overcontrolled from without) or as resentful and insubordinate (undercontrolled from within), we still tend to locate them on the negative side of the individual/society dichotomy. We often portray Japanese as the opposite of our ideal selves: as concrete thinkers, particularistic moralists, situational conformists, unintegrated selves; as intuitive rather than rational, animistic (undivided from their environment), and unable to separate body and mind. The temptation of such general conclusions continually bedevils Western-trained scholars of Japan.[12]

Ruth Benedict's pioneering World War II study of Japanese culture and psyche, *The Chrysanthemum and the Sword*, exemplifies the dichotomous thinking that Rosenberger critiques and suggests how difficult it is to understand the matter using such thinking:

> All these contradictions . . . are true. . . . The Japanese are, to the highest degree, both aggressive and unaggressive, both militaristic and aesthetic, both insolent and polite, rigid and adaptable, submissive and resentful of being pushed around, loyal and treacherous, brave and timid, conservative and hospitable to new ways. They are terribly concerned about what other people

will think of their behavior, and they are overcome by guilt when other people know nothing of their misstep. Their soldiers are disciplined to the hilt but are also insubordinate.[13]

Such thinking persists even when the anthropologist or sociologist tries to comprehend the subject from within the Japanese perspective: The result is a list of dichotomous vernacular Japanese terms—*giri* and *ninjo*,[14] *tanin* and *enryo*,[15] *omote* and *ura*,[16] *tatemae* and *honne*[17]—that continue to make the Japanese person seem both incomprehensible and utterly unlike a Western person.

Lebra characterizes these views as follows:

Many observers of Japanese, while they differ in specific emphases, concur that the Japanese self (or personhood) is socially defined, contextualized, or embedded. To the extent that the social construction of the self is a universal fact, it may be restated that the Japanese person not only acts in response to but also perceives him/herself as contingent upon a given social nexus. The result is the consciously socialized self. If viewed through the Western lens for perceiving the self as non-contingent, autonomous, or intrinsic, the Japanese self indeed appears situationally circumscribed or on/giri bound (Benedict 1946); dependency prone (Doi 1971), rank conscious, and group-oriented (Nakane 1967); empathic (Aida 1970), differentiated into uchi and soto or omote and ura as pointed out by Doi and many other authors; mindful of sekentei (Inoue 1977); indeterminate (Smith 1983); relativistic (Lebra [1976]); hanging "between" persons (Kimura 1972; Hamaguchi 1977); uncertain, multiple, moving, or shifting (Minami 1983; Rosenberger 1989; Kondo 1990; Bachnik 1992). All these characterizations correspond to the linguistic absence of the fixed "I" (or "you") as well as the lexical variety of "I" substitutes.[18]

The limitations of these views have been ably pointed out by Lebra in her essay "Self in Japanese Culture."[19]

As a critical framework, the recognition of autonomy within Japanese culture is indeed a matter of some complexity. At the very least, we would need to recognize Lebra's three levels of self—the social/interactional self, the inner/reflexive self, and the boundless, or chaotic, self—since exclusive focus on the first of them, the socially defined (or outer-directed or group-identified) self, often leads to misunderstanding.

But we also would want to have some notion of how these levels relate to one another, a problem Lebra solves as follows:

The point . . . is that the three levels are far from undercutting one another. The higher levels of self sustain the basic, social self not only by compensating, remedying, or counterbalancing the excess of the social self but [also by] reenergizing it when it is deemed deficient. Thus the Japanese emphasis upon *seishin* (spirit), singled out by Befu (1980) as a proof of Japanese individualism, is in fact mobilized in group training, as witnessed by Rohlen (1973).[20]

Religious Views

Buddhism

The collective and ritual nature of much of Shinto, and its emphasis upon practice rather than belief or theory, has left it relatively impervious to debate over the meaning of selfhood. But Buddhism is quite a different matter![21] The originary acts of Buddhism—breaking away from home, family, and expected social roles for the sake of an individual "salvation" dependent solely upon the individual's own actions (*karma*) and mental states ("Enlightenment"), acts attributed to the historical Buddha but replicated by his followers—are acts taken by an individual, rejecting social role as a means of personal definition. As personal decisions they seem to presuppose the existence of a self. But as active rejections of the traditional routes for human life, they also require courage and personal conviction, and thus seem to presuppose, as well, a strong *experience* of selfhood. As such, they have led—by an almost natural, or at the very least logical, process—to a concern with the nature of the individual person and the fate of the individual soul.

This concern has expressed itself in rigorous debate over a number of distinct issues for close to twenty-five hundred years. The concern arises not only from the practical aspects of Buddhism just mentioned but also, and equally, from the philosophical decision to reject existing forms of *philosophical* understanding and to create a new formulation constituting the philosophical "Middle Way." The philosophical debates current at the time of the historical Buddha, Gautama, framed in terms of existence (*sat, astitva*) and nonexistence (*asat, nastitva*), had questions about the nature of the self at their base, especially the nature of the immutable self (*atman*) and its relation to the universal self (*Atman*).[22] The rejection of these two poles of the dichotomy by Gautama required, among other things, new ways of thinking about the self, the adumbration of which continues to this day.

In addition to this initial formulation of the Middle Way as a rejection of existing dichotomous views of the self are the debates in the Pure Land Sects of tenth- through twelfth-century Japan over what or who is the source of a person's "salvation," one's own power (literally "self power," Jp. *jiriki*) or the Buddha (literally "other power," Jp. *tariki*).[23] The intricacies of such debates, as well as the reliance upon personal experience (a reliance very different from the usual Western experience), make it impossible to do them justice here. Nor is their explication necessary for our argument.

Suffice it to say that nearly all Buddhist versions of selfhood are problematic for nearly all Western philosophies. Two common Buddhist versions of selfhood, for example, hold either that (a) there is no self, and what appears to be a self is merely a delusion, and/or (b) something "internal" to a person continues after death in another body, and therefore the relation it bears to the current body is not an essential one (in terms of reincarnation). Each of these views, that the self is a delusion and that the self continues after death (in various reincarnations), would be incompatible with most Western perspectives.[24] Speaking, for example, of the numerous philosophical writings that have explored various possible cases of "the same person (or what is alleged to be the same person) . . . not [being] the same live human body," John Perry clarifies the relation of personal identity to the body in modern Western philosophy as follows:

> Why are such cases puzzling, and why is the puzzlement of philosophical interest? Because they seem to disprove the view that a person is just a live human body. If we can have the same person on two different occasions when we don't have the same live human body, then it seems that a person cannot be identified with bodily identity. This is puzzling simply because the assumption that the two go together plays a large role in our daily lives.[25]

The contradictions and paradoxes of Buddhist views toward the self are not resolved exclusively through debate or by the splitting into factions based on different self-consistent positions. Rather, two alternative approaches are frequently taken, prototypically in Zen. The first is the position that the apparent contradiction makes no sense, that both ends of the dichotomy are identical. In regard to the *jiriki/tariki* controversy, for example, the Matsunagas point out that

> [i]n the end the individual must either discover or create the awakening within himself. Whether or not he personally takes credit for this discovery is irrelevant, for if he attains true Enlightenment, the wisdom he achieves with that experience will make any form of egotism or spiritual pride impossible. And this is why at the level of Ultimate truth, self-power (*jiriki*) and Other-power (*tariki*) can be viewed as identical.[26]

In other cases the contradiction is between doctrine or belief, on the one hand, and behavior or symbolic form, on the other, and may simply be accepted. Zen paradoxically combines theoretical (and practical) adherence to the notions of "no-self" and "no-mind" with a number of artistic and literary forms that would seem to depend upon strong and highly developed individual selves. Zen's deeply subtle naturalistic portraiture of individual abbots, its tradition of calligraphy and painting that are stylistically highly individual (as well as stylistically close to, and influenced by, Taoism and neo-Confucianism), and its history of narratives about the lives and enlightened sayings of individual masters[27]—all bespeak a high degree of individuation and sensitivity to the individuality of persons.

Confucianism

Confucian views of selfhood also differ from Western views, but in ways different from the Buddhist ones. In Confucianism, unlike Buddhism, the *existence* of the self is never denied, nor is there much challenge to the idea of determining personal identity by its relation to a single body; indeed, the ancestor cult depends upon an established relation between person and a single body. For both the Confucianist and Western traditions, personhood continues after death, and in neither case is there assumed to be more than one body at issue. The main disagreement with Western views, therefore, hinges not on the identification of self with body but, rather, on the degree to which the self is identified with others and on the value ascribed to the self. The value that Western philosophies ascribe to autonomous selves, the necessary relations they perceive between autonomy and virtue/goodness in ethics, and the recognition of the individual as the foundation of the polity are all quite foreign to Confucianism, which perceives individuals as most fully "self-actualizing" when most deeply connected to society.

The foregoing leads, first, to an ontological difference: The Confucian self is inherently relational. I would make a distinction here between relational and relative selves, borrowing the latter term from the vernacular usage and from physics and philosophy. In other words, something is relative if it can be understood or valued only in relation to other things, especially to the perspective from which it is viewed. The frequent example is the elephant viewed by five blind men, who understand it variously as resembling a rope, a wall, and so on, depending upon which part of the elephant they contact. This claim is primarily an epistemological one; although in its radical form it has ontological implications, these do not follow necessarily. The understanding of a self as relative is complicated by the fact that selves are formed in part by self-reflection—that is, by the understanding of the self by itself— such that relative selves come to be so not only in being viewed variously by *others* but also in being viewed by themselves (taking one's own self as an object of reflection and knowledge) and/or in recognizing themselves as viewed by others.

On the one hand, the relative self is seen to be different relative to different perspectives, as the same tree will be seen—literally and metaphorically—to be different by a bird or a squirrel in search of a home, by a person in search of fuel or of shelter from rain or lightning, by a lumberjack, by an artist (and even then, by a fifteenth-century Dutch wood-block artist, an Impressionist, a Confucian literati painter), and so on.[28] As William James puts it, "A man has as many social selves as there are individuals who recognize him and carry an image of him in their mind."[29]

To call a self relational, on the other hand, is to make a claim that is primarily ontological, and to reject essentialism. On this view what is (in some sense essentially) one organism may have different aspects or parts that come into their own, do different things, or act or appear differently in relation to different things (forces, other beings, etc.) in their environment. So a tree is different depending on its environment: Again, on this view there is no single essential version of a pine tree, no ideal pine tree, no idea of a pine tree, independent of realization in an actual environment, and the tree—or parts or aspects of the tree, such as roots, root hairs, branches, and needles—interacts differently with different parts of the environment (sun, water, wind, nutrients, supporting soil, etc.). The good life for a tree depends upon interaction, and it depends upon different kinds of interaction. A self, by analogy, is inherently interdependent. Indeed, the interactions through which it most clearly realizes itself are the Five Human Relationships: between father and son,[30] between ruler and subject, between husband and wife, between older and younger brother, and between friends.

In practice, the relative and the relational views of persons are not always distinct, and both have been developed—sometimes but not exclusively under the influence of Confucianism—in Japan. The story of the five blind men is, after all, from India, and all of Asia shares a degree of comfort with relativism and with perspectivalism that is rare in the West—a comfort that has been transmitted by Buddhism throughout Asia, where it is quite explicit in such practices and doctrines as "expedient means."

At the same time, the perception of Confucianist selfhood as relative rather than relational does not do justice to the radical nature of the Confucian view; it is simply a coloring of the phenomenon by the filtered glasses of Western views. We have little history for understanding things as *being* different depending on context; we have a long history of essentialisms and idealisms.

The Confucian self is relational in two separate respects. First, like a tree, it is dependent upon sociohistorical context and environment for its development. Second, it is different (not only from others, as in the West, but also "from itself") depending upon its relations with others, as summed up in the Five Human Relationships—both because each type of relationship calls for different responsibilities, responses, types of behavior, and so on, and because each relationship will affect the evolving self differently.[31]

The Five Human Relationships are not, as they are often interpreted, five contexts in which an essential or ideal self is to obey but five contexts in which the self develops and becomes itself. As Kasulis explains: "From the Japanese point of view, the person is not primarily an individual subsequently placed within the world. Rather, as indicated by the very structure of the word for 'human being,' the person is always in a context, in a necessary relationship with what is around him or her."[32] One of Japan's foremost twentieth-century philosophers, Watsuji Tetsurô, also speaks of a trans-individual self, and of the "between-ness between persons" (*hito to hito to no aidagara*).[33]

Neither the relational nor the relative self, let it be noted, is the view commonly ascribed to Confucianists by Americans, in which a person is defined by a single relation of primary importance: A person is a Mitsubishi worker, say, or a mother. At the very least, Confucianist relational selves are multiple and multivalent. (This is not to claim that Confucianism has never been abused by men in power to gain obedience for purely selfish purposes.)

We now consider a second difference, the value ascribed to autonomy. From the Western perspective, the Confucian person seems to be put in one of two positions: either fulfilling a role or obeying; obedience seems to be given preeminent value. Of course, this isn't how it always works out—and not simply because individuals of any culture sometimes place their own desires ahead of the common good. Confucianists, as it happens, have been very good at recognizing conflicts between obedience to authority and fulfilling other principles; they have also been good at acknowledging the frequent conflicts between obedience to conflicting authorities and at recognizing that such conflicts may require of the individual agonizing decisions and autonomous acts.

Let me give two illustrations. One of the side panels on the Chinese sarcophagus at the Nelson/Atkins Gallery in Kansas City illustrates a Confucianist parable that shows how the classic Confucian virtue of filial piety might under certain circumstances require not obedience but the admonishment of a father (though the restrictions on disobedience demand that the admonishment be by example rather than verbal):[34] A young man is summoned by his father to help him carry the grandfather up a mountain to die. The young man is reluctant to do this, but ought to obey his father. As they leave the mountaintop, the young man picks up the litter before starting down, and his father tells him not to bother with it. The son, however, insists that it will come in handy for the next trip up the mountain; the father realizes the next trip will be for him and, now able to put himself in the grandfather's place, brings the grandfather back down the mountain.[35]

Such stories, which are common, make it clear that unquestioned obedience is not a Confucian virtue. The young man is singled out as an example of filial piety, yet he has challenged his father's commands. It would be superficial to see this as simply a dilemma of conflicting duties to two different authorities, the father and the grandfather. But it is true that one way in which the Confucian self develops is through resolving the dilemmas of conflicting duties—and Confucian arts are full of stories illustrating such conflicts. Nor is this simply a conflict between duty to obey and a "higher" duty to abstract principles, another theme often encountered in Confucian literature. Rather, the young man here is choosing a vision of life and an interpretation of the significance of the relationship between father and son that allows for the fullest possibility of human growth.[36]

In a more civic and verbally explicit vein, we have the chastising letter written to the Japanese Shogun Minamoto Yoriie in 1200 C.E. by Mongaku, a close adviser to Yoriie's father. Though a Shingon monk, and evincing Buddhist principles as adviser (and subject), Mongaku had a Confucianist's responsibility to obey the ruler. But he also clearly thought he had a responsibility to point out the leader's moral obligations as ruler.[37] In general, such acts of reproval of authorities are a positive responsibility of ministers. One might indeed understand the principle of Mandate of Heaven as a recognition of the greater importance of virtue in general over obedience to authority.

It is also worth noting that even obedience per se does not lead to elimination of the self—it may in fact increase the self's awareness of itself, for either (or both) of two reasons. First, the self that truly tries to put its acts at the will of others may find itself in intellectual disagreement or emotional rebellion with those others, and this may lead to the point where knowledge of one's own feelings and desires and ambitions becomes exceptionally keen, and self-awareness and self-reflection are intensified. Second, obedience often requires a very strong will, which is a kind of self-development, and there can be a great deal of personal satisfaction in the exercise of such individual will power. (These reasons are of course not unknown in the West, where religious traditions and monastic orders in particular have long used obedience for training of the soul.)

Anthropologist Robert Smith has suggested that Japanese and Americans have diametrically opposed views of individuality and individualization: that Americans see persons as fundamentally alike and needing to work at the cultivation of the desirable ends of individuality, autonomy, and creativity, whereas Japanese understand persons as inherently different and needing to work at the cultivation of similarity and self-discipline.[38]

This brings us to a third area of difference between (many) Western views and Confucianist ones: the difference in ways of understanding the relation between the individual person and her individuality, creativity, or autonomy, and the implications of this difference for education and action. The latter may be summed up in terms of the various kinds of emphasis put on "self-cultivation." Note that we have been considering a number of different types of differences: differences between Western and Japanese views, differences among the various Japanese schools of thought, and differences between those Japanese views and American misconceptions or oversimplifications. The current problem, like the problem of obedience, falls within the last category. This is the simplistic view of Confucianism as ignoring the claims of the individual or devaluing the self. The same category of differences has bearing on the perception of the relation between autonomy and originality/creativity in the arts. It's not that originality is not valued but, rather, that it is *realized* differently.

Both painting and calligraphy are frequently done "in the style of" a famous artist. This process, however, does not involve copying or blind imitation. From the Confucianist point of view, perfect copying is not only undesirable, it may even be impossible.[39] The reason is that a work of art can arise only from the individuality of a given person in a particular environment at a particular time. Recall the view of the individual as *not essentially the same* at different times and in different circumstances but relative to a particular time and place and situation. (In other words, the situation comprises your own mood and psychological and physical states as well as the friends you are with and the persons you are painting for, etc.)

Another reason, however, has to do with the technology of Confucian painting. Both Buddhist painting technology (with the above-mentioned exception of Zen) and Western oil paints differ greatly from Confucian painting, which is done with a very soft, pliant brush and indelible black ink. As a result of the brush's pliancy, the lines reflect every nuance of the painter's movement, including breath. And as a result of the ink's indelibility, there is no chance to go back and correct, or to do over. Whatever has been done, stays. Therefore, to do good painting (or calligraphy for the technology and principles are the same) requires both years of training and practice—both in control over the media and in control over one's own mind, mood, hand, and breathing.

But it is one's own mind and mood that one works with. Therefore, the same or identical works of art *cannot* actually be made by two different people—or even by the same person at different times in his or her life. In this sense, originality need not be striven for—it will arise naturally out of the circumstances. And identical works of art cannot arise under different circumstances.

It goes without saying, however, that none of these considerations implies that Confucianism finds the exercise of the individual will per se, or the flourishing of individual passions and desires, to be either an essential inherent good or the grounding for a just or justifiable society. James Cahill's crucial insight about the differences between Western and Confucian attitudes toward the individual—namely, that in Confucianism the individual is strongly in evidence without, however, being used either as the foundation within moral and political theory or as the justification for it—is extremely helpful here.[40]

Philosophical Aspects of Natural Language

The obvious differences between Western and Japanese senses of the self show up brilliantly in the natural languages of each culture. Indo-European sentence structure requires subjects (implicit though they may be) for all sentences; Japanese sentence structure does not. Indeed, well-formed sentences in Japanese frequently (though not always) turn out, upon analysis, to be ambiguous, in the sense of having more than one possible "subject"—although the grammatical and logical differences are great enough that linguists eschew the term *subject* for the Japanese case in favor of *topic*.[41]

An analog in English might be "Hot, huh?" where the presumed subject might be either the empty subject "it" (as in the full disambiguated sentence "It's hot, isn't it?") or "you" (as in "You're hot, aren't you?"). But notice that the ambiguity is preserved in this English case only as long as the verb is omitted, too. As soon as the speaker supplies a verb—"isn't" or "aren't"—the implied subject has been disambiguated. In Japanese, by contrast, there are no inflections for person or number of verbs, and so the presumed subject remains unconstrained. (The Japanese language does feature two distinct but integrated frameworks for verbs that help to indicate who's doing what and to whom, called "politeness" and "formality," but these function quite differently and do not specify a subject.)

An example of this unconstrained subject is the famous opening sentence of Yasunari Kawabata's novel *Snow Country*, "Kokkyoh no nagai tonneru o nukeru to yukiguni de atta," translated by Edward Seidensticker as "The train came out of the long tunnel into the snow country." In the English sentence, the subject *train* has been supplied by the translator. There is no train in the Japanese sentence, which could just as easily be "When *we* came out of the long tunnel, *we* were in [or *there was* the] snow country" but literally would be more like "Upon coming out of the long tunnel at the frontier,[42] [it] was [the] snow country."

Equally unnerving can be the customs regarding personal names, which seem more free-floating in Japanese than in Indo-European linguistic usage. In classical literature, for instance, personal names are unknown for most of the characters, who are referred to by sobriquets or nicknames, by their ranks or titles, or, in the case of women, by the ranks and titles of their husbands and fathers. So we have the slightly odd situation whereby the same characters—in the country's most famous work of fiction, *The Tale of Genji*—are known in English by two different names, depending on the translator, and the same "name" or title refers to different persons at different times, since the original novel used no particular "name" with any consistency. Accordingly, William J. Puette's *Guide to the Tale of Genji by Murasaki Shikibu* has a twenty-page appendix that cross-indexes the names, titles, and sobriquets to the Waley and Seidensticker translations.[43] (Even with this index, the task of keeping track of characters in the novel and of who is speaking to [or about] whom is quite difficult—not only for us today but also for Japanese readers at least by the mid-seventeenth century.)[44]

This example, though somewhat extreme, is of a piece with the larger fabric of Japanese personal nomenclature, which often varies depending on the situation or the social role or the capacity within which a person is momentarily functioning. Emperors take new names when they accede to the throne. Artists and performers, if they "inherit" a particular lineage, are given the right to use the previous master's name (or sometimes a modification of it). And monks, artists, and writers routinely adopt new names or *go* that reflect their new identities; they may even adopt several different *go* to reflect variations in their self-image or in their approach to their work.[45] Because westerners experience a tighter coupling between name and personal identity, and even between name and sense of self (indeed, a name change often reflects our sense that a new self is being born),⁴⁶ the Japanese customs seem to destabilize the subject. In the context of this language difference, Kasulis's caution, about not looking for absolute differences but instead recognizing the relative emphasis placed by each culture on the foregrounding and backgrounding, is very helpful.

Even more distressing to the native Indo-European speaker is the fact that, in Japanese, the combination of topics with no subjects and the complex verbal system—which places the same value on the identification of the speaker and the listener as on the subject/topic [and object or objects]) of the sentence—renders pronouns completely unnecessary.⁴⁷ Consequently, there has (historically) been no consistent way in this language to refer, for example, to *oneself* or to distinguish *I* from *me,* and no customary or easy way to refer to *I* versus *you* versus *she.*

This dearth of pronouns, the use of sentence topics rather than subjects, and the variability of naming have fueled the flames of theories positing that there is no—or little, or only an undeveloped—sense of self among Japanese. But two further features of the Japanese language may also have contributed to this impression. First, because persons are indicated not by pronouns but through endings added to predicates as well as through special diction, both of which locate all persons involved on the two social frameworks of politeness and formality, there is no greater value put on the subject (of the sentence) than on the speaker and the listener, all of whom must equally be assigned a place on the two frameworks. Second, the absence of a connecting link (or copula) between subject and predicate in the Indo-European sense seems to entail that one can posit the predicate of a topic without implying the existence of the topic.

Together, the absence of pronouns, the systems of formality and politeness, and the necessity to take into account the nuances of social rank and intimacy in the relationship not only between speaker and addressee but also between both of them and any listeners, results in a situation where a Japanese speaker cannot determine her own levels of speech (in terms of formality and politeness) by the speech levels of her speech partner but, instead, must speak independently. (That is, while paying attention to the cues of the other, she cannot imitate the other's speech levels.) Perhaps nowhere in ordinary life, then, is autonomy more requisite than in speaking Japanese.

In sum, biases toward certain versions of selfhood have blinded westerners to the existence of important forms of selfhood in Japan. In spite of trends within the Buddhist and Confucianist traditions that explicitly devalue the self, at least in those respects highly valued in the West, certain self-related values, particularly autonomy and originality, exert a very strong presence in Japanese culture.

Notes

1. Catherine MacKinnen, "Feminism, Marxism, Method and the State: An Agenda for Theory," in *Feminist Theory: A Critique of Ideology*, ed. Nannerl O. Keohane, Michelle Z. Rosaldo, and Barbara C. Gelpi (Chicago: University of Chicago Press, 1982).

2. I would caution, however, that they are not necessarily identical, nor causally related. After all, persons may hold erroneous views of the kind of self they (or others) have.

3. Two early anthologies are useful in this connection: Arthur F. Wright, ed., *The Confucian Persuasion* (Stanford: Stanford University Press, 1960), and William Theodore de Bary and the Conference on Ming Thought, *Self and Society in Ming Thought* (New York: Columbia University Press, 1970). More recently, Tu Wei-ming has focused on the issues related to self-cultivation in *Centrality and Commonality: An Essay on Confucian Religiousness* (Albany: State University of New York Press, 1989); *Way, Learning and Politics: Essays on the Confucian Intellectual* (Albany: State University of New York Press, 1993); and, especially, *Confucian Thought: Selfhood as Creative Transformation* (Albany: State University of New York Press, 1985).

4. Here, I am thinking of studies such as Stephen J. Greenblatt's groundbreaking *Renaissance Self-Fashioning: From More to Shakespeare* (Chicago: University of Chicago Press, 1980).

5. Louis Althusser, "Ideology and Ideological State Apparatuses (Notes Towards an Investigation)," in *Lenin and Philosophy* (New York: Monthly Review Press, 1971); Peter L. Berger and Thomas Luckmann, *The Social Construction of Reality: A Treatise in the Sociology of Knowledge* (New York: Doubleday Anchor, 1966, 1967); Jacques Derrida, "Structure, Sign and Play in the Discourse of the Human Sciences," in *Modern Literary Theory: A Reader*, ed. P. Rice and P. Waugh (London: Edward Arnold, 1966, 1989).

6. Mara Miller, "Art and the Construction of Self and Subject in Japan," in *Self as Person in China, Japan, and India*, ed. Wimal Dissanayake (Albany: State University of New York Press, 1996).

7. Takie Sugiyama Lebra, "Migawari: The Cultural Idiom of Self-Other Exchange in Japan," in *Self as Person in Asian Theory and Practice*, ed. Roger T. Ames, with Wimal Dissanayake and Thomas P. Kasulis (Albany: SUNY Press, 1994), p. 108.

8. This idea was developed by Thomas Kasulis in lectures at a National Endowment for the Humanities summer seminar in Japanese philosophy, directed by Kasulis and held at Ohio State University in June and July 1994.

9. Mara Miller, *The Garden as an Art* (Albany: State University of New York Press, 1993).

10. See, for example, Carol Gilligan, *In a Different Voice: Psychological Theory and Women's Development* (Cambridge, Mass.: Harvard University Press, 1982).

11. Nancy R. Rosenberger, *Japanese Sense of Self* (Cambridge: Cambridge University Press, 1992), p. 2.

12. Ibid.

13. Ruth Benedict, *The Chrysanthemum and the Sword: Patterns of Japanese Culture* (Boston: Houghton Mifflin, 1946), p. 2.

14. According to Takie Sugiyama Lebra and William P. Lebra, *giri*, "a duty to a specific person," or "socially contracted dependence," and *ninjo*, literally "human feeling" (in Doi's words, "spontaneously arising feeling"), are related in that both entail "consideration of other persons" that motivates a moral actor (see *Japanese Culture and Behavior: Selected Readings*, rev. ed. [Honolulu: University of Hawaii Press, 1974, 1986], p. 4). *Giri* is frequently paired with *on*, a moral or social debt.

15. *Tanin* and *enryo* refer to self-discipline or self-restraint.

16. Takeo Doi tells us that "*omote* and *ura*, which Japanese use to indicate the contrasting attitudes in dealing with social situations . . . like the English equivalents 'front' and 'rear,' literally refer to the fore and back sides of things. Apart from this literal use, however, they are sometimes used in naming things to suggest the social function of the thing thus named. For instance, *omote-guchi* (front door) is the main entrance to Japanese houses which is of use for the members of a family or their guests, but the maid or the shopmen who call either to take orders or to deliver things use only *ura-guchi* (kitchen-door). *Omote-dori* or *omote-kaido* is a busy street and *ura-dori* or *ura-kaido* a lonely alley, hence these two words may be used to imply a success or the lack of it. . . . *[O]mote* is the appearance one would show to others. In this respect it is interesting to note that *omote* means 'face' and ura 'mind' in old literary Japanese. That one is able to build up omote is a commendable thing in Japan. It means that one is finally on one's own. It is different from a similar English expression, 'to put up a front,' which has the bad connotation of making a show." See Takeo Doi, *Omote to ura* (Tokyo: Kobundo, 1985), translated by Mark A. Harbison as *The Anatomy of Self: The Individual Versus Society* (Tokyo/New York: Kodansha International, 1986), p. 158.

17. "[D]ictionary definitions of *tatemae* define it as a type of principles or rules that have been established as natural and proper. . . . [T]hese rules or conventions are established by people and can therefore be overturned by people. . . . *Tatemae* refers to conventions created by people on the basis of consensus. . . . In short, *tatemae* always implies the existence of a group of people in its background who assent to it. . . . In contrast to this, *honne* refers to the fact that the individuals who belong to the group, even while they consent to the tatemae, each have their own motives and opinions that are distinct from it, and that they hold these in the background" (from Harbison, trans., *The Anatomy of Self*, pp. 35–37).

18. Lebra, "Migawari," p. 107. Of the works cited in this passage, two are articles: Jane Buchnik's "The Two 'Faces' of Self and Society in Japan," *Ethos* 20(1992): 3–32, and Nancy R. Rosenberger's "Dialectic Balance in the Polar Model of Self: The Japan Case," *Ethos* 17(1989): 88–113. The other works are books listed in the Bibliography of the present volume.

19. Lebra, "Self in Japanese Culture," in Rosenberger, ed., *Japanese Sense of Self*.

20. Ibid., p. 108. Regarding the two works cited in this passage: Thomas Rohlen's "Spiritual Education in a Japanese Bank" is reprinted in *Japanese Culture and Behavior*, ed. T. S. Lebra and W. P. Lebra (Honolulu: University of Hawaii Press, 1986), and Harumi Befu's book is listed in the Bibliography.

21. The differences are more than coincidental; they reflect the profoundly different natures of the two religions. According to Talcott Parsons's theoretical framework, for example, Shinto is particularistic, whereas Buddhism is universalistic. For an application of Parsons's theory to Japanese religion, see Robert N. Bellah,

Tokugawa Religion: The Values of Pre-Industrial Japan (Glencoe, Ill.: Free Press, 1957; Boston: Beacon Press, 1970).

22. David Kalupahana, *Nagarjuna: The Philosophy of the Middle Way* (Albany: State University of New York Press, 1986).

23. For an analysis of the *jiriki/tariki* debate, a good introduction is Daigan and Alicia Matsunaga's *Foundation of Japanese Buddhism*, especially the chapter in Volume 2 entitled "Pure Land Sects" (Los Angeles/Tokyo: Buddhist Books International, 1976).

24. I won't even begin to go into the "nothingness" debate here. The reader can, however, consult Keiji Nishitani, *Religion and Nothingness,* trans. Jan van Bragt (Berkeley/Los Angeles: University of California Press, 1982).

25. John Perry, ed., *Personal Identity* (Berkeley/Los Angeles: University of California Press, 1975), p. 5.

26. Matsunaga and Matsunaga, *Foundation of Japanese Buddhism*, p. 205.

27. Of course, this apparent paradox ought not to be taken at face value. It indicates, perhaps among other things, that language itself is being used differently here than in normal discourse. Though masked in descriptive or narrative syntax, such pronouncements are actually closer to speech acts.

28. The selection of a tree as an analog for the Confucian self is not arbitrary, for this use of trees has a long history in Confucianism.

29. William James, *The Principles of Psychology* (New York: Henry Holt and Co., 1890; Cambridge, Mass.: Harvard University Press, 1983), p. 294.

30. But in *Confucian Thought* Tu Wei-ming interprets this relationship to include father-daughter and mother-child relationships as well.

31. Tu Wei-ming, *Confucian Thought*, chapter 7: "Selfhood and Otherness: The Father-Son Relationship in Confucian Thought."

32. T. P. Kasulis, *Zen Action, Zen Person* (Honolulu: University of Hawaii Press, 1981).

33. Tetsuro Watsuji, "The Significance of Ethics as the Study of Man," trans. David A. Dilworth, in *Monumenta Nipponica*, Vol. 26, pp. 3–4; see also chapter 1 of *Rinrigaku (Ethics)*, Vol. 1, rev. ed. (Tokyo: Iwanami Shoten, 1965; originally published in 1937), pp. 11–31.

34. This piece has been attributed variously to the Han (206 B.C.E.–220 C.E.) and Northern Wei (386–535 C.E.) dynasties.

35. The sarcophagus, but not this episode, is illustrated in Sherman Lee's *History of Far Eastern Art*, 4th ed. fig. 342; and in the *Handbook of the Collections in the William Rockhill Nelson Gallery of Art and Mary Atkins Museum of Fine Arts, Kansas City, Missouri, Vol. II: Art of the Orient* (Kansas City, 1973), p. 44.

36. Another wonderful example can be found in Tu's analysis of the story of Sage-King Shun in *Confucian Thought*.

37. "Letter of the Priest Mongaku to Shogun Yoriie 1200," in *Sources of Japanese Tradition,* Vol. 1, compiled by Ryusaku Tsunoda, William Theodore de Bary, and Donald Keene (New York: Columbia University Press, 1964), pp. 165–171.

38. Robert Smith, *Japanese Society: Tradition, Self, and the Social Order* (Cambridge: Cambridge University Press, 1983).

39. Nonetheless, both copying in the sense of forgery (for illegal purposes) and copying in order to gain as close as possible a reproduction of a much-loved work did exist.

40. James Cahill, "Confucian Elements in the Theory of Painting," in *The Confucian Persuasion,* Arthur F. Wright, ed. (Stanford: Stanford University Press, 1960).

41. Charles N. Li, ed., *Subject and Topic* (New York/San Francisco/London: Academic Press, 1976).

42. Here I am supplying the preposition "at"; the Japanese uses a genitive which sounds quite peculiar in English: "the frontier's long tunnel," or "the long tunnel of the frontier."

43. William J. Puette, *Guide to the Tale of Genji by Murasaki Shikibu* (Rutland, Vt./Tokyo: Tuttle, 1983).

44. Richard Bowring reports that Kitamura Kigin's edition with commentary, *Kogetsushoh* (1675), "is full of notations which help the reader to identify who is talking to whom at any given point, and who is the subject of any given sentence. This was a major development." See *The Tale of Genji* (Cambridge/New York: Cambridge University Press, 1988), p. 92.

45. Thus Laurance P. Roberts's *A Dictionary of Japanese Artists* (Tokyo/New York: Weatherhill, 1976) includes a thirty-page "Index of Alternate Names."

46. Clearly, the adoption of new names is far from unknown in the West where, in some cultures, women frequently take the surname of their husbands' families, persons taking religious orders assume new personal names, writers and actors often adopt noms-de-plume, and the use of nicknames may indicate the degree of intimacy or length of the history of the person using it. It is also the case, however, that these instances in the West tend to indicate either marginalized social status, as in the case of actors or religious persons, or differences in social hierarchy, especially those relating to gender: Women, not men, change their names upon marriage, and nuns, not priests or monks, take new personal names—further evidence of the Western belief that name bears an inherent relation to the self.

47. This grammatical phenomenon began to change with the close interaction between Japan and the West in the late nineteenth century.

Bibliography

Abe Jirô. *Niichie no Tsuaratsusutora kaishaku narabi ni hihyô* [Nietzsche's *Zarathustra*: Interpretation and critique]. Tokyo: Kadokawa Shoten, 1919.

Aboulafia, Mitchell. *The Mediating Self: Mead, Sartre, and Self-Determination*. New Haven: Yale University Press, 1986.

Adams, E. M. *The Metaphysics of Self and World*. Philadelphia: Temple University Press, 1991.

Aida Yuji. *Nihonjin no ishiki kozo*. Tokyo: Kodanasha, 1970.

Allen, Douglas. *Structure and Creativity in Religion*. The Hague: Mouton, 1978.

_____. *Mircea Eliade et le phénomène religieux*. Paris: Payot Editions, 1982.

_____. *Mircea Eliade on Myth and Religion*. New York: Garland Publishers, 1997.

Allen, Douglas, ed. *Religion and Political Conflict in South Asia: India, Pakistan, and Sri Lanka*. Westport, Conn.: Greenwood Publishers, 1992; Delhi: Oxford University Press, 1993.

Allinson, Robert E. *Understanding the Chinese Mind: The Philosophical Roots*. Hong Kong/New York: Oxford University Press, 1989.

Allport, G. *The Person in Psychology*. Boston: Beacon Press, 1968.

Althusser, Louis. *Lenin and Philosophy*. New York: Monthly Review Press, 1971.

Ames, Roger T., with Wimal Dissanayake and Thomas P. Kasulis, eds. *Self as Person in Asian Theory and Practice*. Albany: State University of New York Press, 1994.

Ayer, A. J. *The Concept of a Person*. London: Macmillan, 1963.

Bachnik, Jane, and Charles Quinn. *Situated Meaning: Inside and Outside in Japanese Self, Society, and Language*. Princeton: Princeton University Press, 1994.

Befu, Harumi. *The Group Model of Japanese Society and an Alternate Model*. Houston: Rice University Studies Series 66, 1980.

Beidler, William. *The Vision of Self in Early Vedanta*. Delhi: Motilal Banarsidass, 1975.

Bellah, Robert N. *Tokugawa Religion: The Values of Pre-Industrial Japan*. Glencoe, Ill.: Free Press, 1957; Boston: Beacon Press, 1970.

Benedict, Ruth. *The Chrysanthemum and the Sword: Patterns of Japanese Culture*. Boston: Houghton Mifflin, 1946.

Berger, Peter L., and Thomas Luckmann. *The Social Construction of Reality*. New York: Doubleday, 1967.

Bharati, A. *The Tantric Tradition*. London: Rider and Co., 1965.

Bilimoria, Purushottama. *Sabdapramana, Word and Knowledge: A Doctrine in Mimamsa-Nyaya Philosophy*. Dordrecht/Boston: Kluwer Academic, 1988.

_____. *The Self and Its Destiny in Hinduism*. Victoria: Deakin University, 1990.

Bockover, Mary I., ed. *Rules, Rituals, and Responsibility: Essays Dedicated to Herbert Fingarette*. La Salle, Ill.: Open Court, 1991.

Brinthaupt, Thomas M., and Richard P. Lipka, eds. *The Self: Definitional and Methodological Issues.* Albany: State University of New York Press, 1992.

_____. *Changing the Self: Philosophies, Techniques, and Experiences.* Albany: State University of New York Press, 1994.

Buber, Martin. *Between Man and Man.* New York: Macmillan, 1965.

_____. *I and Thou.* New York: Charles Scribner, 1955; New York: Touchstone, 1996.

Bynum, Caroline W., Steven Harrell, and Paula Richman, eds. *Gender and Religion: On the Complexity of Symbols.* Boston: Beacon Press, 1986.

Carrithers, Michael, Steven Collins, and Steven Lukes, eds. *The Category of the Person: Anthropology, Philosophy, History.* Cambridge: Cambridge University Press, 1985.

Chan, Wing-tsit. *A Source Book in Chinese Philosophy.* Princeton: Princeton University Press, 1963.

Chang, Chung-Yuan. *Original Teachings of Ch'an Buddhism.* New York: Vintage Books, 1971.

Chisholm, Roderick M. *Person and Object: A Metaphysical Study.* La Salle, Ill.: Open Court, 1976.

Chodorow, Nancy. *The Reproduction of Mothering.* Berkeley: University of California Press, 1978.

Chuang Tzu. *The Complete Works of Chuang Tzu*, trans. Burton Watson. New York: Columbia University Press, 1968.

Cole, James Preston. *The Problematic Self in Kierkegaard and Freud.* New Haven: Yale University Press, 1971.

Colli, Giorgio and Mazzino Montinari, eds. *Friedrich Nietzsche: Sämtliche Werke, Kritische Studienausgabe.* Berlin/New York: de Gruyter, 1980.

Collins, Steven. *Selfless Persons: Imagery and Thought in Theravada Buddhism.* Cambridge: Cambridge University Press, 1982.

Conze, Edward. *Buddhist Thought in India.* Ann Arbor: University of Michigan Press, 1962.

Da Silva, Padmasiri. *An Introduction to Buddhist Psychology.* New York: Barnes and Noble, 1979.

Dastidar, Koyeli G. *Conceptions of Individual Autonomy and Self-Responsibility.* Burdwan, India: University of Burdwan, 1992.

De Bary, William Theodore, and the Conference on Ming Thought. *Self and Society in Ming Thought.* New York: Columbia University Press, 1970.

De Beauvoir, Simone. *The Second Sex*, trans. H. M. Parshley. New York: Random House/Vintage Books, 1974.

Dennett, Daniel C. *Consciousness Explained.* Boston: Little, Brown, 1991.

Desai, Mahadev. *The Gita According to Gandhi.* Ahmedabad: Navajivan Publishing House, 1946.

Descartes, René. *Discourse on Method.* New York: Library of Liberal Arts, 1956.

_____. *Meditations on First Philosophy.* Indianapolis, Ind.: Hackett Publishing Co., 1979; Cambridge/New York: Cambridge University Press, 1986.

Dissanayake, Wimal, with Thomas P. Kasulis and Roger T. Ames, eds. *Self as Image in Asian Theory and Practice.* Albany: State University of New York Press, 1995.

Doi, Takeo. *Amae no kozo*. Tokyo: Kobundo, 1971. Translated by John Bestor as *The Anatomy of Dependence*. Tokyo/New York: Kodansha International, 1973.
_____. *Omote to ura*. Tokyo: Kobundo, 1985. Translated by Mark A. Harbison as *The Anatomy of Self: The Individual Versus Society*. Tokyo/New York: Kodansha International, 1986.

Dumont, L. *Essays on Individualism*. Chicago: University of Chicago Press, 1986.

Dupré, Louis K. *Passage to Modernity: An Essay in the Hermeneutics of Nature and Culture*. New Haven: Yale University Press, 1993.

Eccles, J. C. *Evolution of the Brain: Creation of the Self*. London: Routledge, 1989.

Elster, Jon. *The Multiple Self*. Cambridge/New York: Cambridge University Press, 1986.

Erikson, Erik. *Childhood and Society*, 2nd ed. New York: W. W. Norton. 1963.
_____. *Identity, Youth and Crisis*. New York: W. W. Norton, 1968.

Evans, Cedric Oliver. *The Subject of Consciousness*. London: Allen and Unwin; New York: Humanities Press, 1970.

Fingarette, Herbert. *Confucius—The Secular as Sacred*. New York: Harper Torchbooks, 1972.

Fromm, Erich. *Marx's Concept of Man*. New York: F. Ungar Publishing Co., 1961.
_____. *The Art of Loving*. New York: Harper and Brothers, 1970.

Garfield, Jay. *The Fundamental Wisdom of the Middle Way*. New York: Oxford University Press, 1995.

Garry, Ann, and Marilyn Pearsall, eds. *Women, Knowledge, and Reality*. Boston: Unwin Hyman, 1989.

Geertz, Clifford. *The Interpretation of Cultures*. New York: Basic Books, 1973.

Geras, Norman. *Marx and Human Nature: Refutation of a Legend*. London: Verso Editions, 1983.

Gergen, K. *The Concept of Self*. New York: Holt, Rinehart and Winston, 1971.

Giddens, Anthony. *Modernity and Self-Identity: Self and Society in the Late Modern Age*. Stanford: Stanford University Press, 1991.

Gillespie, Michael Allen. *Nihilism Before Nietzsche*. Chicago: University of Chicago Press, 1995.

Gilligan, Carol. *In a Different Voice: Psychological Theory and Women's Development*. Cambridge, Mass.: Harvard University Press, 1982.

Glover, Jonathon, ed., *Philosophy of Mind*. Oxford: Oxford University Press, 1976.

Gordon, C., and Gergen, K., eds. *The Self in Social Interaction*, Vols. 1 and 2. New York: John Wiley, 1968.

Gould, Carol C., and Marx W. Wartofsky, eds. *Women and Philosophy: Toward a Theory of Liberation*. New York: Perigee Books/G. P. Putnam's, 1980.

Greenblatt, Stephen J. *Renaissance Self-Fashioning: From More to Shakespeare*. Chicago: University of Chicago Press, 1980.

Griffith, Paul. *On Being Mindless: Buddhist Meditation and the Mind-Body Problem*. La Salle, Ill.: Open Court, 1986.

Griffiths, M., and M. Whitford, eds. *Feminist Perspectives in Philosophy*. Bloomington: Indiana University Press, 1988.

Grimshaw, J. *Philosophy and Feminist Theory*. Minneapolis: University of Minnesota Press, 1986.

Guntrip, Harry. *Schizoid Phenomena, Object-Relations, and the Self*. New York: International Universities Press, 1969.

_____. *Psychoanalytic Theory, Therapy, and the Self*. New York: Basic Books, 1971.

Hamaguchi, Eschun. *Nihon rashisa no saihakken*. Tokyo: Nihon Keizai Shinbunsha, 1977.

Hamilton, N. Gregory. *Self and Others: Object Relations Theory in Practice*. Northvale, N.J.: Aronson, 1988.

Harding, M. Esther. *The "I" and the "Not-I": A Study in the Development of Consciousness*. Princeton: Princeton University Press, 1965.

Harding, Sandra. *The Science Question in Feminism*. Ithaca, N.Y.: Cornell University Press, 1986.

Harre, Rom. *Personal Being: A Theory For Individual Psychology*. Cambridge, Mass.: Harvard University Press, 1984.

Hasan, Zoya, ed. *Forging Identities: Gender, Communities, and the State*. New Delhi: Kali for Women, 1994; Boulder, Colo.: Westview Press, 1994.

Hegel, G.W.F. *The Phenomenology of Mind*, trans. J. B. Baillie. New York: Harper and Row, 1967.

Heidegger, Martin. *Being and Time*, trans. John Macquarrie and Edward Robinson. New York: Harper and Row, 1962.

Hofstadter, Douglas R. *Metamagical Themes: Questing for the Essence of Mind and Pattern*. New York: Basic Books, 1985.

Hofstadter, Douglas R., and Daniel Clement Dennett. *The Mind's I: Fantasies and Reflections of Self and Soul*. New York: Basic Books, 1981.

Holland, Ray. *Self and Social Context*. New York: St. Martin's Press, 1977.

Horner, Althea J. *Object Relations and the Developing Ego in Therapy*. Northvale, N.J.: Aronson, 1984.

Hume, David. *A Treatise on Human Nature*, ed. L. A. Selby-Bigge and P. H. Nidditch. Oxford: Clarendon Press, 1978.

Husserl, Edmund. *Cartesian Meditations*, trans. Dorian Cairns. The Hague: Martinus Nijhoff, 1970.

_____. *Ideas: General Introduction to Pure Phenomenology*, trans. W. R. Boyce Gibson. New York: Collier Books, 1975.

Ilie, Paul. *Unamuno: An Existential View of Self and Society*. Madison: University of Wisconsin Press, 1967.

Inada, Kenneth K., ed. *East-West Dialogues in Aesthetics*. Buffalo: State University of New York at Buffalo, 1978.

Inada, Kenneth K., and Nolan P. Jacobson, eds. *Buddhism and American Thinkers*. Albany: State University of New York Press, 1983.

Inoue, Tadashi. *Sekentei no kozo*. Tokyo: Nippon Hoso Shunppankai, 1977.

Jackson, Helene. *Using Self Psychology in Psychotherapy*. Northvale, N.J.: Aronson, 1991.

Jacobson, Edith. *The Self and the Object World*. New York: International Universities Press, 1964.

Jaggar, Alison M. *Feminist Politics and Human Nature*. Totowa, N.J.: Rowman and Allanheld, 1983.

James, William. *The Principles of Psychology*. New York: Henry Holt and Co., 1890; Cambridge, Mass.: Harvard University Press, 1983.

Johnstone, Henry W. *The Problem of the Self*. University Park: Pennsylvania State University Press, 1970.

Jung, C. G. *The Undiscovered Self*. Boston: Little, Brown, 1958.

Kakar, Sudhir. *The Inner World: A Psychoanalytical Study of Childhood and Society in India*. Delhi: Oxford University Press, 1978.

_____. *Shamans, Mystics and Doctors*. New York: Alfred A. Knopf, 1982.

_____. *The Analyst and the Mystic: Psychoanalytic Reflections on Religion and Mysticism*. New Delhi: Penguin Books, 1991.

_____. *Intimate Relations: Exploring Indian Sexuality*. Chicago: University of Chicago Press, 1991.

Kakar, Sudhir, ed. *Identity and Adulthood*. Delhi: Oxford University Press, 1979.

Kalupahana, David. *Nagarjuna: The Philosophy of the Middle Way*. Albany: State University of New York Press, 1986.

Kasulis, Thomas P. *Zen Action, Zen Person*. Honolulu: University of Hawaii Press, 1981.

Kasulis, Thomas P., with Roger T. Ames and Wimal Dissanayake, eds. *Self as Body in Asian Theory and Practice*. Albany: State University of New York Press, 1993.

Keller, Catherine. *From a Broken Web: Separation, Sexism, and Self*. Boston: Beacon Press, 1986.

Kenny, Anthony. *The Self*. Milwaukee: Marquette University Press, 1988.

Keohane, Nannerl O., Michelle Z. Rosaldo, and Barbara C. Gelpi, eds. *Feminist Theory: A Critique of Ideology*. Chicago: University of Chicago Press, 1982.

Kerby, Anthony Paul. *Narrative and the Self*. Bloomington: Indiana University Press, 1991.

Kessel, F. S., P. M. Cole, and D. L. Johnson, eds. *Self and Consciousness: Multiple Perspectives*. Hillsdale, N.J.: Lawrence Erlbaum, 1992.

Kimura, Bin. *Hito to hito to no aida*. Tokyo: Kobundo, 1972.

Kittay, Eva Feder, and Diana T. Meyers, eds. *Women and Moral Theory*. Totowa, N.J.: Rowman and Littlefield, 1987.

Klossowski, Pierre. *Nietzsche et le cercle vicieux*. Paris: Mercure de France, 1969.

Kohut, Heinz. *Analysis of the Self*. New York: International Universities Press, 1971.

_____. *Restoration of the Self*. New York: International Universities Press, 1977.

Kondo, Dorinne. *Crafting Selves: Power, Gender, and Discourses of Identity in a Japanese Workplace*. Chicago: University of Chicago, 1990.

Kotarba, Joseph A., and Andrea Fontana. *The Existential Self in Society*. Chicago: University of Chicago Press, 1984.

Krausz, Michael, and Jack Meiland, eds. *Relativism: Cognitive and Moral*. Notre Dame, Ind.: Notre Dame University Press, 1982.

Laing, R. D. *Self and Others*. New York: Pantheon Books, 1969.

Larson, G. J. *Classical Samkhya: An Interpretation of Its History and Meaning*, 2nd ed. Delhi: Motilal Banarsidass, 1979.

Lasch, Christopher. *The Culture of Narcissism*. New York: Warner Books, 1979.

_____. *The Minimal Self: Psychic Survival in Troubled Times*. New York: W. W. Norton, 1984.

Lebra, Takie Sugiyama. *Japanese Patterns of Behavior*. Honolulu: University of Hawaii Press, 1976.

Lebra, Takie Sugiyama, and W. P. Lebra, eds. *Japanese Culture and Behavior*. Honolulu: University of Hawaii Press, 1986.

Lee, Benjamin, ed. *Psychosocial Theories of the Self*. New York: Plenum, 1982.

Levin, J. D. *Theories of the Self*. Washington, D.C.: Hemisphere, 1992.

Levinas, Emmanuel. *The Levinas Reader*, ed. Sean Hand. New York: B. Blackwell, 1989.

_____. *Outside the Subject*. Stanford: Stanford University Press, 1994.

Levine, George. ed. *Constructions of the Self*. New Brunswick, N.J.: Rutgers University Press, 1992.

Levita, David Joel de. *The Concept of Identity*. Paris: Mouton, 1965; New York: Basic Books, 1967.

Lifton, Robert Jay. *The Protean Self: Human Resilience in an Age of Fragmentation*. New York: Basic Books, 1993

Li Guohao et al., eds. *Explorations in the History of Science and Technology in China*. Shanghai: Shanghai Chinese Classics Publishing House, 1982.

Locke, John. *An Essay Concerning Human Understanding*. Oxford: Clarendon Press; New York: Oxford University Press, 1979.

Lyons, John O. *The Invention of the Self: The Hinge of Consciousness in the Eighteenth Century*. Carbondale: Southern Illinois University Press, 1978.

Magnus, Bernd, and Kathleen M. Higgins, eds. *The Cambridge Companion to Nietzsche*. Cambridge/New York: Cambridge University Press, 1996.

Malhotra, Ashok K. *Jean Paul Sartre's Existentialism as Literature and Philosophy*. Oneonta, N.Y.: Oneonta Philosophy Series, 1995.

Marcel, Gabriel. *The Mystery of Being*. Chicago: Henry Regnery, 1960.

Marriott, McKim. *India Through Hindu Categories*. New Delhi/London: Sage Publications, 1990.

Marsella, Anthony J., George De Vos, and Francis L. K. Hsu, eds. *Culture and Self: Asian and Western Perspectives*. New York: Tavistock Publications, 1985.

Marx, Karl. *The Ethnological Notebooks of Karl Marx*, ed. Lawrence Krader. Assen, the Netherlands: Van Gorcum, 1972.

_____. *Grundrisse*, trans. Martin Nicolaus. New York: Random House/Vintage Books, 1973.

_____. *Capital*, Vol. 1, trans. Ben Fowkes. New York: Random House/Vintage Books, 1977.

Marx, Karl, and Frederick Engels. *The Marx-Engels Reader*, ed. Robert C. Tucker. New York: Norton, 1972.

_____. *Marx-Engels: The Individual and Society*. Moscow: Progress Publishers, 1984.

Masavisut, Nitaya, George Simson, and Larry E. Smith, eds. *Gender and Culture in Literature and Film East and West: Issues of Perception and Interpretation*. Honolulu: University of Hawaii Press, 1994.

Materson, James F. *The Real Self: A Developmental Self and Object Relations Approach*. New York: Brunner/Mazel, 1985.

Matsunaga, Daigan, and Alicia Matsunaga. *Foundation of Japanese Buddhism*, 2 vols. Los Angeles/Tokyo: Buddhist Books International, 1974–1976.

May, Rollo. *Man's Search for Himself.* New York: Norton, 1953.

Mead, George Herbert. *Mind, Self and Society from the Standpoint of a Social Behaviorist*, ed. Charles W. Morris. Chicago: University of Chicago Press, 1934.

_____. *The Individual and the Social Self*, ed. David C. Miller. Chicago: University of Chicago Press, 1982.

Merleau-Ponty, Maurice. *The Primacy of Perception*, trans. and ed. James M. Edie. Evanston, Ill.: Northwestern University Press, 1964.

_____. *Phenomenology of Perception*, trans. Colin Smith. London: Humanities Press, 1978.

Meyers, Diana T. *Self, Society and Personal Choice.* New York: Columbia University Press, 1989.

Meyers, Diana T., ed., *Feminists Rethink the Self.* Boulder, Colo.: Westview Press, 1997.

Mikhailov, F. T. *The Riddle of the Self.* New York: International Publishers, 1980.

Mill, John Stuart. *Utilitarianism.* Indianapolis, Ind.: Hackett Publishing Co., 1979. Originally published in 1861.

Miller, Mara. *The Garden as an Art.* Albany: State University of New York Press, 1993.

Minami, Hiroshi. *Psychology of the Japanese people.* Toronto: University of Toronto Press, 1971.

_____. *Nihon teki jiga.* Tokyo: Iwanami Shoten, 1983.

Mindell, Arnold, Sisa Sternback-Scott, and Becky Goodman. *Dreambody: The Body's Role in Revealing the Self.* Santa Monica, Calif.: Sigo Press, 1982.

Mischel, Theodore, ed. *The Self: Psychological and Philosophical Issues.* Totowa, N.J.: Rowman and Littlefield, 1977.

Moghadam, Valentine M., ed. *Gender and National Identity: Women and Politics in Muslim Societies.* Karachi: Oxford University Press, 1994.

_____. *Identity Politics and Women: Cultural Reassertions and Feminisms in International Perspective.* Boulder, Colo.: Westview Press, 1994.

Mohanty, Jitendra Nath. *Essays on Indian Philosophy Traditional and Modern*, ed. Purushottama Bilimoria. Delhi/New York: Oxford University Press, 1993.

Moore, Charles A., ed. *The Status of the Individual in East and West.* Honolulu: University of Hawaii Press, 1968.

Mukerju, A. C. *Self, Thought, and Reality.* Allahabad: Indian Press, 1957.

Munro, Donald. *The Concept of Man in Early China.* Stanford: Stanford University Press, 1969.

_____. *The Concept of Man in Contemporary China.* Ann Arbor: University of Michigan Press, 1977.

Nakane, Chie. *Tate shakai no ningen kankei.* Tokyo: Kodansha, 1967.

Nandy, Ashish. *The Intimate Enemy: Loss and Recovery of Self Under Colonialism.* Delhi: Oxford University Press, 1983.

_____. *The Savage Freud and Other Essays on Possible and Retrievable Selves.* Princeton: Princeton University Press, 1995.

Natanson, Maurice. *The Journeying Self: A Study in Philosophy and Social Role.* Reading, Mass.: Addison-Wesley, 1970.

Niebuhr, Reinhold. *The Self and the Dreams of History.* New York: Scribner, 1955.

Nietzsche, Friedrich. *Werke: Grossoktavausgabe.* Leipzig: C. G. Naumann, 1901.

_____. *Twilight of the Idols*. Harmondsworth, England: Penguin Books, 1968.

_____. *Beyond Good and Evil*. New York: Vintage Books, 1966; London/New York: Penguin Books, 1990.

_____. *Thus Spoke Zarathustra*. Harmondsworth, England/New York: Penguin Books, 1978; New York: Modern Library, 1995.

Nishitani Keiji. *Religion and Nothingness*, trans. Jan Van Bragt. Berkeley: University of California Press, 1982.

_____. *The Self-Overcoming of Nihilism*, trans. Graham Parkes with Setsuko Aihara. Albany: State University of New York Press, 1990.

_____. *Nishida Kitaro*, trans. Yamamoto Seisaku and James W. Heisig. Berkeley: University of California Press, 1991.

Noddings, Nel. *Caring: A Feminine Approach to Ethics and Moral Education*. Berkeley: University of California Press, 1984.

Noonan, Harold W. *Personal Identity*. London/New York: Routledge, 1989.

Odin, Steve. *The Social Self in Zen and American Pragmatism*. Albany: State University of New York Press, 1996.

Ogilvy, James A., ed. *Self and World: Readings in Philosophy*. New York: Harcourt Brace and Jovanovich, 1981.

Ohnuki-Tierney, Emiko. *Rice as Self: Japanese Identities Through Time*. Princeton: Princeton University Press, 1993.

Ollman, Bertell. *Alienation: Marx's Conception of Man in Capitalist Society*. Cambridge: Cambridge University Press, 1971.

Organ, Troy W. *Philosophy and the Self: East and West*. Selinsgrove, Pa.: Susquehanna University Press, 1987.

Oster, A, L. Fruzzetti, and S. Barnett, eds. *Concepts of Person: Kinship, Caste, and Marriage in India*. Cambridge, Mass.: Harvard University Press, 1982.

Padel, Ruth. *In and Out of the Mind: Greek Images of the Tragic Self*. Princeton: Princeton University Press, 1992.

Parfit, Derek. *Reasons and Persons*. Oxford: Oxford University Press, 1984.

Parkes, Graham. *Composing the Soul: Reaches of Nietzsche's Psychology*. Chicago: University of Chicago Press, 1994.

Parkes, Graham, ed. *Heidegger and Asian Thought*. Honolulu: University of Hawaii Press, 1987.

_____. *Nietzsche and Asian Thought*. Chicago: University of Chicago Press, 1991.

Parsons, T. *Social Structure and Personality*. New York: Free Press, 1964.

Pearsall, Marilyn, ed. *Women and Vlaues: Readings in Recent Feminist Philosophy*. Belmont, Calif.: Wadsworth Publishing Co., 1986.

Perry, John, ed. *Personal Identity*. Berkeley: University of California Press, 1975.

Popper, Karl, and John Eccles. *The Self and Its Brain*. New York: Springer International, 1977.

Rachels, James. *The Elements of Moral Philosophy*, 2nd ed. New York: McGraw-Hill, 1993.

Radhakrishnan, Sarvepalli, and Charles A. Moore, eds. *A Source Book in Indian Philosophy*. Princeton: Princeton University Press, 1957.

Rahula, Walpole. *What the Buddha Taught*. New York: Grove Press, 1959.

Ramanan, K. Venkat. *Nagarjuna's Philosophy: As Presented in the Maha-Prajna-paramita-Sastra*. Delhi: Motilal Banarsidass, 1966.

Ricoeur, Paul. *Oneself as Another*, trans. Kathleen Blamey. Chicago: University of Chicago Press, 1992.

Roberts, Laurance P. *A Dictionary of Japanese Artists*. Tokyo/New York: Weatherhill, 1976.

Roland, Alan. *In Search of Self in India and Japan: Toward a Cross-Cultural Psychology*. Princeton: Princeton University Press, 1988.

_____. *Cultural Pluralism and Psychoanalysis: The Asian and North American Experience*. New York: Routledge, 1996.

Ropp, Paul S., ed. *Heritage of China*. Berkeley: University of California Press, 1990.

Rorty, Amelie O., ed. *The Identities of Persons*. Berkeley: University of California Press, 1976.

Rosemont, Henry, Jr. *A Chinese Mirror: Moral Reflections on Political Economy and Society*. La Salle, Ill.: Open Court, 1991.

Rosemont, Henry, Jr., ed. *Chinese Texts and Philosophical Contexts: Essays Dedicated to Angus C. Graham*. La Salle, Ill.: Open Court, 1991.

Rosenberg, J. F. *The Thinking Self*. Philadelphia: Temple University Press, 1986.

Rosenberg, M. *Conceiving the Self*. New York: Basic Books, 1979.

Rosenberger, Nancy R., ed. *Japanese Sense of Self*. Cambridge: Cambridge University Press, 1992.

Rouner, L. S., ed. *Selves, People, and Persons*. Notre Dame, Ind.: Notre Dame University Press, 1992.

Roy, Ramashray. *Self and Society: A Study in Gandhian Thought*. New Delhi: Sage Publications, 1985.

Said, Edward W. *Orientalism*. New York: Vintage Books, 1979.

Sartre, Jean-Paul. *Being and Nothingness: An Essay on Phenomenological Ontology*, trans. Hazel E. Barnes. New York: Philosophical Library, 1956.

_____. *The Transcendence of the Ego*, trans. Forrest Williams and Robert Kirkpatrick. New York: Noonday Press, 1957.

_____. *Critique of Dialectical Reason*, Vol. 1. London: New Left Books; Atlantic Highlands, N.J.: Humanities Press, 1976.

_____. *Critique of Dialectical Reason*, Vol. 2. London/New York: Verso, 1991.

Schmitt, Richard. *Beyond Separateness: The Social Nature of Human Beings—Their Autonomy, Knowledge, and Power*. Boulder, Colo.: Westview Press, 1995.

Sengupta, P. K. *Freedom, Transcendence and Identity: Essays in Memory of Kalidas Bhattacharya*. New Delhi: Motilal Banarsidas, 1988.

Shoemaker, Sydney. *Self-Knowledge and Self Identity*. Ithaca, N.Y.: Cornell University Press, 1963.

Shotter, John. *Social Accountability and Selfhood*. Oxford/New York: B. Blackwell, 1984.

Shrader, D., and A. Malhotra, eds. *Pathways to Philosophy: A Multidisciplinary Approach*. Upper Saddle River, N.J.: Prentice-Hall, 1996.

Shweder, Richard A., and Robert A. Levine, eds. *Culture Theory: Essays on Mind, Self, and Emotion*. Cambridge: Cambridge University Press, 1984.

Sinari, R. A., ed. *Concept of Man in Philosophy*. New Delhi: B. R. Publishing Co., 1991.

Sivin, N., ed., *Science and Technology in East Asia*. New York, 1977.

Smith, Robert J. *Japanese Society: Tradition, Self, and the Social Order*. Cambridge: Cambridge University Press, 1983.

Strawson, P. F. *Individuals: An Essay in Descriptive Metaphysics*. Garden City, N.Y.: Anchor Books, 1963.

Suzuki, Daisetz T. *Zen and Japanese Culture*. Princeton: Princeton University Press, 1959.

Symonds, Percival Mallon. *The Ego and the Self*. New York: Appleton-Century-Crofts, 1951.

Taylor, Charles. *Sources of the Self: The Making of the Modern Identity*. Cambridge, Mass.: Harvard University Press, 1989.

_____. *The Ethics of Authenticity*. Cambridge, Mass: Harvard University Press, 1992.

Taylor, Mark C. *Journeys to Selfhood: Hegel and Kierkegaard*. Berkeley: University of California Press, 1980.

Tsunoda, Ryusaku, William Theodore de Bary, and Donald Keene, comps. *Sources of Japanese Tradition*, Vol. 1. New York: Columbia University Press, 1964.

Tucker, Robert C., ed. *The Marx-Engels Reader*. New York: Norton, 1972.

Tu Wei-ming. *Confucian Thought: Selfhood as Creative Transformation*. Albany: State University of New York Press, 1985.

_____. *Centrality and Commonality: An Essay on Confucian Religiousness*. Albany: State University of New York Press, 1989.

_____. *Way, Learning and Politics: Essays on the Confucian Intellectual*. Albany: State University of New York Press, 1993.

Unger, Peter K. *Identity, Consciousness, and Value*. New York: Oxford University Press, 1990.

Varela, F. J., E. Thomson, and E. Rosch. *The Embodied Mind*. Cambridge, Mass.: MIT Press, 1991.

Warren, Henry Clarke, ed. *Buddhism in Translations*. New York: Atheneum, 1963.

Watsuji Tetsurô. *Niichie kenkyû* [A study of Nietzsche]. Tokyo: Iwanami Shoten, 1913.

Watts, Alan. *Ego*. Millbrae, Calif.: Celestial Arts, 1975.

Weitz, Morris, ed. *Twentieth Century Philosophy: The Analytic Tradition*. New York: Free Press, 1966.

Westen, Drew. *Self and Society: Narcissism, Collectivism, and the Development of Morals*. New York: Cambridge University Press, 1985.

White, M., and S. Pollak, eds. *The Cultural Transitions: Human Experience and Social Transformation in the Third World and Japan*. London: Routledge and Kegan Paul, 1986.

Williams, Bernard. *Problems of the Self*. Cambridge: Cambridge University Press, 1973.

Winnicott, Donald W. *Collected Papers*. New York: Basic Books, 1951.

Wright, Arthur F., ed. *The Confucian Persuasion*. Stanford: Stanford University Press, 1960.

Zaner, Richard M. *The Context of Self: A Phenomenological Inquiry Using Medicine as a Clue*. Athens: Ohio University Press, 1981.

About the Book and Editor

Traditional scholars of philosophy and religion, both East and West, often place a major emphasis on analyzing the nature of "the self." In recent decades, there has been a renewed interest in analyzing self, but most scholars have not claimed knowledge of an ahistorical, objective, essential self free from all cultural determinants. The contributors of this volume recognize the need to contextualize specific views of self and to analyze such views in terms of the dynamic, dialectical relations between self and culture.

An unusual feature of this book is that all of the chapters not only focus on traditions and individuals, East and West, but include as primary emphases comparative philosophy, religion, and culture, reinforcing individual and cultural creativity. Each chapter brings specific Eastern and Western perspectives into a dynamic, comparative relation. This comparative orientation emphasizes our growing sense of interrelatedness and interdependency.

Douglas Allen is professor of philosophy at the University of Maine. He is the author of *Structure and Creativity in Religion; Mircea Eliade: An Annotated Bibliography* (with Dennis Doeing); *Mircea Eliade et le phénomène religieux; Coming to Terms: Indochina, the United States, and the War* (coedited with Ngo Vinh Long and published by Westview Press); and *Religion and Political Conflict in South Asia*. He is also an editor of *Bulletin of Concerned Asian Scholars* and has received Fulbright and Smithsonian Institution grants to teach and study in India.

About the Contributors

Ananyo Basu, assistant professor of philosophy at the University of Massachusetts at Boston, is also Visiting Scholar in the Afro-American Studies Department at Harvard University. Educated in Hong Kong and India, and at Dartmouth College, he received his Ph.D. in philosophy from Duke University. In addition to his work in Asian philosophy, he does research on African and African-American philosophy, philosophy of mind, and ethical and political theory.

Mary I. Bockover, associate professor of philosophy at Humboldt State University, received her Ph.D. in philosophy from the University of California at Santa Barbara. She is editor of *Rules, Rituals, and Responsibility: Essays Dedicated to Herbert Fingarette.* In addition, she has published in such journals as *Philosophy East and West,* the *Journal of Asian Studies,* and the *Journal of the American Academy of Religion.* Her "The Concept of Emotion Revisited" appears in the anthology *Emotions in Asian Thought.*

Kenneth K. Inada, Distinguished Service Professor, Emeritus, State University of New York at Buffalo, is a past president of both the Society for Asian and Comparative Philosophy and the International Society for Chinese Philosophy. He also served as editor of the State University of New York Series in Buddhist Studies. He is the author, translator, and editor of numerous books on Buddhism and comparative philosophy. His current interest is Oriental aesthetics.

Ashok K. Malhotra, professor of philosophy at the State University of New York at Oneonta, received his Ph.D. from the University of Hawaii and is a past vice president, secretary-treasurer, and symposium chair of the Society for Asian and Comparative Philosophy. He is the author of *Jean-Paul Sartre's Existentialism as Literature and Philosophy, Pathways to Philosophy: A Multidisciplinary Approach* (with Douglas Shrader), and *The Transcreation of the Bhagavad Gita.*

Mara Miller, a Mellon Post-Doctoral Fellow in East Asian Art and Religion at Emory University, received her Ph.D. in philosophy from Yale University. She has studied Japanese language and culture at Cornell and at Michigan's Center for Japanese Studies. The author of *The Garden as an Art,* she is completing a study of the position of women in Japanese culture *(Desiring Women: Gender, Power and Personal Identity in Ukiyo-e Prints)* and is editing an anthology on East Asian aesthetics.

Graham Parkes, professor of philosophy at the University of Hawaii, was Visiting Scholar at the Reischauer Institute of Japanese Studies, Harvard University. He is the author of *Composing the Soul: Reaches of Nietzsche's Psychology* and *Strategies for Reading Japanese* (with Setsuko Aihara). In addition, he has edited *Heidegger and Asian Thought* and *Nietzsche and Asian Thought* and has translated *Secret Doctrines of the Tibetan Books of the Dead* and *The Self-Overcoming of Nihilism* (with Setsuko Aihara).

Alan Roland, a practicing psychoanalyst in New York City, is a Senior Member and Faculty Member of the National Psychological Association for Psychoanalysis. He is the author of *In Search of Self in India and Japan: Toward a Cross-Cultural Psychology* and *Cultural Pluralism and Psychoanalysis: The Asian and North American Experience.* A recipient of grants from the American Institute for Indian Studies, he has conducted clinical psychoanalytic research in India and in Japan.

Henry Rosemont, Jr., professor of philosophy at St. Mary's College of Maryland and Distinguished Consulting Professor at Fudan University, Shanghai, is the author of *A Chinese Mirror* and the forthcoming *Classical Confucianism and Contemporary Ethics.* Among his edited and/or translated works is *Leibniz: Writings on China* (with Daniel J. Cook). He is a past president of the Society for Asian and Comparative Philosophy and has held NEH, ACLS, NSF, and Fulbright fellowships.

Index

Abe Jirô, 132
Absolutism, 69, 85
Abstract rationality, 15
Affects, 35
Aggregates, 88
Ahamkara, 111, 118, 119–120, 123, 127
Allen, Douglas, xii
Altruism, 100
Amae. See Dependency relationships
Analects (Confucius), 53, 57, 64
Analytic philosophy, xi
Anatta (no-self), xii, 4, 11, 22
Anitya, 87
Anthropology, xii, 29, 30–31, 148, 155
Anupalambha-yoga, 106, 108
A posteriori, 49
A priori, 49, 50
Aristotle, 51, 57–58, 64
  and self, 45
Arjuna, 9
Ashoka (emperor of India), 108(n4)
Asiatic mode of perception, 86, 87,
  93(n3)
Assorted Opinions and Maxims
  (Nietzsche), 134
Autonomous individual. *See* Individual,
  autonomous
Autonomy, xv, 15, 28

Baier, Annette, 77
Balint, Michael, 32
Basho (poet), 92
Bastow, David, xiv, 97, 101–104
Basu, Ananyo, xiv
Becoming, xiii, xiv, 85, 86, 87, 88, 89,
  93(n4)
Befu, Harumi, 149
Being, xiii, xiv85, 86, 87, 89, 93(n4), 113,
  122, 125, 128(n1)

*Being and Nothingness: An Essay on
  Phenomenological Ontology*
  (Sartre), xiv, 111, 112, 113, 117, 123,
  126, 128
Benedict, Ruth, 148
Bentham, Jeremy, 46, 50
Beyond Good and Evil (Nietzsche), 132
Bhagavad-Gita, xii, 5–6, 16. *See also
  Karma yoga* path
Black, Alison, 66, 67
Bockover, Mary I., xiii
Body as self, 114–116, 120–121, 123,
  127–128
Book of Changes (Yi Ching), 87
Buddha, xii, 3, 10–11, 16, 99, 103, 107,
  150
Buddhi, 111, 118, 119, 120, 123, 127
Buddhism, 16, 139, 141, 160–161(n21)
  and becoming, 86, 87, 93(n4)
  middle way, 150. *See also*
    Madhyamika school
  schools, xiv, 100, 102, 104, 105
  and self, xii, xiii, 10–12, 17, 88, 102,
    104, 106, 146, 150–151. *See also
    Anatta;* Self, reductionist view of
  texts, 5, 6, 11

Cahill, James, 156
Calligraphy, 155
Capital (Marx), 13
Capitalism, 7, 13, 69, 71, 74, 79. *See also*
  Marxism, and self
Caring, xiii, 15
Cartesianism
  post-, xii, 22, 23(n3)
  and self, xii, 7, 50, 92–93(n2), 99
Categorical Imperative, 45–46, 47, 49
Chemical accidents, 20
China, xii, 78, 86, 106

and Great Britain, 83–84
and the West, 78
and women, 65–67
See also Buddhism; Confucianism;
    Taoism
Chitta, 120, 127
Chodorow, Nancy, 15, 65
Chrysanthemum and the Sword, The:
    Patterns of Japanese Culture
    (Benedict), 148–149
Chuang Tzu, 89
Cixous, Hélène, 18
Colonialism, 37
"Commonality with differences"
    principle, xii, 5, 18–20
Community, 35, 38
Comprehensive harmony, 84–85
Conditioned/relational organization, 88
Confucianism, 139
    elitism, 73, 74, 78, 79
    ethics, 53–57, 59–60(n18), 60–61(n27),
        77
    and feminism, xiii, 63, 66, 68, 72–73,
        75, 78, 79
    and hierarchy, 73–74
    neo-, 151
    parable, 154
    and PEI, 45
    and self, xii, xiii, 45, 54, 56,
        60(nn21&22), 71, 72–73, 77–78,
        146, 151–156
    and particularism, 75, 77, 78
    and universalism, 75, 77
    and Western ethics, xiii, 53, 54,
        59(n17), 79
    and Western gender attitudes, 65–66
    and Western tradition compared,
        151–156
Confucius, 64
Confucius—The Secular as Sacred
    (Fingarette), 55
Conscience, 30, 34
Consciousness, 102, 111, 114, 124
    prereflective, 113, 117, 118, 122–123,
        124
    pure, 118, 119, 120, 121, 127
Contextualization, 27–28, 35

Creativity, xv, 19, 141, 147
Critique of Pure Reason (Kant), 64
Cultural anthropology, xii, 29
Cultural diversity, 17, 27
Cultural relativism, 18, 31
Culture, xii, 5, 27–28, 29, 31, 70, 131
    and tradition, 131, 133, 140
    Western, 68–71
    Western and Eastern, 83–84
    See also under Self

Daniels, Norman, 100
Dao De Jing, 66
Death, 126, 150–151
De Beauvoir, Simone, xii
    and self, 4, 14, 16, 17, 22, 25(n21)
Declaration of Independence, 69
Declaration of the Rights of Man, 69
Deconstructionism, 18
Degeneration, 134
Dependency relationships, 32, 33, 34, 35
Derrida, Jacques, 18
Descartes, René, 4, 50, 51, 58(n9). *See*
    also Cartesianism
Desires, 87, 88, 101, 119120, 125–126
Developmental stages, 35
Dewey, John, 92–93(n2)
Dharma, 9, 27–28, 87, 104
Diachronic unity, 100–101
Dialectics, 20
Doi, Takeo, xii, 32–34, 35, 149
Donne, John, 79
Dostoevsky, Fedor, 140
Dream-analysis, 35
Drive theory, 28, 35

Ebrey, Patricia, 66
Ecological damage, 20
Ego, 10, 16–17, 28
    boundaries, 35–36, 37, 132
    conscious, 132
    -ideal, 35, 36
    -less self, 117
    as self, 113–114
    -sense, 111, 118, 119–120, 123, 127
    underdeveloped, 30

See also Self, Western and Eastern comparisons of

Egoism, 10, 12, 16, 100

Ego psychology, 28, 31, 33

Einsteinian physics, 85, 86, 93(n3)

English (language), 156–157, 158

Enlightenment, 28, 30, 37, 69, 79, 126, 150

Erikson, Erik, 28, 39(n5)

"Ennoblement through degeneration," 134

Ethical indeterminacy, xiii. *See also* Problem of ethical indeterminacy

Ethics, xiii, 43–44
  comparative, 45, 52
  and impartiality, 59(n13)
  Kantian, 44, 46, 47, 49, 50
  paradox, 51–52, 56, 57
  and real confrontation, 47, 48, 52
  speculative, 50
  universal, 44, 48, 49, 52, 57
  Western, 45–52, 53
  See also Problem of ethical indeterminacy; *under* Confucianism

Ethnocentrism, 18

Ethnological Notebooks of Karl Marx, The (Marx), 12

Eudaemonia, 57, 58

Evolutionism, xii, 29–30

Ewing, Catherine, xii, 30–31

Existentialism, xi, 14, 117–118, 124

Experimentation, 135

Family relationships, 35, 37, 38

Fang, Thome H., 84

Fate, 135, 137–138

Feminism, 18, 25(n19)
  defined, 63–64
  perspectives, 63
  postmodern, 18
  and self, xii, 4, 8, 14–15, 16, 17, 18, 22, 147–148
  See also under Confucianism

Fingarette, Herbert, 55

Five Human Relationships, 153

Franciscans, 78

Freedom, 46, 49, 50, 124–125

Free spirit, 134

Free will, 47

Freud, Sigmund, 15, 28

Fuller, Buckminster, 92

Functionalist, 99

Fundamentalism, 20

Gandhi, Mohandas K., 5, 6, 10, 19

Gautama, Siddhartha. *See* Buddha

Geertz, Clifford, 27

"German Ideology" (Marx), 13

Gilligan, Carol, 14–15, 65

Gita. See Bhagavad-Gita

Globalism, 20, 86

Goblet words, 89, 93(n10)

God, 126

Groundwork of the Metaphysic of Morals (Kant), 45

Group relationships, 35, 37, 38

Guide to the Tale of Genjii by Murasaki Shikibu (Puette), 157

Haiku, 92

Han Dynasty, 67

Happiness, 46–47, 50
  and virtue, 51

Harding, Sandra, 64

Hartsock, Nancy, 15

Hegel, G.W.F., 20

Heidegger, Martin, 139, 140

Hinduism, 16, 27–28
  and self, xii, 4, 9–10, 11–12, 17, 22, 23(n2). *See also* Samkhya-Yoga
  texts, 5, 16

Historical materialism, 13

History, 133–135. *See also under* Self

Hobbes, Thomas, 4, 7

Homophobia, 73

Hua, 87

Huang Di Nei Jing, 67

Humankind unity and oneness, 17, 19, 27

Human nature, xii, 27, 29, 112

Human rights. *See* Individual, rights-bearing

Hume, David, 4, 72, 87, 97, 98, 99, 100,
    101
"Hundred Schools," 78

Ichimaru, Totoro, 36
Ideal, 57
Imputed words, 89
Inada, Kenneth K., xiii–xiv
*In a Different Voice: Psychological
    Theory and Women's Development*
    (Gilligan), 14
India, xii, 6, 86, 106
    neurosis, 37
    psychoanalytic studies, xii–xiii, 29–30,
        34
    and self, 23(n4), 17–18, 21, 35–36
Individual
    abstract, xiii
    atomistic, 7–8, 9, 13, 20
    autonomous, xii, xiii, 8, 9, 70, 152
    caring, xiii
    recognition and respect for, 15
    rights-bearing, xiii, 68–71
    as social being, xiii, 20
Individualism, 12, 28, 29, 30, 38(n4), 68,
    146
Individuality, 99, 155
Indriyas, 111, 118, 119
*Inner World, The: A Psychoanalytical
    Study of Childhood and Society in
    India* (Kakar), 30
Intelligence, 111, 118, 119, 120, 123, 127
Interdependence, 15, 20
Internal object world, 35
Irigaray, Luce, 18

James, William, 109(n18), 152
Japan, xii, 106, 139, 154–155
    neurosis, 37
    and Nietzsche, interpretations of,
        132, 139
    postwar, 140
    psychoanalytic studies, xii–xiii, 32–34,
        36–37
    and self, 36, 147, 155, 156–158,
        160(nn14–17)
    selfhood in, xv, 145–149

Japanese (language), 156–158
Japanese Sense of Self (Rosenberger),
    147, 148
Jen, 53, 54–55, 56, 57, 58, 60(n23),
    60–61(n27)
Jesuits, 78
Joyful Science, The (Nietzsche), 136, 139

Kaccayana-gotta sutta, 107
Kakar, Sudhir, xii, 29–30
Kant, Immanuel, 28, 45–46, 49, 64, 71
    and self, 44, 100, 102
Kardiner, Abraham, 28
Karma, 9, 88, 150
Karma yoga path, xii, 4, 5, 9–10, 22
Kasulis, Thomas P., 147–148, 153, 158
Kawabata , Yasunari, 157
Keller, Catherine, 72
Khandas, 102, 103, 104
King, Martin Luther, Jr., 19
Klein, Melanie, 28
Kohlberg, Lawrence, 14–15
Kohut, Heinz, 28
Korsgaard, Christine, 100–101
Krishna, 9, 12, 16
Kristeva, Julia, 18
Kshanika, 87
Kyoto School, xiv, 140

Lacan, Jacques, 18
Lakshanas, 105
Lebra, Takie Sugiyama, 147, 149
Li, 53–54, 55, 56, 60(n20), 60–61(n27),
    77
Lienu Zhuan, 67
Lie Zi, 66
Locke, John, 4, 7, 69
Logical positivism, xi
Lun Yu, 64–65, 74

MacIntyre, Alasdair, 8
Madhyamika school, xiv, 104, 106–107,
    108
Magic-cosmic world of personal destiny,
    38
Mahasanghika school, 105, 109(n21)

Mahayana Buddhism, 100, 105, 139–140, 141
Malhotra, Ashok Kumar, xiv
Manas, 111, 118, 119, 120, 123, 127
Mandate of Heaven, 155
Marx, Karl, xii, 12, 16
Marxism, 78
  and self, xii, 4, 12–14, 16, 17, 22
Masculinist self, xii, 4, 8, 14, 17, 25(n18)
Materia Medica, 67
Maternal empathy, 34
Matsunaga, Alicia, 151
Matsunaga, Daigan, 151
Maya, 10, 16
Mead, George H., 92–93(n2)
Meditative exercises, 124–125
Mencius, 64
Metaphysics, 85, 86–87, 93(n4)
Mill, John Stuart, 46, 50
Miller, Mara, xv
Minamoto Yoriie (shogun), 154–155
Mind, 111, 118, 119, 120, 123, 127
Ming Dynasty, 67
Mirroring, 34
Missionaries, 78
Mohanty, Jitendra Nath, 7
Mongaku (monk), 154–155
Moral action, 51, 54
Moral development, 14–15, 25–26(n23)
Moral falsity, 44
Morality, xiii, 46, 49–50, 51, 52, 53, 56, 57, 60(n19), 76
Moral relativism. *See* Relativism, moral
Moral Truth, 43, 44, 48, 49, 56, 58(nn6–8)
  empirical approach, 50
  "higher," 47
  as indeterminate, 48, 49–50, 51, 57, 59(nn11&15)
Multiculturalism, 18
Myths, 19

Nagarjuna, 106
Nagasena (monk), 88
Names, 157–158, 162(n46)
Nausea (Sartre), 123
Needham, Joseph, 67

Newtonian physics, 85, 86
Nicomachean Ethics (Aristotle), 51, 64
Nietzsche, Friedrich, xiv, 131
  on history, 133–135
  and self, xii, xiv–xv, 132, 133, 134, 136, 137, 138
  See also Nihilism
Nietzsche contra Wagner (Nietzsche), 135
Nihilism, xiv–xv, 105, 131, 132–133, 135–136, 138, 139–140
  European, 131, 134, 139, 140
Nirvana, 87
Nishitani Keiji, xiv, xv, 131, 133, 135, 136, 137–141
Noddings, Nell, 65
"No man is an island. . . ," 79
Non-being, xiii–xiv, 84, 86, 89–90, 91, 92
Nonclinging, 106, 108
No-thing, 124
Nothingness. *See* Consciousness, prereflective
No-self. *See* Anatta
Noumena, 49
Nuclear accidents, 20
Nujie qian shi, 67

Object, 116, 118
Object relations theory, 28
Omote/ura. See Self, dual
Oriental dynamics, 84, 89, 92
Orientalism, 18
Otherness, 18. *See also* Self, -other

Painting, 155–156
Pakistan, 30–31
Pali Canon, 5, 6, 11, 103
Parfit, Derek, xiv, 97–101, 105, 107
Parkes, Graham, xiv
Passions and desires, 87, 88
Patriarchal self. *See* Masculinist self
PEI. *See* Problem of ethical indeterminacy
Perception, 86–87, 93(n3), 102
Person, 7, 23(n4), 60(n22)
Personhood, 101
Phenomenology, xi, 123–124

Phenomenology of the Mind, The (Hegel), 20
Philosophy, xi
Physics, 85, 86, 87, 93(n3), 106
Plato, 85
Poetics (Aristotle), 64
Politics (Aristotle), 64
Positivism, xi
Postmodernism, 18
Power, 150, 151
Pragmatism, 107
Prakriti, 118, 119, 121, 122, 124, 125, 126
Pratitya-samutpada, 88, 102–103
Private self. *See* Self, dual
Problem of ethical indeterminacy (PEI), 43, 44, 45, 48, 49, 51–52, 56
  and Truth, 50
Psychoanalysis
  and Asian societies, 29–34
  atheoretical approach, 33
  comparative, 35–38
  and evolutionism, 29–30, 31
  and human nature, 29
  and relativism, 32–34
  and universalism, xii–xiii, 27, 29, 30–32, 33, 35, 38
  as Western, 28, 30
Psychoanalytic anthropology, 29, 30–31
Psychological connectedness, 98–99
Psychopathology, 29, 31, 34, 36–37, 38
Public self. *See* Self, dual
Puette, William J., 157
Pure Land Sects, 150
Purusha, 111, 118, 119, 120–123, 124, 125, 126

Quasi-memories, 98, 99
Queen's Bridge (Cambridge, England), 83–84, 92
Questions of King Milinda, The, 88

Rachels, James, 59(n13)
Ramanujan, A. K., 27–28
Ramayana, 6
Raphals, Lisa, 67
Rational agent, 100
Rationality, 15, 28

Reason, 46, 49, 50
Reasons and Persons (Parfit), 97, 98
Reincarnations, 151
Relation R, 99, 105
Relativism, xii, 3, 18, 29, 31, 32–34, 85, 107, 152, 153
  ethical, xiii, 44
  moral, 43–44, 47–48, 49, 58(n6)
  truth in, 47, 48, 58(n7)
Religion, 30, 126
Religion and Nothingness (Nishitani), 140
Repeated words, 89
Resistance, 35
Ricardo, David, 7
Rohlan, Thomas, 149
Roland, Alan, xii–xiii
Role-carrying person, xiii, 71–72, 76
Rosemont, Henry, Jr., xiii
Rosenberger, Nancy R., 147
Rupa, 102

Samkhya-Yoga, 5, 10, 118
  and self, xii, xiv, 111, 119–128
Samsara, 11, 16
Sankhara, 102
San-lun, 106
Sanna, 102
San-ron, 106
Sartre, Jean-Paul, 14
  and self, xii, xiv, 111, 112–118, 122–128
Sarvastivadins, 104–105, 109(n21)
Sautrantikas, 105, 109(n21)
Second Sex, The (de Beauvoir), 14
Second Treatise on Civil Government (Locke), 69
Seidensticker, Edward, 158
Self
  abstract, 44, 50, 51, 58(n9), 59(n12)
  -alienation, 20
  anti-essentialist view of, xiv, 14, 104, 107
  authentic, 3, 7, 8, 23(n2)
  capitalist. *See* Marxism, and self
  -constitution, 19, 20, 21, 22–23

-creation, 103–104, 105, 115, 117, 123, 127, 146
and culture, xi–xii, xiii, xiv, 3, 4, 8–9, 10, 12–14, 15, 16, 30, 111, 121, 123
development, xii, 20, 136, 137
and differences, 18–19
dual, 32, 33, 35, 37
empirical, 88, 122
enlightened, 122
essential, 7, 14, 15, 101
and history, xi, xii, 3, 4, 8–9, 10, 12–14, 15, 16, 134
I-, 31, 114, 127
levels of, 149
moral, 51, 57
and name, 158, 162(n46)
-other, 14, 26, 30, 31, 35–36, 115, 116, 136, 152
and person, 7, 23(n4), 60(n22)
relational. *See* Confucianism, and self
religious, 126
reductionist view of, xiv, 97, 99–100, 101–108
transcending, 13, 14, 19, 20, 132
true, 123
value, 117, 136, 152
we-, 31, 116–117
Western, critiques of, 5, 7, 8, 15–18, 112
Western and Eastern comparisons of, xii, xiii–xiv, xv, 4, 8, 12–15, 20, 23(n3), 85–87, 122–128, 145–149, 150–158
See also under Buddhism; Cartesianism; Confucianism; Feminism; Hinduism; Japan; Nietzsche, Friedrich; Sarte, Jean-Paul; Taoism
Self and object representations, 35
"Self-Construction in Buddhism" (Bastow), 101
Selfhood, xv, 101, 145–149
Self-esteem, 34
Self-identity, 35–36, 72, 74, 97–98, 100
false, 121, 123, 125, 128
Self-images, 3–4, 31
"Self in Japanese Culture" (Lebra), 149

Self-interest, 99–100
Self-object relationships, 28, 35
Self-Overcoming of Nihilism, The (Nishitani), 135, 139
Self psychology, 28, 34, 105
Sense-motor organ complex, 118, 119, 120–121
Shankara Vedanta, 5, 6
Shi Jing, 65
Shinto, 150, 160–161(n21)
Shoemaker, Sydney, 98
Sivin, Nathan, 67, 74
Skandhas, 88
Smith, Adam, 7
Smith, Robert J., 155
Snow Country (Kawabata), 157
Social being, xiii, 54, 116, 123, 152
Social etiquette, 36, 37
Sociocentric/organic societies, 38
Soul, 74, 150
Spiritual experiences and disciplines, 37–38
Spiritual substance, 125
Sri Lanka, 6
Stirner, Max, 139
Structural theory, 28
Subject, 116, 118, 146
Suffering, 137. *See also* Self-identity, false
Superego, 35
Symbols, 19
Symmetry/asymmetry, 90–91, 92
Synchronic unity, 100

Tale of Genji, The (Murasaki), 146, 157
Tao, 56, 60(n23), 84, 90
Taoism
and becoming, 86, 87, 89, 90, 93(n4)
doctrines, 84, 88–89
and self, xii, xiii, 91, 92, 151
Tao Te Ching, 90
Te, 53
Thus Spoke Zarathustra (Nietzsche), 136, 137, 138
Transference, 35, 36–37
Transitional objects, 29

Treatise on Human Nature, A (Hume), 72
Triadic relationship, 84, 89
Trishna-upadana, 87, 88
Truth, 45, 107. *See also Dharma;* Moral Truth
"Truth in Relativism, The" (Williams), 47, 59(n17)
Twilight of the Idols (Nietzsche), 133–134

Unconscious, 28, 118, 122
United Nations Declaration of Human Rights, 70
Universalism, xii–xiii, 27, 28, 29, 30–32, 75, 76, 77
   "postconventional," 15
   See also Ethics, universal
Untimely Meditations (Nietzsche), 133
Utility principle, 44, 46–47, 50, 99, 101

Vedana, 102
Vedanta, xii, 6
Vinnana, 102

Virginia Declaration of Rights, 69
Virtue, 51, 155

Walker, Margaret, 75
Wang Pi, 90
Wars, 20
Watsuji Tetsurô, 132, 153
Wheel of life, 87, 88
Williams, Bernard, xiii, 47–48, 59(n17)
Will to power, 132
Winnicott, D. W., 28–29
Wittgenstein, Ludwig, 99
Word types, 89

Xun Zi, 64

Yi, 87
Ying/Yang, 66–67, 74, 90

Zen, xiv, 136, 151
Zhuang Zi, 66